From Roman Basilica to Medieval Market

Museum of London

From Roman Basilica to Medieval Market

ARCHAEOLOGY IN ACTION IN THE CITY OF LONDON

edited by Gustav Milne

LONDON: HMSO

© Copyright the Board of Governors of
the Museum of London 1992

Applications for reproduction should be made
to HMSO

First published 1992

ISBN 0 11 290446 7

British Library Cataloguing in Publication Data
A CIP catalogue record for this book is available from the
British Library

HMSO

HMSO publications are available from:

HMSO Publications Centre
(Mail, fax and telephone orders only)
PO Box 276, London, SW8 5DT
Telephone orders 071-873 9090
General enquiries 071-873 0011
(queuing system in operation for both numbers)
Fax orders 071-873 8200

HMSO Bookshops
49 High Holborn, London, WC1V 6HB
(counter service only)
071-873 0011 Fax 071-873 8200
258 Broad Street, Birmingham, B1 2HE
021-643 3740 Fax 021-643 6510
Southey House, 33 Wine Street, Bristol, BS1 2BQ
0272 264306 Fax 0272 294515
9-21 Princess Street, Manchester, M60 8AS
061-834 7201 Fax 061-833 0634
16 Arthur Street, Belfast, BT1 4GD
0232 238451 Fax 0232 235401
71 Lothian Road, Edinburgh, EH3 9AZ
031-228 4181 Fax 031-229 2734

HMSO's Accredited Agents
(see Yellow Pages)

and through good booksellers

FRONT COVER
Prestigious architecture: the remains of London's Roman
Basilica, once the largest building in Britain, are discovered
in the shadow of the new Lloyds building during the
Leadenhall Court excavations in 1986. Inset: digging deeply
into London's past on the Leadenhall Court site.

BACK COVER
Fifteenth-century civic pride: this cut-away reconstruction
of the north-west corner of the Garner at Leadenhall shows
the decorated facade the public market presented to
London.
(Reconstruction by Mark Samuel)

Printed in the United Kingdom for HMSO
Dd 295258 5/92 C15 531/3 12521

Contents

Preface		vii
Acknowledgements		xi
Notes and conventions		xii
List of illustrations		xiii
1	The patient discovery of London's past Gustav Milne	1
2	From fields to Forum Chrissie Milne, Gustav Milne and Trevor Brigham	9
3	New towns Gustav Milne	34
4	The 'Ledene Hall' and medieval market Mark Samuel and Gustav Milne	39
5	The archaeologist as alchemist Gustav Milne	51
6	An absolute chronology Barbara Davies with Jenny Hall and Gustav Milne	60
7	Inner city living Gustav Milne, Chrissie Milne and Paul Wootton	73
8	Civic centre redevelopment Trevor Brigham	81
9	Reconstructing the Basilica Trevor Brigham with Naomi Crowley	96
10	Basilica studies Trevor Brigham	106
11	Reconstructing the medieval market at Leadenhall Mark Samuel	114
12	London viewed from Leadenhall Trevor Brigham, Gustav Milne and Mark Samuel	126

Appendices

    A: **Whittington Avenue excavations: a summary**   **135**
         Gary Brown and Brian Pye

    B: **Public archaeology**   **138**
         Gustav Milne and Chrissie Milne

Bibliography   **140**

Colour Plates   *between pages* **66** *and* **67**

Preface

This book began as a report on a Roman basilica, but grew into a wider study of London's history. That, at least, is the present hope and intention. It is based primarily upon the results of an extensive programme of rescue excavations in 1985–6 at Leadenhall Court, which sits in the heart of the ancient City, on the crest of the hill overlooking the road leading down to Old London Bridge. The site was more particularly distinguished by overlying part of the eastern half of the Basilica (or town hall) built to serve the Roman town of Londinium in the early 2nd century AD. As such, the site obviously held considerable archaeological potential.

Once it was known that redevelopment was imminent, trial holes were dug in the basement of a derelict building in Gracechurch Street prior to demolition to establish the degree of preservation of the ancient levels. This exercise, apart from providing welcome confirmation of the survival of the Roman public building, was also prepared to 'expect the unexpected', an essential component of all such project designs (Barker 1977, 37). At Leadenhall Court in February 1985, the unexpected results took two forms. Beneath the remains of the Basilica was a long sequence of earlier Roman buildings, dating back to the very birth of the settlement of Londinium. However, an even greater surprise awaited the archaeologists examining the shell of the Victorian building in which they were excavating. Once the plaster was stripped away from the back wall, it revealed not stock bricks but a massive masonry wall some 14m high. This proved to be a substantial section, from basement to roof line, of the western range of the 15th-century Leadenhall market. That building was thought to have been entirely demolished by the 1880s, but this section had survived to its full height of four storeys, encased within the fabric of the buildings which superseded it.

The true potential of the project thus began taking shape. Here was an opportunity to compare the rise and fall of two important civic buildings: both incorporated ranges of rooms set around a courtyard and both were directly related to the commercial life of the City. Was it just a coincidence that both should have occupied the same site, although 1,000 years apart? In addition, there was evidence of occupation and development of a different character in the preceding period, represented by the traces of early Roman buildings of a much more modest type. Taken together, it was clear that the site could provide a remarkable insight into the changing fortunes of London, and could focus on the contrasting roles of public and private redevelopments in that story. The evidence lay in the fabric of the ancient buildings themselves and in the significant changes in the layout and topography of the site over a 2,000 year period. Study of the private buildings will tell us much about the first Londoners, while study of the public buildings reveals the aspirations of the City's civic authorities: the fate of both is the story of London itself.

Yet the opportunity to record that evidence would have been lost forever had a major programme of excavations not been mounted. Thanks to the generosity of the developer, Legal & General Assurance Company, and of English Heritage together with the special appeal launched by the City of London Archaeological Trust Fund, much of the site was recorded before redevelopment began, a considerable tribute to the excavation teams. As might be expected, quantities of finds and other samples were recovered and subsequently processed, enabling features to be dated and functions suggested. Detailed reports have been prepared, of which some have been published, while others may be consulted in the Museum of London archive, filed under the site code LCT84.

Much of that work is summarised in this book. The project highlights the problems of attempting large-scale excavation in a busy city, constrained by demolition and redevelopment schedules, shoring requirements and finite resources. The necessarily piecemeal excavation programme provided its own problems of integration and correlation. The results then had to be related to work conducted on neighbouring sites, which were excavated to varying standards at a variety of dates between 1880 and 1989. This point serves as a reminder that any interpretation of London's past based on archaeological evidence depends on the data available at that particular moment: each new site excavated provides new evidence for assessment and for reassessing the old. As a consequence, the picture of Roman development presented here is in many respects significantly different from that compiled in 1985 by Peter Marsden in his appraisal of the Roman Forum for example, for he had less information to draw upon, at least in regard to the Basilica itself (Marsden 1987).

By the same token, reappraisals of the 1985–6 material or further excavations in the Gracechurch Street area could allow equally significant reinterpretations of the evidence. Indeed, the discoveries made on the neighbouring Whittington Avenue site just two years later (Fig 2, site 2) proved too noteworthy to ignore. Even though the detailed post-excavation research for that site has yet to be completed, it became clear that some of the results of particular relevance to the interpretation of the Basilica and the Leadenhall could not be overlooked, and they were therefore incorporated in Chapters 4, 8 and 9 at the eleventh hour. In addition, the site supervisors were kind enough to prepare the summary of this important excavation which is included in Appendix A.

The model around which this book is based has yet to be tested: further work may contradict the broad thrust of its argument, or the fine detail of the case as presented. Nevertheless, whatever its failings, this book tries to present a coherent archaeological history of an important area of the City. But such a study has a wider relevance for several reasons, of which the following are among the more significant. The project incorporates the largest area of contiguous Roman buildings examined on one site in London: the picture of 1st-century urban topography drawn in Chapters 2 and 7 is therefore as yet unique. By definition, a detailed understanding of the Basilica, or town hall, is crucial to our appreciation of the status, aspirations and prosperity of Londinium, and these excavations were able to establish the form, function, date and development of that building (Chapters 2, 7 and 8). The relevance of this sequence to basilica excavations elsewhere in the country cannot be stressed too highly, as Chapter 10 tries to show. The assessment and reconstruction of the 15th-century Leadenhall Garner and market complex outlined in Chapter 11 represents the first exercise of the kind conducted on such a scale on material from London, and provides a fine example of the happy integration of excavated, cartographic and pictorial evidence with that derived from the detailed examination of discarded moulded stones. The methods and result of that reconstruction may be profitably compared with the equally ambitious reappraisal of the Basilica presented in Chapter 9.

Such detailed reconstructions are an essential component of archaeological interpretation for they force us to think of the past in three dimensions, to move from plans towards the physical realities of the ancient City.

Finally, this report represents a deviation from the recent trend of archaeological publication in London in which the Roman part of a site sequence is published separately from the later levels. It is contended here that the sequence as a sequence is important to our understanding of the City's growth. The nature of the interface between each major period is a crucial element in the story, determining how the elements of one phase did or did not influence subsequent developments (Chapters 2,

3 and 4). As a consequence, it is hoped that this study of the changing fortunes of these specific public and private buildings has produced a story which, while particular to Leadenhall Court, says much about London in general. This is not to say that the old approach is without virtue: indeed, those who require reports devoted exclusively to a particular period of activity will find articles already published on the early Roman buildings (Milne & Wootton 1990), the Basilica (Brigham 1990a) and the 15th-century Garner at Leadenhall (Samuel 1989). In addition, a more detailed study of the material from the 1st-century buildings is being prepared for publication as a London and Middlesex Archaeological Society Special Paper, while an additional paper on the medieval Leadenhall will hopefully be published by the London Topographical Society.

Gustav Milne
Project Co-ordinator
Department of Urban Archaeology
Museum of London

Pl 1 Class of '86: project team pose next to a Basilica wall fragment, at the end of the excavations in September 1986. (Area S)

Acknowledgements

This report on the Leadenhall Court project was made possible by the support, expertise, advice or hard labour of many individuals and institutions. Legal & General Assurance Company, English Heritage (Historic Buildings and Monuments Commission) and the City of London Archaeological Trust generously provided the funding for the excavation and post-excavation analysis reported in this book. Tony Dyson, Francis Grew and Philip Glover gave invaluable advice and assistance on matters related to its preparation and production. Additional comments by Dr Hugh Chapman (Society of Antiquaries), Professor Mike Fulford (University of Reading) and Dr Caroline Barron (University of London) have also been gratefully incorporated.

However, responsibility for whatever factual errors and misinterpretation of the evidence remain in this book rests not with them but with the authors credited at the head of each chapter. Of those who bore the brunt of the field work, particular mention must be made of Simon O'Connor Thompson, who set the project on its feet. Of the rest of the team, Trevor Brigham, Gary Brown, Chrissie Milne, Mark Samuel, and Paul Wootton all made major contributions in the field as well as to this report.

The photography is principally the work of Jon Bailey and Jan Scrivener, and the majority of the illustrations were drawn by Susan Banks, aided by Alison Hawkins, from material prepared by Chrissie Milne and Trevor Brigham. However, Figs 21, 23, 24, 42–48, and the back cover illustration were prepared by Mark Samuel; Tables 1–9 are by Chrissie Milne, and Figs 37 and 38 are by Nigel Harriss. Figs 1–3 and 22 are based on Ordnance Survey maps, by permission of the Controller of HMSO.

Naomi Crowley kindly supplied details on wall plaster, Barbara Davies on Roman pottery, Julie Edwards on medieval pottery, Angela Wardle on small finds, John Shepherd on Roman glass, Barbara West on environmental matters, Jenny Hall on coins, and Ian Betts on building material. The task of dealing with the finds on site or in the Museum fell mainly to Jo Groves, with help from Penny MacConnoran and her team.

The Area Supervisors on site were ably assisted by Patrick Allen, Julian Ayre, Sasha Barnes, Ryszard Bartkowiak, Nick Bateman, Ian Blair, Olwen Bleazley, Josephine Brown (née Batteson), Robin Brown, Mark Burch, Peter Cardiff, Julie Carr, Robert Chester, Prince Chitwood, Siriol Collins, Rebecca Coombs, Mike Copper, James Drummond-Murray, Peter Durnford, Sarah Gibson (née Ford), Damian Goodburn, Chris Goode, Susan Greenwood, Valerie Griggs, Ron Harris, Julian Hill, Mark Holmes, Mike Inzani, Queta and Anna Kaye, Lynne Keys, Duncan Lees, Wendy Locker, Paul McCulloch, Frank Meddens, Gavin Morgan, Jane Murray, Marie Nally, Stefania Perring, Patricia James (née Price), Brian Pye, Peter Rowsome, Duncan Schlee, Jo Stevenson (née Coombs), Tony Tynan, Simone Warr, Bruce Watson, Andrew Westman, Hester White and Mark Wiggins. Support was also provided by many volunteers, including students from the Institute of Archaeology (University College) and particularly our many friends from the City of London Archaeological Society, who also manned the viewing gallery with such enthusiasm.

It is customary to comment that archaeological projects are multi-disciplinary exercises. As such they demand a team approach, a point proved by the length of this list of acknowledgements, incomplete as it is. This book is therefore dedicated to the many who made it possible.

Notes and conventions

A number of conventions have been adopted in this book, and these are summarised here. Recent excavations in the City of London are often referred to by their site codes, which are usually a unique three-letter reference followed by an indication of the year the project began: thus LCT84 refers to the Leadenhall Court project which commenced in 1984; FEN83 the Fenchurch Street site excavated in 1983; WIV88 the Whittington Ave site which ran from 1988–9 and so forth. The location of some of these excavations is shown on Fig 2. In this book, 'the site' usually refers to all the Leadenhall Court (LCT84) area investigated from 1985–6, whereas work on, for example, Area N refers to the excavations in a particular part of that site, in this case the northern trench shown on Fig 4. To the west and south lay Areas W and S respectively, while the other smaller trenches were cut in the basements of the buildings previously known as the Metal Exchange (subsequently termed Area M, here) and Dominion House (Area D).

The term 'Brickearth' with a capital B refers to the natural, undisturbed strata underlying the Roman occupation levels, whereas the term 'brickearth' with a small b refers to the redeposited, reworked material used in building construction. As for the Roman buildings, the use of upper case initials for the Basilica refers to the 2nd- to 3rd-century structure in London, while upper case initials for Nave, Apse, Northern Range, etc, refer to particular rooms within that particular building, as shown on Figs 14 and 15 for example.

The adjective 'medieval' refers to features or activity datable from $c.$ AD 450 to $c.$ 1500, 'mid-Saxon' to $c.$ AD 600 to $c.$ 850, and 'late Saxon' to $c.$ 850 to $c.$ 1100. OD or Ordnance Datum refers to the sea level at Newlyn, Cornwall, the national benchmark upon which the Ordnance Survey (OS), the body responsible for mapping in Great Britain, base their calculations of absolute level. Thus a figure in our text such as 14.35m OD means that the feature was 14.35 metres above Mean Sea Level. However, most of the levels and measurements quoted represent approximate values, and are given to aid comparison: more detailed measurements can be found in the archive reports listed in the Bibliography.

Other terms used include *opus signinum*, a pink-red mortar mixture which provided a hard-wearing floor surface in Roman buildings; an *insula* is a square or rectangular building plot bounded by streets; pers comm refers to an unpublished personal communication to the author; while RCP and MCP are abbreviations for Roman or Medieval Ceramic Phase respectively, terms used by those concerned with the dating of pottery from the site (see Chapter 6).

Illustrations

Plates

1 Project team
2 Working conditions on site
3 Collecting the data
4 Washing the pots
5 Marking and measuring
6 Demolition of the medieval wall
7 Birth of Londinium
8 Mid-1st-century cremation urn
9 Unstable Basilica foundations
10 Hoofprints preserved
11 Roman mortar-mixing pit
12 Roman scaffolding
13 Roman piped water supply
14 Roman Basilica systematically demolished
15 Basilica foundations unsystematically quarried
16 2nd-century London street
17 Late 3rd- early 4th-century London street
18 Dark Age fields and a medieval market
19 15th-century foundations on 13th-century remains
20 Elizabethan Leadenhall
21 15th-century Garner: west face
22 15th-century Garner: east face
23 Air-dried mud bricks
24 Roman timber-framed building
25 Building the Basilica: first phase
26 Building the Basilica: second phase
27 Garner revealed in a 19th-century building
28 Internal ashlar face of the Garner
29 18th-century cellar built of stone from Garner
30 Reused moulded stones in the 18th-century cellar
31 Dismantling the cellar wall
32 18th-century engraving of the Garner's north facade
33 Fragments of a marble plaque

Figures

1 Plan of the City showing Leadenhall Court excavations, 1985–6
2 The Forum Study Area
3 Leadenhall Project Study Area
4 Leadenhall Court Excavations: position and numbering of trenches
5 Site development in the mid-1st century
6 1st-century cemetery and ditched enclosures
7 Ribbon development c.AD 70
8 Building 4 within its own yard
9 Urban expansion c.AD 75
10 Urban occupation c.AD 80
11 Urban expansion c.AD 85
12 Urban occupation c.AD 90
13 Inner city redevelopment c.AD 95
14 Work on new Basilica c.AD 100
15 London Basilica: second phase of construction
16 London Basilica early 2nd century
17 London Basilica 2nd century: rebuilding and a fire
18 London Basilica late 2nd to early 3rd century
19 Demolition of the Basilica c.4th century
20 A new town plan: Saxo-Norman buildings
21 13th-century Leadenhall
22 London with medieval features shown in relation to Leadenhall
23 15th-century Garner
24 Protracted demolition of Garner
25 Comparative plans of early Roman buildings 1–6
26 Comparative plans of early Roman buildings 7–10
27 Comparative plans of early Roman buildings 11–15
28 Comparative plans of early Roman buildings 16–23
29 Comparative plans of 2nd- to 4th-century buildings
30 Basilica development 2nd and 3rd centuries
31 Forum development 1st and 2nd centuries
32 Monumental gateway in the Forum

33	Reconstruction of the Forum and Basilica 2nd to 3rd century
34	Reconstructed elevations of the Forum and Basilica
35	Development of north-east corner of Basilica
36	Moulded brick manufactured for Basilica
37	Interior decoration in Basilica: wall-plaster fragments
38	Interior Decoration in Basilica: painted figure
39	Provincial basilicas and fora
40	Basilicas and fora in Romano-British towns
41	Romano-British towns
42	Elevations and profile of Garner west wall
43	15th-century moulded stones
44	15th-century Garner: north wall
45	Spiral stair detail and helix
46	Reconstruction of Garner north range with stair turret
47	Reconstructed ground plan of the Garner
48	Reconstructed north elevation of the Garner
49	Whittington Avenue excavations 1988–9

Tables

1	Field matrix represented by context numbers
2	Context groups from Area N
3	'Grouptrix': relationships of Groups in each Area and trench
4	Group Dating Table
5	Coin histogram
6	Roman pottery types and date range
7	Samian pottery forms and date range
8	Leadenhall Court site pottery forms and date range
9	Pottery types from the Basilica

Colour Plates

A	Living room: 1st-century artisan dwellings
B	Vernacular architecture in 1st-century London
C	Interior decoration in Building 6
D	1st-century fitted kitchen
E	Inside the 2nd-century Basilica
F	Construction level of the Basilica
G	2nd-century Basilica: masonry walls with brick corners
H	The Eastern Portico
I & J	Arcade piers in the redesigned Basilica
K, L, M & N	Wall plaster details
O	Life in the Basilica
P	Rebuilding after a Basilica fire

1 The patient discovery of London's past

Gustav Milne

Although much of the popular press would wish it otherwise, modern archaeological excavation is no more than measured, methodical earth-moving, with little room for sensational headlines. The point of real discovery comes not in the field, but in the assessment of the excavation record in libraries and laboratories, often years after the site work finished. This obvious and simple truth needs to be stressed, for it is not understood by most of the public or many television producers, who equate archaeology solely with excavation. The actual act of digging up and recording raw data is just the first of many stages in the protracted study of any archaeological site. In addition, for the study of a town like London, the information recovered from one site, once it has been assessed, must then be compared with results from neighbouring projects before lasting conclusions can be drawn: archaeological discovery is therefore an accumulative, patient process. Nevertheless, conclusions reached while sifting piles of plans and paperwork can often be dramatic, overturning former theories and extending our insights into the past in previously unconsidered ways. Archaeologists do make sensational discoveries, but not usually while digging.

The search for the Roman civic centre
(Figs 1, 2)

The discovery of the Roman civic centre in London is a prime example of this process, for the recovery of the relevant information incorporated in this report spans a period of more than a century. In c. AD 50, the Romans founded the settlement they called Londinium. The site chosen was an excellent one for communications and administration, for it was set on high ground on the north bank of the Thames, at a point where that wide tidal river could be bridged. The settlement prospered and by the time it was enclosed by the town wall in c. AD 200 it was the largest in the country. Roman London would have had an extensive civic centre with a forum, a market and meeting place; and a basilica, the offices of local government or 'town hall'. These would have been set within a framework of streets and other buildings such as shops and temples. However, no contemporary record of the civic centre survived and no fragment of the forum was visible above ground, unlike Lincoln or Wroxeter. If the London forum plan was to be recovered, it would only be revealed piecemeal, as redevelopment in the City fortuitously exposed parts of it.

The ancient remains which were uncovered in this way might well have escaped detection but for a series of outstanding achievements on the part of London's 19th- and early 20th-century rescue archaeologists. It is wholly thanks to them that the site of the Basilica was identified. Appropriately enough for this report, the earliest significant discoveries were made on and to the south of the Leadenhall Court site in the early 1880s, as the area was subjected to major redevelopment with the construction of the elegant Leadenhall Market buildings. The drawings and paintings produced by Henry Hodge and William Miller present an admirably detailed record of part of a major Roman building. Such is the quality of this record that, over a century later, we were able to

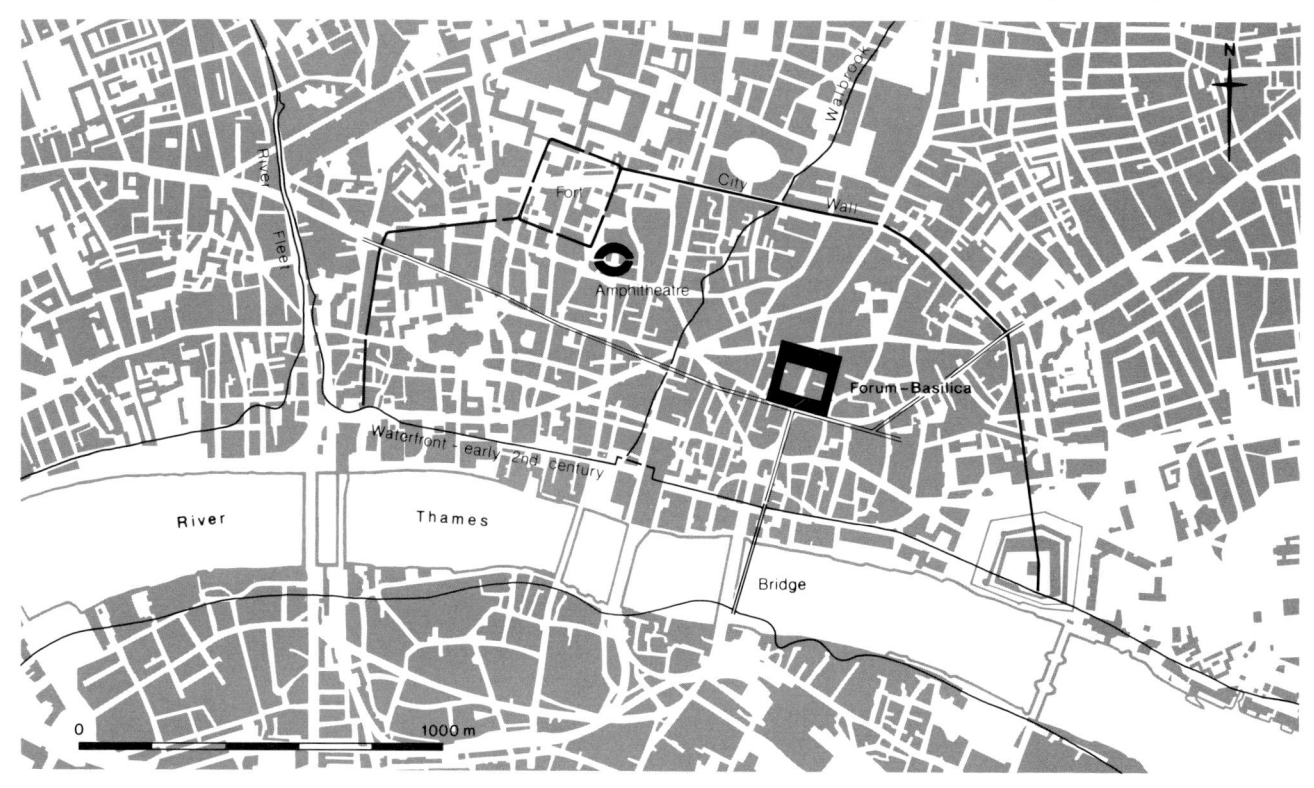

Fig 1 Plan of the present-day City showing position of 2nd- to 3rd-century Forum with Basilica to the north in relation to the early 3rd-century city wall and other Roman features. Scale 1: 20,000

incorporate much of it with confidence in the reconstructions considered in this report.

The chronology of subsequent excavations in the area of the forum has recently been published by Peter Marsden, who catalogues 20 sites investigated principally between 1930 and 1984 (Marsden 1987, 79–150). Those examined before 1976 were, in the main, observations rather than excavations, a reflection of the resources made available for archaeological work rather than of the potential importance of the sites themselves. To that list must be added Brian Philp's major site at 168–170 Fenchurch Street in 1968–9, one of the first large-scale rescue excavations in the City (Philp 1977), a watching brief at 1 Gracechurch Street in 1984, the Leadenhall Court project of 1985–6 (the substance of this book), and the Whittington Avenue site of 1988–9 (Appendix A). How this accumulating body of data has been interpreted, developed and reinterpreted is of some interest, as a brief summary of the published data shows.

The walls which Hodge and Miller drew with such objective precision in the 1880s were not identified as part of the Basilica until 40 years later (Lethaby 1923). In 1928, Dr Mortimer Wheeler accepted that interpretation and suggested it had been rebuilt at least once, but had no evidence to date the building's construction closely (RCHM 1928). Just two years later Gerald Dunning recovered pottery from beneath the western end of the Basilica, none of which he thought need be later than *c*.AD 90 (Dunning 1931). The implication was that the Basilica itself was erected in *c*.AD 100. By 1965, Ralph Merrifield brought together much new material, and was able to show that the Leadenhall Basilica was not the first major building in the area since it was preceded by a substantial masonry complex just to the south. It was

OPPOSITE
Fig 2 A century of discoveries in the Forum Study Area: plan showing relationship of:
1 *Leadenhall Court site 1985–6 to other excavations referred to in this report:* **2** *Whittington Avenue 1988–9 (see Appendix A);*
3 *Leadenhall Market 1881–2;* **4** *83–87 Gracechurch Street 1934;*
5 *77–79 Gracechurch Street 1983–4;* **6** *15–18 Lime Street 1932;*
7 *20–21 Lime Street 1990;* **8** *22 Lime Street 1969;*
9 *St Dionis, Backchurch 1878;* **10** *160–62 Fenchurch Street 1976;* **11** *168–170 Fenchurch Street 1968–9;* **12** *Gracechurch Street shaft 1978;* **13** *Gracechurch Street tunnel 1978;*
14 *Lombard Street 1933;* **15** *30–32 Lombard Street 1962;*
16 *54–58 Lombard Street 1960;* **17** *All Hallows, Lombard Street 1939;* **18** *17–19 Gracechurch Street 1934–5;* **19** *19–21 Birchin Lane 1935;* **20** *St Michael's Alley 1933;* **21** *4 Castle Court 1976;* **22** *3–6 Gracechurch Street 1964–6;* **23** *1 Gracechurch Street 1984;* **24** *52 Cornhill 1930;* **25** *66–73 Cornhill 1894–7, 1959, 1981–2. Scale 1: 1,250*

The patient discovery of London's past 3

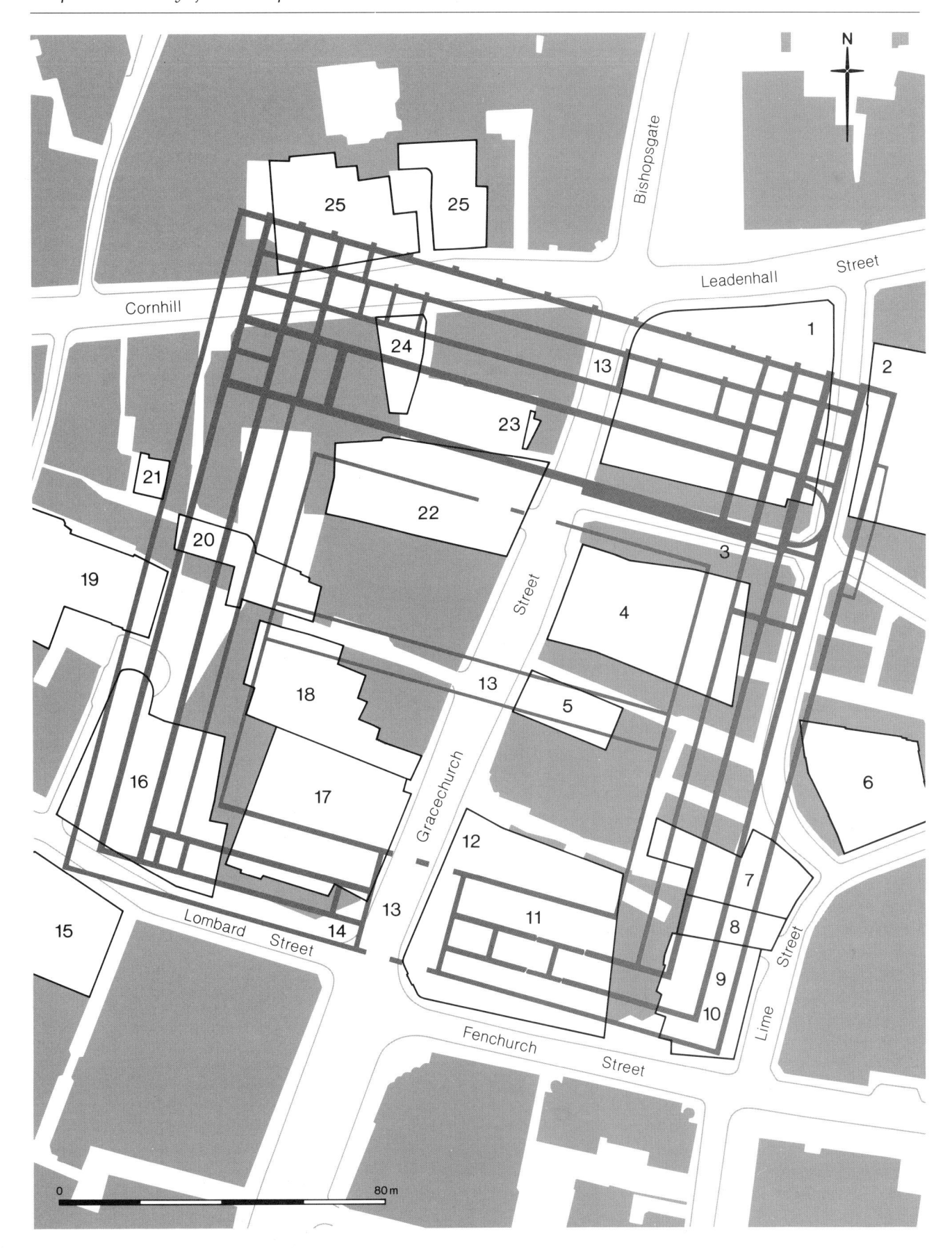

Brian Philp's pioneering work at the end of that decade which provided a series of dates for the development of the civic centre. He argued that the earlier building, which he termed the 'Proto-forum', was erected after the Boudiccan revolt of AD 60, but was demolished between AD 90 and 100, after which the southern range of the much larger forum was built on the site (Philp 1977). Marsden accepted the main thrust of these interpretations, but saw the earlier complex as a forum and basilica in its own right, replaced by the larger version. Initially he argued for a construction date of post *c.*AD 120 for the second Basilica (Marsden 1978), but subsequently agreed with the date of *c.*AD 100 as suggested by Philp (Marsden 1987). To sum up: one hundred years after the initial discovery of the Basilica, it had been established that the first phase of the civic centre was erected in *c.*AD 70 and that it was greatly enlarged in *c.*AD 100, but the exact form and the ultimate fate of that structure, the most important building in Roman London, was still unknown.

The Leadenhall Court project 1983–1990
(Figs 3, 4)

Fortunately, the most recent excavations have at last provided some surprising answers to the crucial questions just posed. However, it must be stressed that the answers were not suddenly revealed during the dig itself, but had to wait until the field records had been assessed and assimilated. Part of this vital work, which is normally invisible to the press and the public, is described in Chapters 5 and 6. As for the collection of the data upon which the conclusions would rest, that too was a long drawn-out process. Serious negotiations between the developers, Legal & General Assurance Company, and the Museum of London began in 1983, but the first excavations did not take place until January 1985. These were confined to five small trenches cut in the basement of a standing building at 91–92 Gracechurch Street (Area D). The work took less than two months, using a team of six highly experienced archaeologists (Pls 2 and 3). The results revealed the richness of the Leadenhall Court site, for they proved to the satisfaction of the Museum, English Heritage and the developers that substantial remains of the Basilica, earlier Roman buildings and the later medieval market had all survived. Clearly, a major archaeological investigation had to be mounted to record the ancient levels

Pl 2 Working conditions: much of the excavation was conducted in deep holes below the basements of standing buildings prior to demolition. (Area D, February 1985)

Pl 3 Collecting the data: every layer was planned, levelled and described before excavation. Here an opus signinum *floor in the Basilica is being measured. (Area D)*

The patient discovery of London's past

before their destruction in the proposed development. Through the good offices of their director, Jeremy Edwards, Legal & General agreed to give generous support in cash and kind to the project, to which English Heritage also promised major contributions. Armed with all this information, the next phase of excavations could now be planned.

The Museum wanted as large an open area as possible to ensure that every part of the site was at least partially examined. The developers, while wishing to co-operate fully, naturally wanted minimal disruption to their demolition and construction programme. A compromise was reached in which we

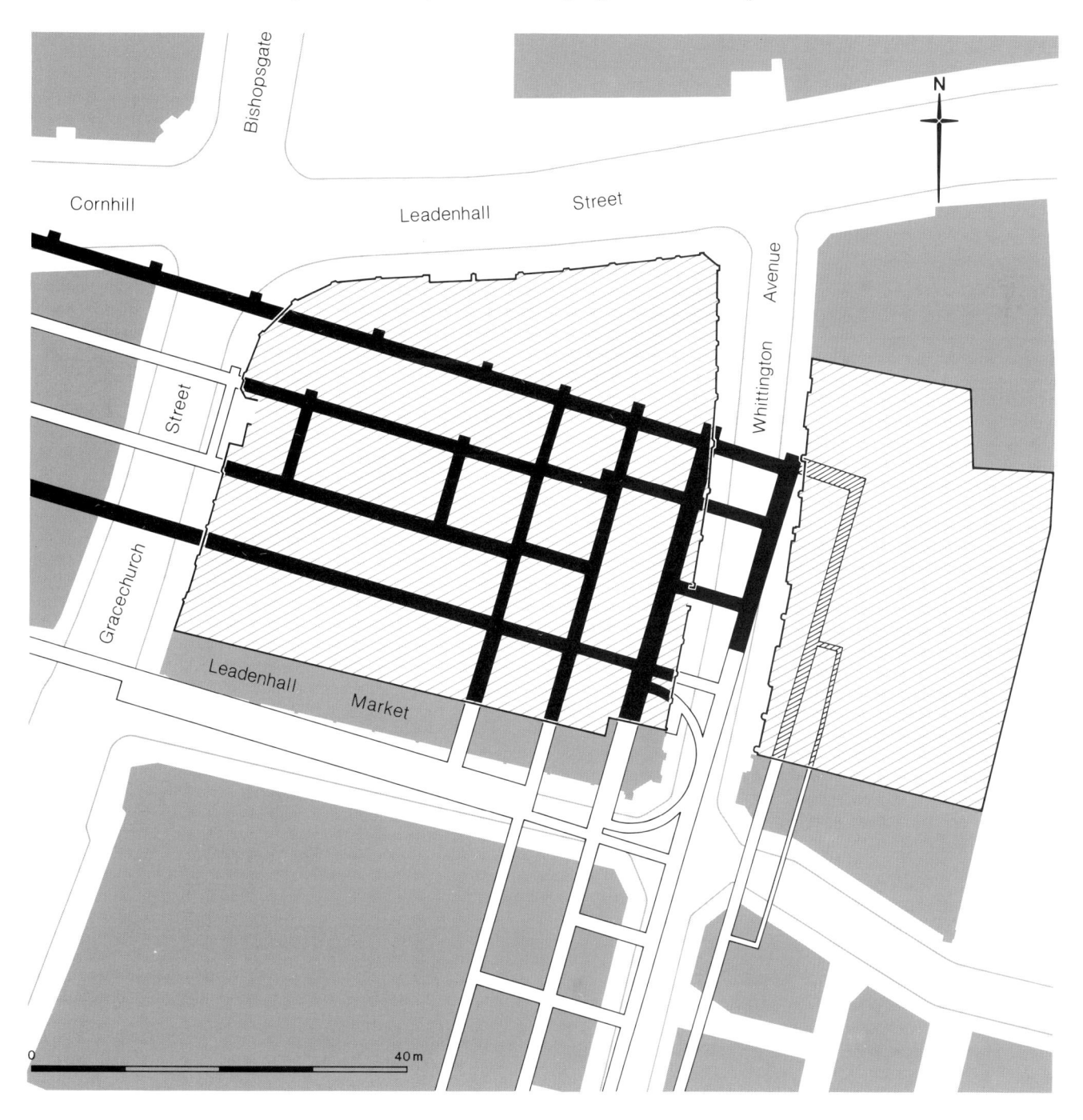

Fig 3 Integrating the results: plan of the Leadenhall Project Study Area showing position of Roman Basilica walls found or conjectured on three adjacent sites. Those found or conjectured from the Leadenhall Court excavations (code LCT84; 1 on Fig 2) marked in black; those from the Whittington Avenue site (code WIV88; 2 on Fig 2) shown hatched; the walls recorded by Henry Hodge and William Miller (3 on Fig 2) shown with open lines

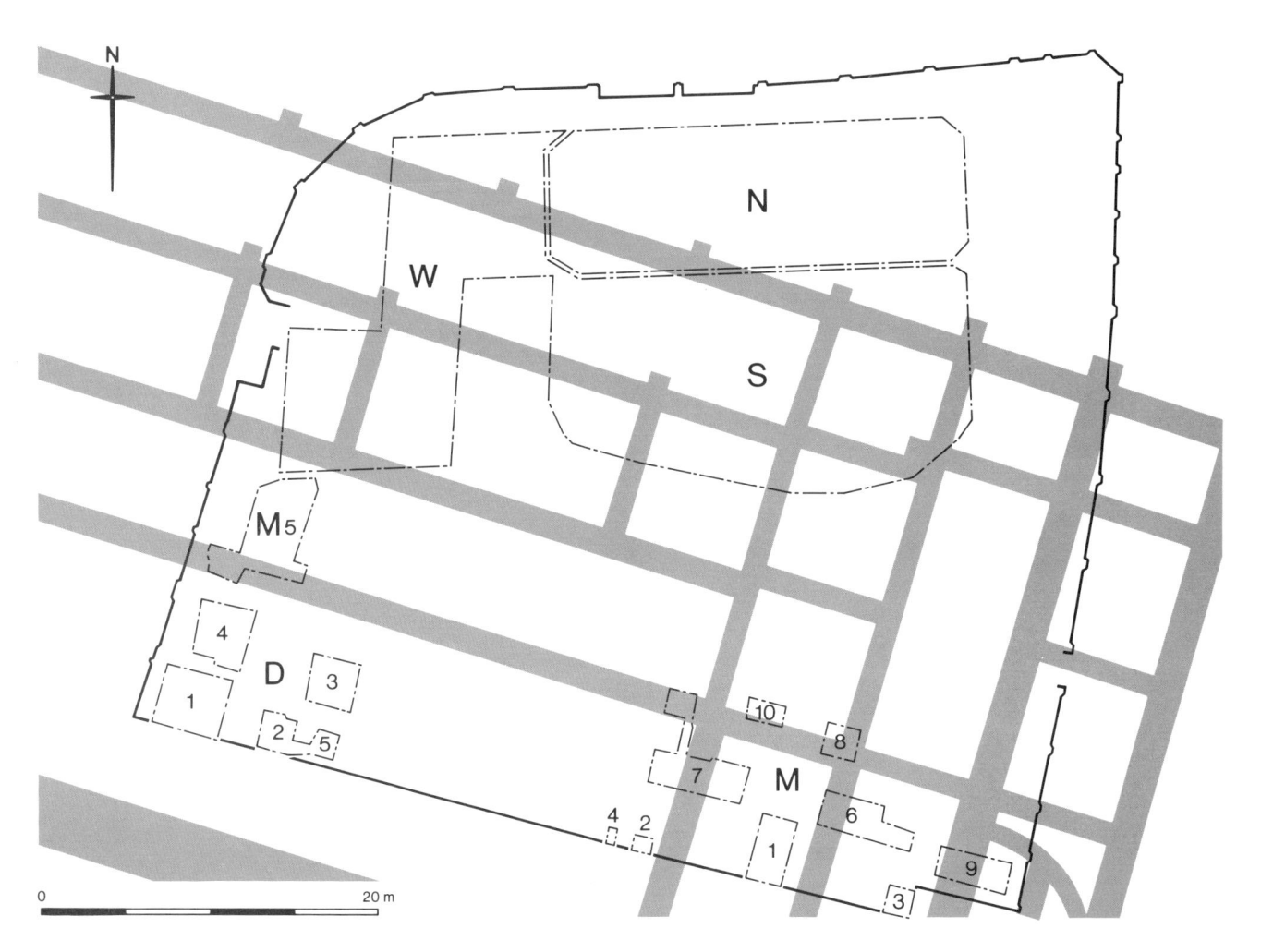

*Fig 4 Leadenhall Court excavations: plan showing position and numbering of trenches excavated under controlled conditions seen in relation to the total area of the redevelopment. The northern, southern and western open area excavations (Areas N, S and W) are labelled N, S and W, while the numbered trenches were dug in the basements of standing buildings: Dominion House (Area D) and the Metal Exchange (Area M). The Roman walls observed elsewhere on the site could only be recorded during the contractor's earth-moving operations in December 1986. Nevertheless, a detailed picture of the 2nd- to 3rd-century Roman Basilica was obtained, and its outline is shown in grey.
Scale 1: 400*

mounted a series of excavations programmed around the demolition schedule. However, this was determined by the speed with which tenants moved out, a factor beyond the control of both the Museum and the developers. As a direct consequence, the programme and scale of our excavations was ultimately determined not by academic criteria, but by the presence or absence of occupants in the 20 discrete properties which formerly occupied the site.

Three large open areas were ultimately excavated after some of the properties were cleared and demolished (Col Pl G), Area N from November 1985 to September 1986, Area W from May 1986 for five months, and Area S from June of that year for four months (Col Pl F). By that date, a three-man team had dug a series of trenches in the basements of the Metal Exchange Buildings to the south (Area M) which were not demolished until after the Museum team left the site in September. During the summer of that year, there were some forty professional archaeologists working on the site, supported by the finds processing team (Pls 4 and 5) and a loyal brigade of volunteers. The Museum team worked a full five-day week, but the site was also open on Sundays, when the City of London Archaeological Society volunteer group turned out in force. During December 1986, a small Museum team returned to the cleared site to monitor the contractor's earth-moving operations. Two large Poclain 190s were working in tandem, lowering the ground surface for the insertion of the new basement, the floor of which lay well below the level of the earliest Roman features. As far as

The patient discovery of London's past

LEFT
Pl 4   Washing the pots: some 4,000 bags of pottery were collected on site; everything had to be washed in this dark basement before it could be examined and dated

ABOVE
Pl 5   Marking and measuring: after washing, the finds were labelled prior to careful study

BELOW
Pl 6   Rescue archaeology: empty office buildings and an upstanding fragment of the 15th-century Leadenhall Garner wall (L) being demolished in October 1986. No sooner had the Museum team withdrawn from the site (Areas N, W and S) than redevelopment began with a vengeance. What had not been recorded then was lost forever

archaeological field work was concerned, it was all over by Christmas (Pl 6).

But then the real work began. The mountains of pottery and other artefacts had to be processed and the plans and written record of nearly 6,000 archaeological features had to be assessed. It took two years of intermittent excavation and observation to collect the raw data, amounting to over 200 person-months work at a cost of about £250,000. A further four years of even more intermittent work by finds staff, environmentalists and site supervisors, some 90 person-months in total, were required to compile the relevant archive reports upon which this study is based. The research, writing, illustrating and editing needed to complete this book represents another 48 person-months work, and was not completed until April 1991. This delay can be partially explained by the fact that several members of the post-excavation team were called upon to work on other urgent rescue projects in the City during this period, such as the sites of Whittington Avenue (Appendix A) and Thames Exchange (Milne & Goodburn 1990), and on other pressing publication projects with imminent deadlines (e.g. Brigham 1990b; Horsman et al. 1988). Nevertheless, by March 1990 the archive reports for the Leadenhall Court project were completed and a series of academic papers written (Samuel 1989, Milne & Wootton 1990; Brigham 1990a), some five years after the first exploratory trench had revealed the remarkable potential of the site. Although learning about London is clearly a slow process, the results are, it is suggested, well worth waiting for.

From fields to Forum

ROMAN DEVELOPMENTS AT LEADENHALL AD 50–450

Chrissie Milne, Gustav Milne and Trevor Brigham

Redevelopment in the City is not a modern problem. London has seen much rebuilding over the last 2,000 years, the scale of such projects varying as much as the motivation behind them. Individual buildings were continually modified by their owners or their occupiers as much in the Roman period as they would be today. At the other end of the scale, whole streets have been torn down and replaced during major projects, perhaps as a result of a catastrophic fire, as part of new, prestigious civic schemes, or as a private landlord bought up several neighbouring properties to erect a larger building. The archaeologists working on the Leadenhall Court site recorded a long sequence of building development stretching back to the foundation of the City in AD 50. It is that material which is summarised in the next three chapters. The evidence for many differing types of redevelopment will be shown, only a few of which lasted for more than a century without further major change. The story includes the rise and fall of domestic dwellings (Milne & Wootton 1990), a Roman Basilica (Brigham 1990a), a Saxon town and a major medieval market (Samuel 1989). But it began inauspiciously in a field on top of a wooded hill which rose steeply beside the untamed Thames.

AD 50–70/75: City limits
(Figs 5–8)

Following the Roman invasion of AD 43, the lines of the rich and ancient British landscape were gradually but comprehensively redrawn. New landowners established new estates, forests were cleared, marshland drained; forts were built and towns developed around a network of roads driven across the country. The lowest north–south crossing over the Thames in the 40s was made in the Westminster area, but by the 50s a second crossing was established just downstream, taking advantage of the islands on the south bank and the well-drained high ground on the northern side. This line is close to that occupied by modern-day London Bridge. A settlement naturally developed around this focal point where major river and land routes met. Although relatively unplanned, it prospered none the less, and became known to the Romans as Londinium.

The earliest surviving documentary reference to that town appears in a description of the Boudiccan Revolt of AD 60. Londinium is referred to in this period as 'a place not indeed distinguished by the title of *Colonia*': that is to say, although it was a settlement of some substance, it did not have the self-governing status which it subsequently acquired. Archaeological research has revealed how extensive the area of contemporary occupation was, for it is all too clearly marked by readily identifiable layers of burnt debris, the graphic evidence of the destruction wrought by the aggrieved British. Such deposits were not encountered on the Leadenhall Court site, which must therefore have lain outside the limits of that first unplanned town. However, there was plenty of evidence to show that the northern boundary of the earliest settlement must have lain immediately to the south of the excavations, and that the town expanded northwards from that point within a generation after the revolt.

Precise details of the layout and use of our site

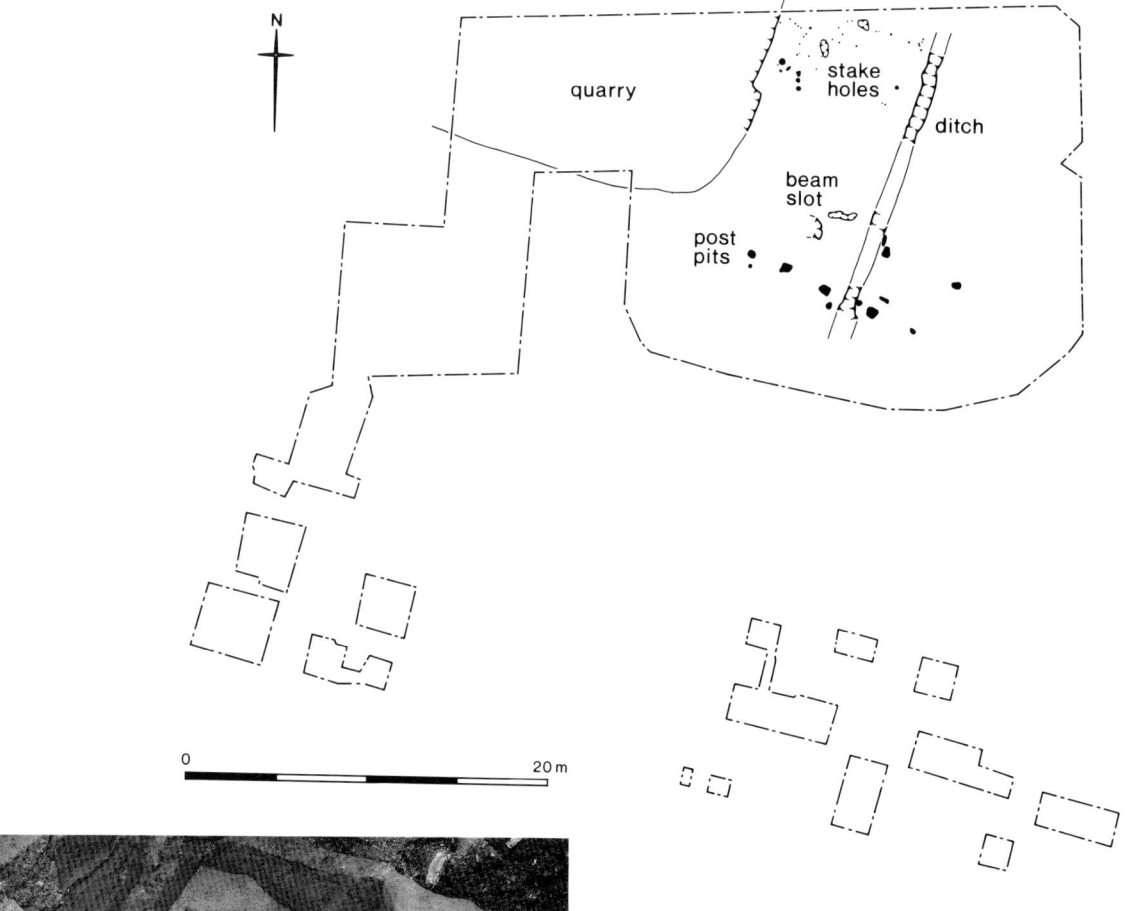

ABOVE
Fig 5   Inauspicious beginnings: plan showing site development in mid-1st century, with ditch and Brickearth quarry. Scale 1: 400

LEFT
Pl 7   Birth of Londinium: irregular holes cut into natural Brickearth (on which 10x100mm scale rests) mark the position of trees and shrubs which the Romans had to dig up before the new settlement could be built. (Area W)

before AD 50 are difficult to establish, for the area had been comprehensively deturfed and levelled by the Romans prior to their subsequent operations. Those actions unfortunately removed the topsoil in which much of the evidence for any former fields and farms would have lain. Among the earliest features which were recorded were the truncated bases of a scatter of stake holes, two shallow beam slots and a line of more substantial post pits which represented a fence line or similar boundary (Fig 5). The majority, perhaps all, of these features are of Roman date: only the stake holes may represent earlier occupation, but there is little evidence to support the suggestion.

The next phase of activity saw the cutting of a series of ditches marking subdivisions of the land.

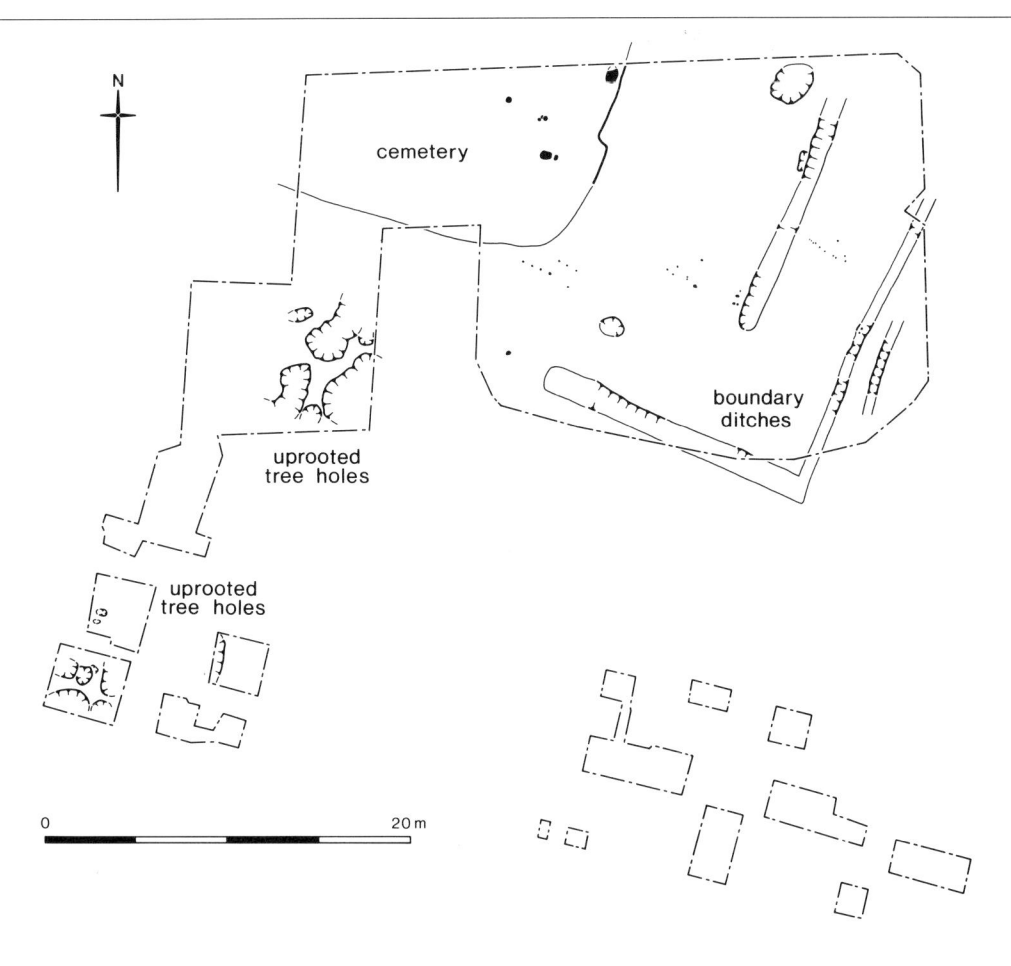

ABOVE
Fig 6 Beyond the town boundary: plan showing site development in mid-1st century, with small cremation cemetery and ditched enclosures. Scale 1: 400

BELOW
Pl 8 Remains of the first Londoners: the 10x10mm scale lies next to a mid-1st-century cremation urn, set into a backfilled quarry. The neck of the pot had been deliberately broken off: was this small cemetery slighted during the Boudiccan Revolt in AD 60? (Area N)

One of the east–west ditches was closely aligned on the post-built fence line mentioned above, on an alignment which is traceable in the topography of the area for the next half-century. This suggests that that particular boundary may represent one of the major land subdivisions of the early settlement. Within the ditched enclosure in the north–west corner of the site was a large quarry dug to extract the natural Brickearth, a substance (as its name suggests) used extensively for building material in the Roman period. The hole was subsequently left open and slowly began to silt up.

A new use was then found for it as part of a small cemetery (Fig 6 and Pl 8). At least five pottery vessels were found, of which one was still *in situ*, set vertically in the ground, and containing burnt bone. It was a shallow-necked jar in a micaceous sand-tempered fabric, of a type known from other sites in London, and dating to the late AD 50s. The neck and rim had been broken off, but the other pots had been even more thoroughly disturbed. It is possible that two small holes might mark the position of more vessels, which rather than just being broken had been dug up. Taken together, it seems that a small

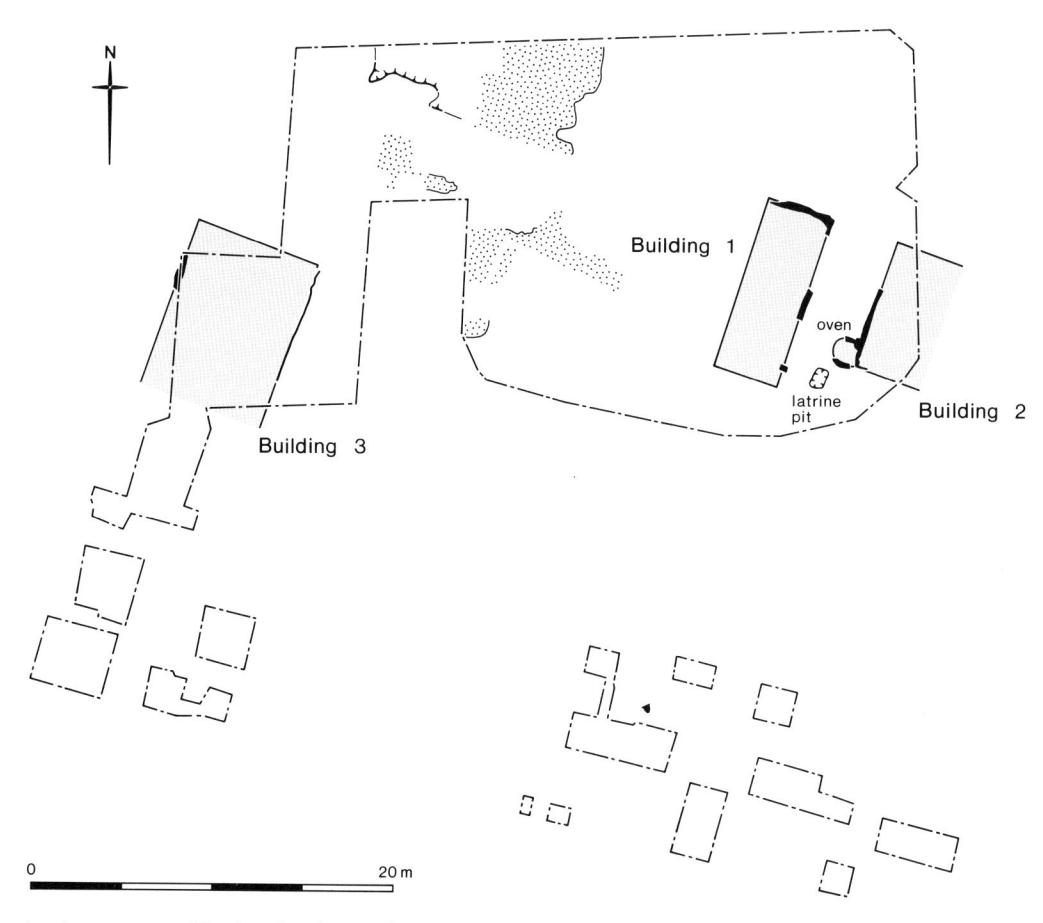

Fig 7 Ribbon development c.AD 70: plan showing settlement encroaching over the former extra-mural area with introduction of Buildings 1, 2 and 3 set in a yard. Middens shown stippled. Scale 1: 400

cemetery had been established here in the mid-1st century, and that it had subsequently been slighted. Whether this action took place during or after the Boudiccan Revolt is not possible to confirm or deny. What is certain is that, by the AD 60s, Londinium had not expanded that far north, since by Roman law cemeteries occupied positions outside the limits of urban settlement, although they often lay close to main roads.

Signs that the settlement was encroaching upon the area now become apparent (Fig 7). First, a number of trees or shrubs were uprooted during general clearance, and the resulting irregular holes infilled (Pl 7). Finds recovered from these tree holes included an iron mount, possibly part of a cart fitting. An extensive slab of brickearth was then spread over much of the site, to prepare the ground for building. Quantities of domestic refuse were dumped over the disused cemetery, perhaps by the occupants of the buildings which had been newly erected in the vicinity. Two such structures, Buildings 1 and 2, were recorded on the east side of the site, their wall lines marked by shallow beam slots, and a small latrine pit lay between them. Remains of a third building (Building 3) were found to the south of the infilled cemetery.

Shortly after Building 1 was demolished, a quarry some 5m in diameter was dug to extract Brickearth, presumably for Building 4 which was then erected to the south (Fig 8). This building was aligned east-west while to the north were wells and a metalled surface which partially sealed the now infilled quarry. The latter had been surrounded by a fence, the line of which was defined by post holes. It is noteworthy that the building development was focused on the east side of the site, and that evidence of horticultural activity next to a main road was recorded on contemporary levels on the Whittington Avenue site (Appendix A) just beyond the eastern limit of our excavation. It is suggested that Buildings 1 to 4 represent widely-spaced ribbon development set back from that main road leading north from the more densely occupied centre of the early Roman settlement.

From fields to Forum

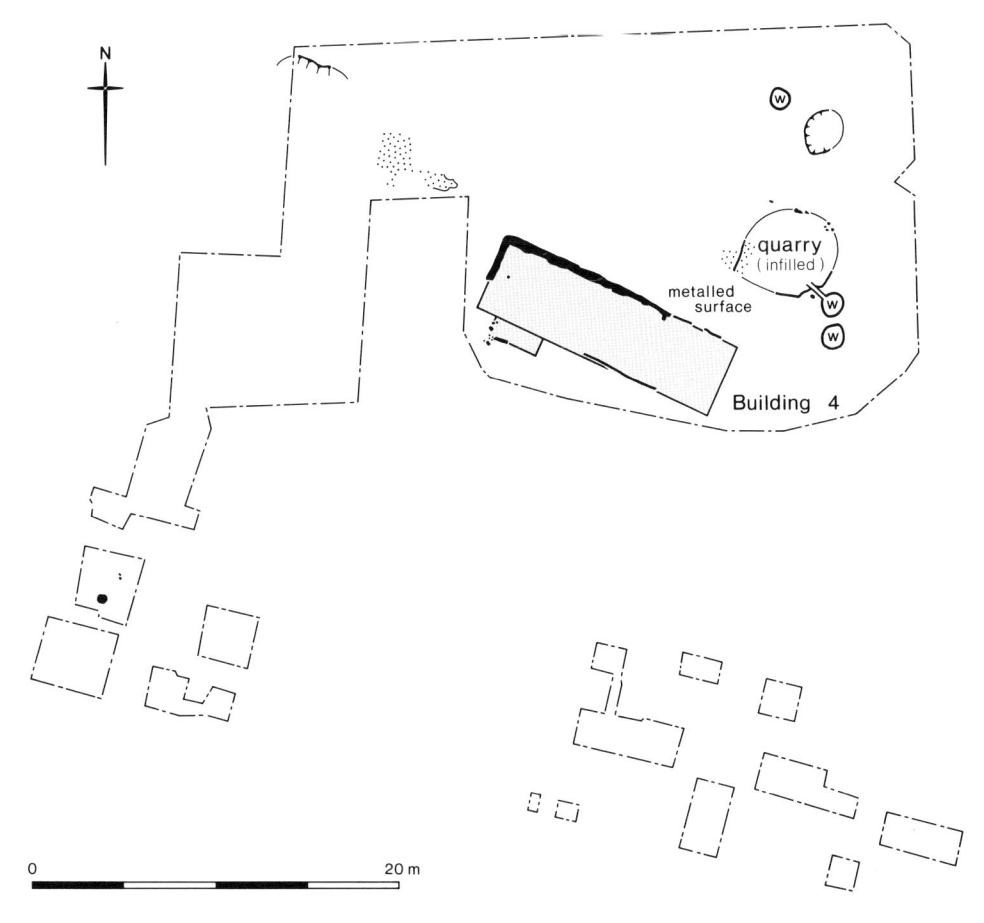

Fig 8 Building 4 within its own yard: Middens shown stippled. W = well. Scale 1: 400

AD 70/75–80/85: The settlement expands
(Figs 9–11)

The major urban development of c.AD 75 established a more formal layout of closely-spaced houses, although it was partially based on alignments set out in the previous phases. The focus of this new plan now faced west; that is to say that the frontage of the new buildings was laid out along the line of the principal north–south road which lay beyond the western limit of excavation, beneath modern Gracechurch Street. This street ran directly north from the waterfront to the forum, the first phase of which was also constructed c.AD 75 (Marsden 1987). A radical replanning had obviously taken place in this part of Londinium, involving the insula which lay immediately north of the town's first basilica. The construction of Roman London's civic centre presumably marks the town's elevation to the status of a self-governing *municipium*. As might be expected, this occasion was marked by major changes in much of the town, with the introduction of public buildings such as bath-houses (Spence & Grew 1989, 10–11) and harbour facilities (Milne 1985), together with substantial developments in domestic accommodation. The decade from c.AD 70 to 80 saw Londinium acquire the appearance and attributes of a major town.

Of the new buildings examined on the Leadenhall Court site (see Chapter 7), Building 6 seems to have been the largest (Fig 9). Its walls were founded on squared timber base-plates and enclosed several interconnecting rooms. By contrast, Buildings 5, 7, 8, 9 and 11 were strip buildings comprising a simpler arrangement of square rooms aligned one behind the other. Access to the rooms was via one of the narrow gravel alleyways which ran from the principal thoroughfare in the west to the back-yards in the east. The area to the rear of the buildings contained single-roomed outhouses, Buildings 13 and 14, and wells, latrine pits and the remains of several refuse middens.

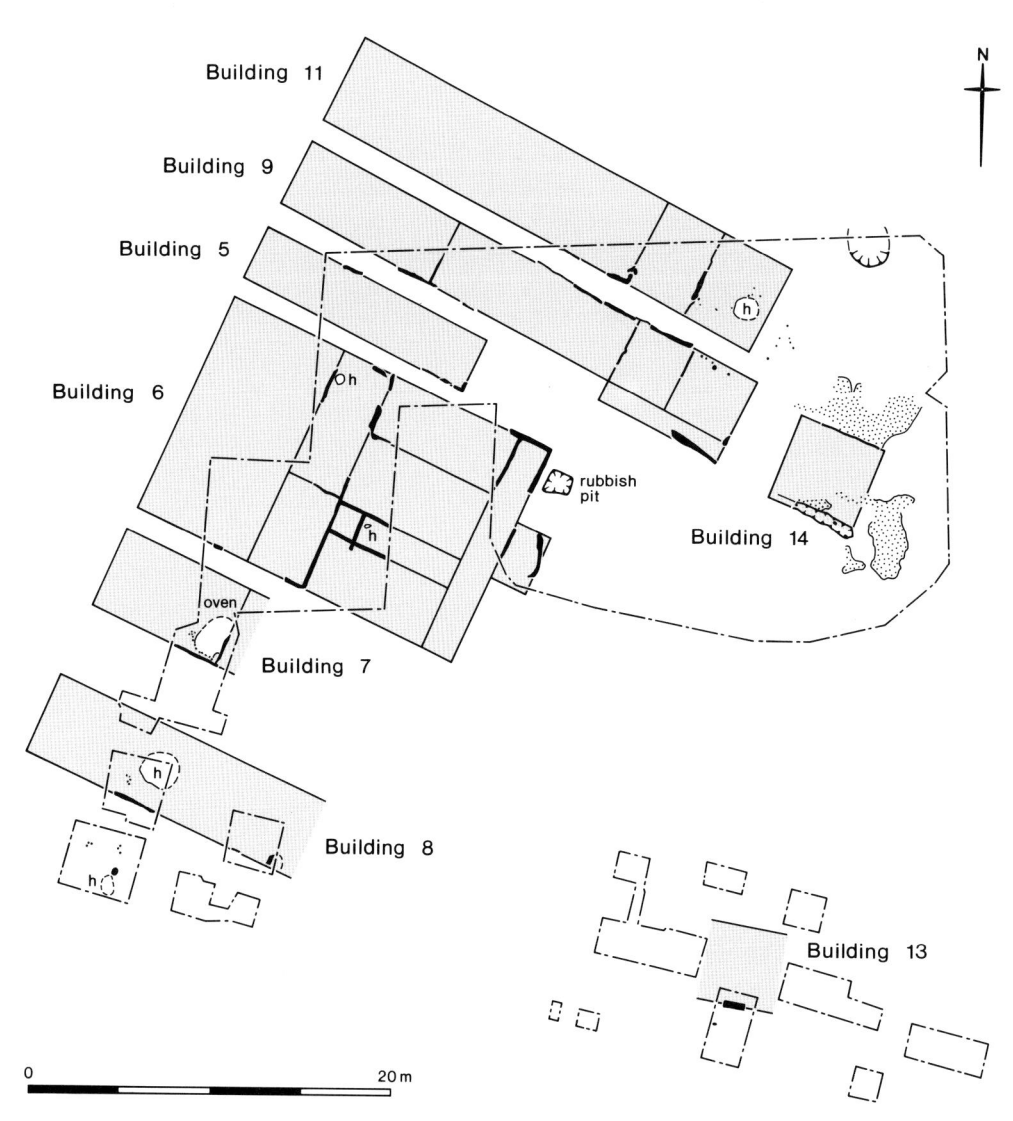

Fig 9 Urban expansion c.AD 75: a new insula laid out with buildings fronting a street just beyond the western limits of excavation. Note middens (stippled) and wells in backyard areas. h = hearth. Scale 1: 400

It is possible to gain some insight into the general lifestyle and status of the occupants of the early Roman buildings recorded on this site by studying the material which they threw out on to the middens. A detailed discussion of the finds and faunal evidence is being prepared (London and Middlesex Archaeological Society Special Paper), and the following summary indicates the potential of such a study. Among the items recovered were quantities of pottery, the majority of which were cooking jars and bowls, flagons and mortaria used for grinding the coarse cereals. Samian tableware, a number of beakers and some oil lamps including one with a winged female figure were also found, together with various Mediterranean amphora fragments from vessels used to store olive oil, fish sauces, dates and wine. The general domestic nature of the assemblage was also evident in the non-ceramic finds. A roughly-worked bone spoon, a tumbler lock slide key, stone mortars and a shale tray were among the items retrieved, together with over 80 fragments of glass representing several vessels including a fine facet-cut beaker. Items of personal adornment were also found, such as a plain copper alloy finger ring, a shale bracelet, a melon bead and spatula fragments. In addition there were several brooches, two of the simple 'Colchester' type and one a more elaborate enamelled 'sawfish' type.

Study of the bones from the middens suggests that beef was of primary importance to the diet of the local inhabitants, followed by pork, mutton and some poultry. Some bones of red and roe deer as well as hare were present, showing that hunting provided

From fields to Forum

some of Roman London's needs. Although horse and dog bones were found, they were probably not part of the diet. The relative paucity of finds from around the house sites may be contrasted with the much larger assemblages of discarded material recovered from the Roman waterfront: presumably much of the midden material was regularly carted away from the occupation areas, perhaps as part of a civic refuse disposal service.

The general lines of the building development were retained for the next 15 to 20 years, although several of the buildings were modified or replaced during that period (Figs 10 and 11 and Col Pl A). Building 9 was demolished and the southern wall of its replacement, Building 10, encroached over the adjacent alley: this access route was now just 1m wide. To the north, Building 12 was built over the site

of Building 11, with a deep latrine pit at its north–east corner. New outhouses, Buildings 16 and 21, were built in the yards behind the street frontage. A large oven was added to the rear of Building 6, just north of which an annexe was extended over the earlier yard. Evidence for an unusual religious practice was discovered here, for the remains of an entire burnt sheep had been buried in a basket directly below the first surface of this new structure. Such ritual deposits have been found elsewhere in Roman London: a young dog had been carefully buried beneath the foundations of a 2nd-century building on the GPO site in Newgate Street (Merrifield 1987, 52–3) for example. At Leadenhall Court, Buildings 7 and 8 were demolished and subsequently replaced by Buildings 17 and 18, which both had large hearths or ovens. Evidence for another hearth was recorded in the south–west of the site, associated with Building 19. Unusual finds from that building were an imported Gaulish figurine and a copper alloy military belt plate with repoussé work depicting a cavalryman spearing

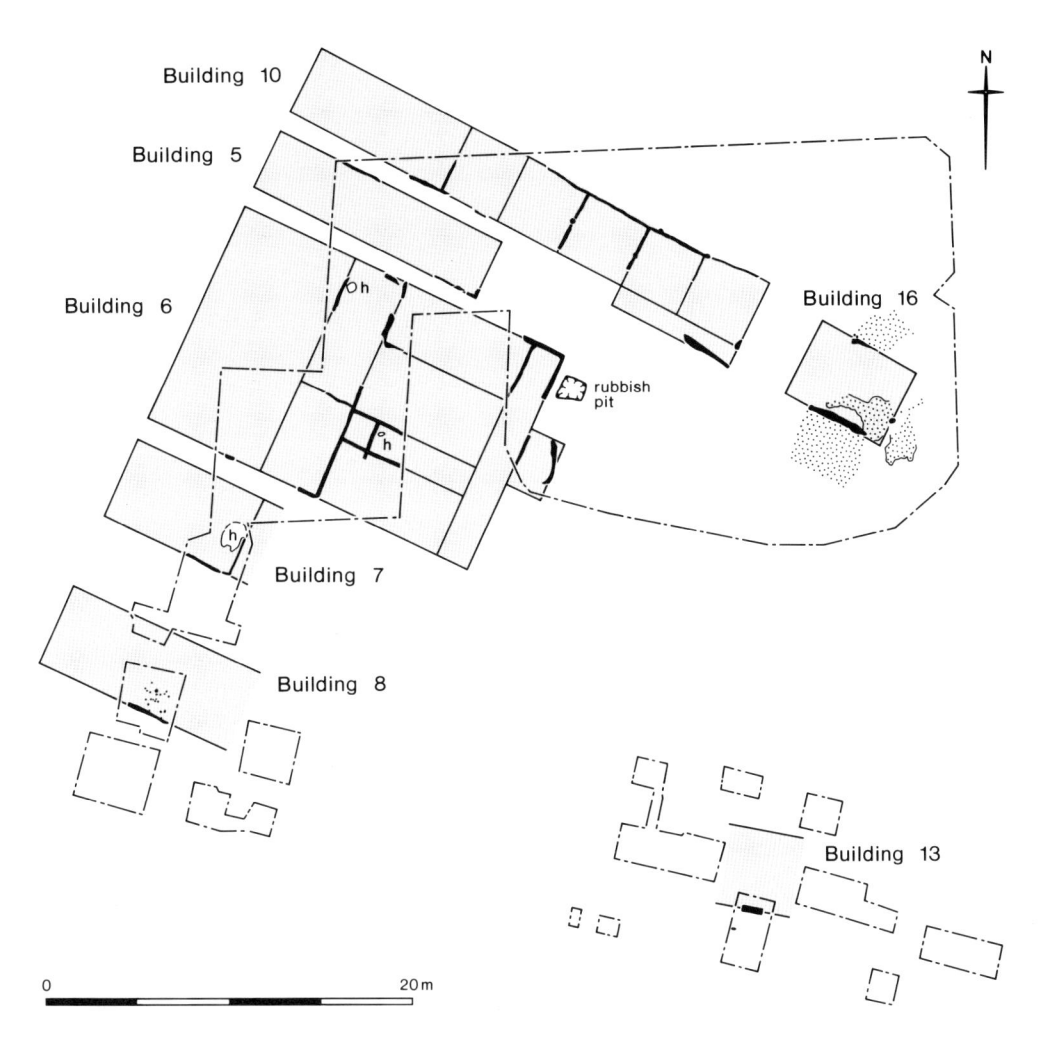

Fig 10 Urban occupation c.AD 80: several of the brickearth and timber buildings shown in Fig 9 repaired or replaced by the buildings shown here. Middens shown stippled. h = hearth. Scale 1: 400

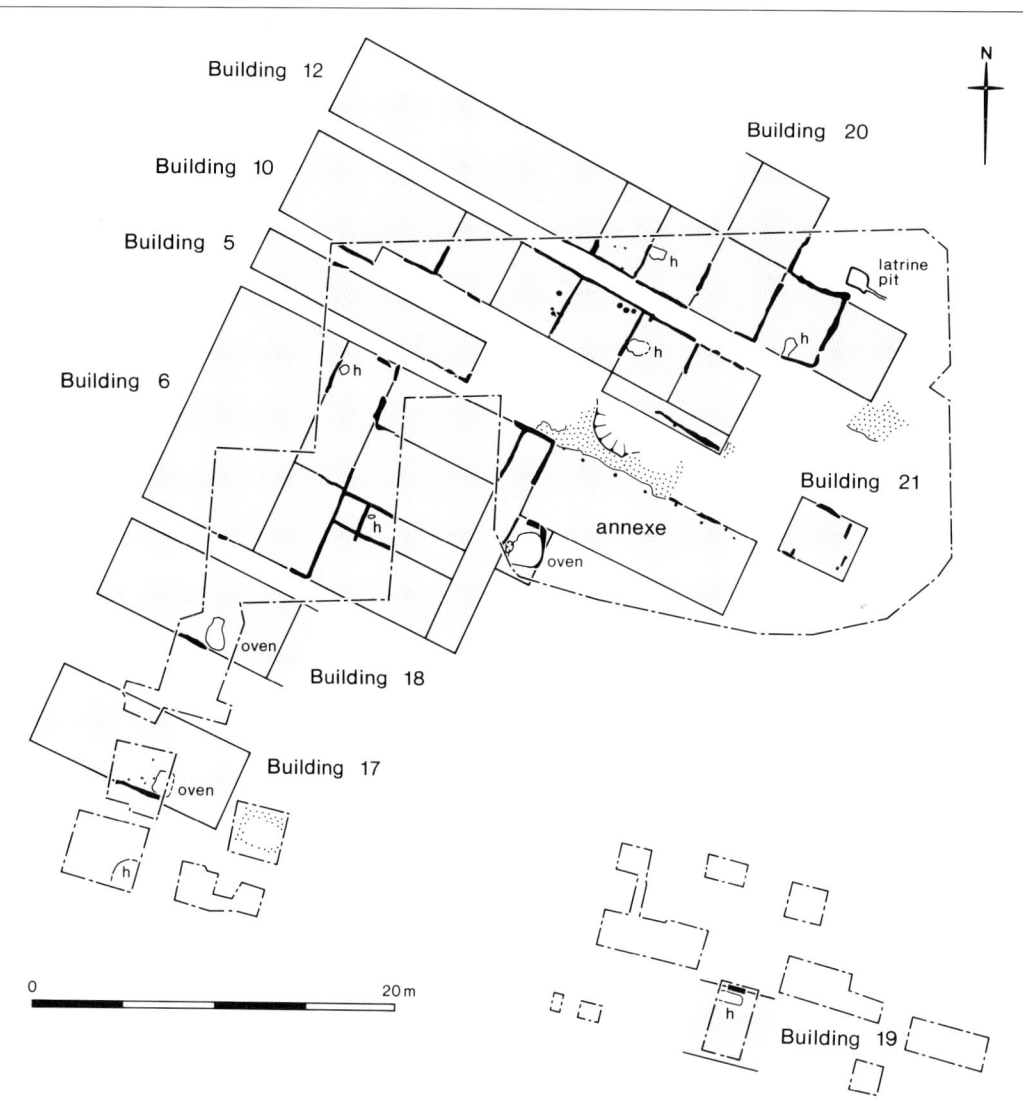

Fig 11 Further developments within the insula c.AD 85: cf. Figs 9 and 10. h = hearth. Scale 1: 400

a fallen enemy, a familiar subject in Roman art. This is one of the surprisingly few objects recovered from the site which had military associations.

AD 80/85–100: Contraction and clearance *(Figs 12, 13)*

The pace of expansion in this area was suddenly arrested at the end of the 1st century. First, the outhouse Building 21 was replaced by Building 22, the annexe on Building 6 was dismantled, and the eastern end of Building 12 contracted with midden deposits accumulating over the demolished rooms. Among the finds from those deposits was part of a lead strip, possibly a curse, inscribed with the name 'Saturninus', a number of mould-blown chariot or gladiator cups, and a well-preserved circular hand mirror.

The next phase saw a more dramatic change with the clearance of Buildings 6, 17, 18 and 19 (Fig 13). The reasons for this reversal in fortunes may be seen in the succeeding development, for it is now clear that the entire insula was in the process of being deliberately emptied of inhabitants and then demolished. The land was now required for an extension to the civic centre, the forum and basilica complex. The next major alteration in the town plan was about to be imposed upon the site, just 30 years after the establishment of the original insula. It is not certain exactly what powers of compulsory purchase or eviction the town council had, but they were clearly effective.

From fields to Forum 17

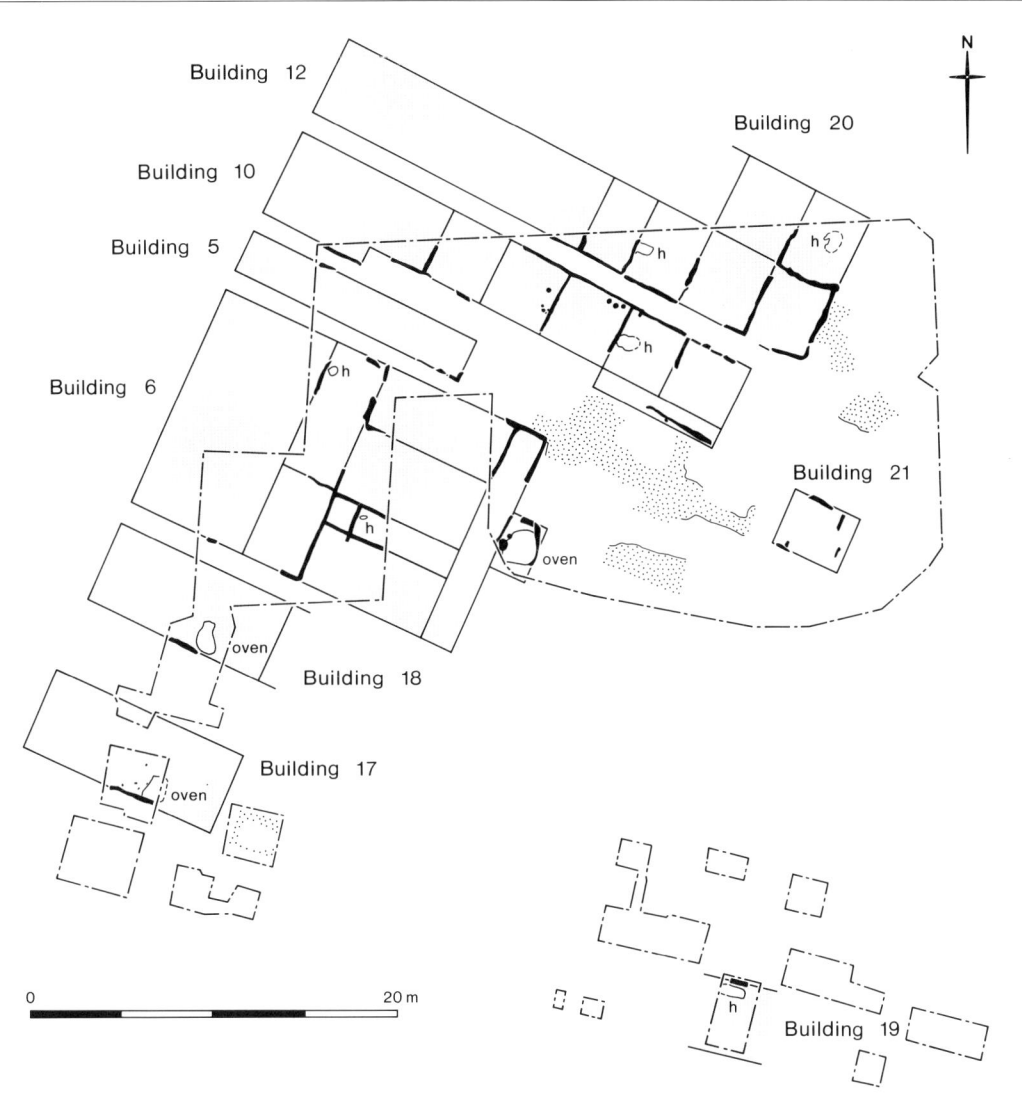

Fig 12 Contraction c.AD 90: buildings 6 and 12 have contracted: cf. Figs 10 and 11. h = hearth. Scale 1: 400

AD 85/90–120+: A new civic centre is built *(Figs 14–16)*

Once those buildings had been demolished, the preparation of the site began. The structures which survived in the north of the area (Buildings 5, 10, 12) were modified, and the new Buildings 15 and 23 erected just to the south and east. This new arrangement would have housed the construction workers, providing site huts, canteens and storerooms, all the paraphernalia to be expected on any major long-term civic building project. To the south and east, the ground was cleared and levelled, and deep foundation trenches dug. Into these were poured ragstone and mortar, the latter prepared in special mortar-mixing pits such as the one dug in the yard surrounded by Buildings 10 and 15. To the east, between the pit and the foundations, was a spread of ragstone chippings, detritus from the construction programme. Work on the new, enlarged Basilica had begun.

This was a massive project and a major investment in time and resources. The first phase of construction took between 20 and 30 years to complete, and the complexities of the full programme are summarised in Chapter 8. What will concern us here is the crucial evidence for the dating, phasing and demise of the Basilica, as recorded on the Leadenhall Court excavations (Brigham 1990a). The study also shed considerable light on aspects of Roman building technology and practice, with the

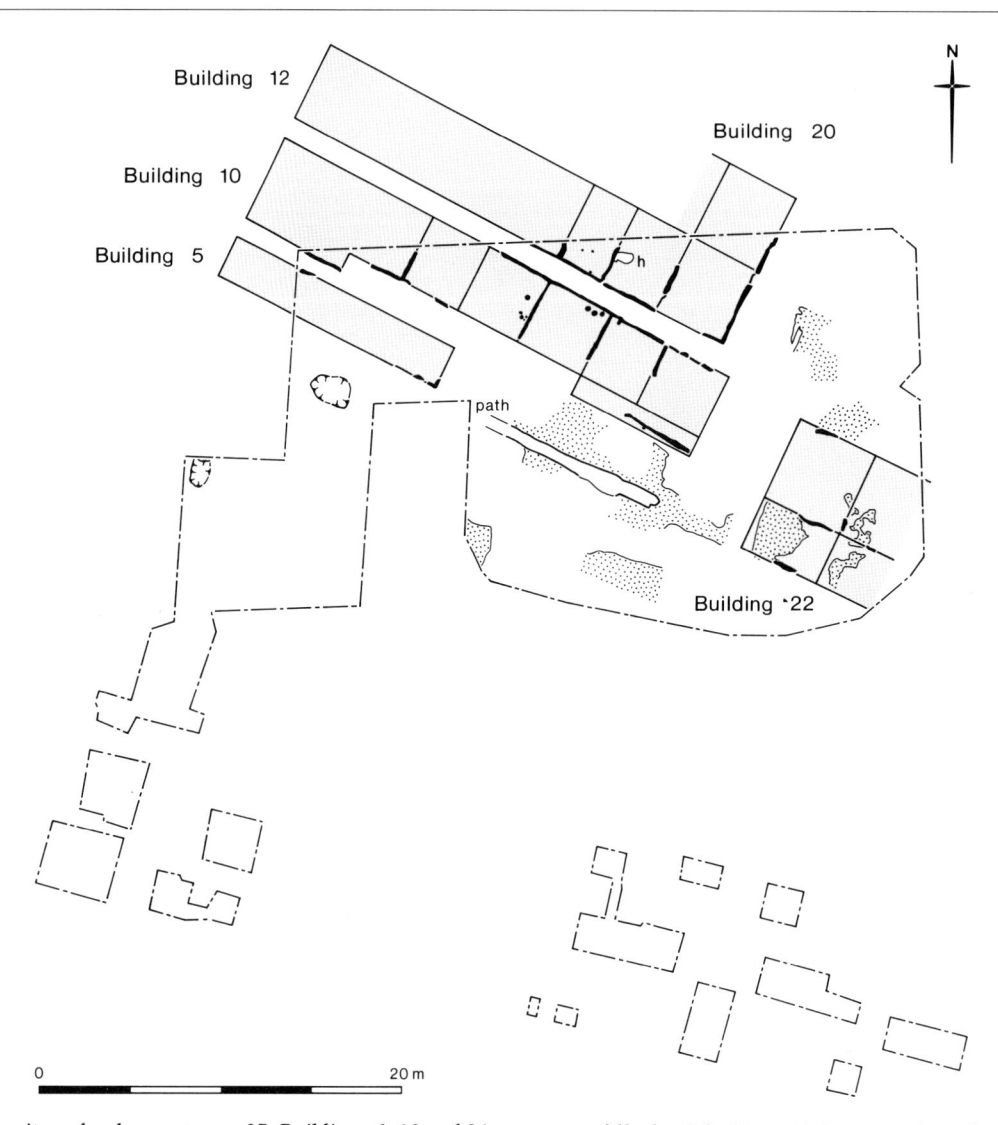

Fig 13 Inner city redevelopment c.AD 95: Buildings 6, 18 and 21 have been demolished in advance of construction work for the enlarged Basilica: cf. Fig 12. h = hearth. Scale 1: 400

recording of features such as the site huts, mortar-mixing pits and scaffolding placements and the careful analysis of the foundations themselves. Our excavations examined much of the eastern end of the Basilica, incorporating parts of Rooms 1 to 11, which were in the Northern Range and the wing north of the Apse, and several of the public rooms – the North Aisle (Room 12), the Nave itself (Room 13), the Western and Eastern Antechambers (Rooms 14 and 15) and the Apse (Room 15).

The structure was not built in one major campaign, but in discrete phases, separated by substantial periods of delay. Construction began in the south and south-east with the Nave, Antechambers, Apse and Rooms 6 and 10 (Fig 14). The foundation trenches were filled with 11 to 12 layers of pitched ragstone set in bands of hard yellow mortar, but the upper courses of the dressed stone footings were carried above the undulating construction horizon to a consistent level of 13m OD. The ground level was then raised to that height across the site, presumably by spreading out the upcast from the foundation trenches. This particular technique had two superficial advantages: it provided a 2.5m-deep foundation while only requiring the effort needed to dig 2m-deep trenches, and simultaneously seemed to solve the problem of what to do with the tons of loose spoil that trench-digging on such a scale produces. However, the use of such large quantities of relatively unconsolidated brickearth as a foundation raft was to have grave consequences for the stability of the building and its floors, as will be considered later.

Only after the first phase of foundations had been laid were the construction trenches for the walls of the

Northern Range dug (Fig 15). Exactly how much time elapsed between the two phases is not known, but the trenches were left open for an extended period, long enough for up to 0.5m of loose debris to erode into them. The masonry foundations were then laid directly over that unconsolidated material, some of which subsequently compacted or was washed out. The consequence was that a series of voids opened up beneath the masonry, causing the foundations to crack as they settled (Pl 9). A significant period of time must have been allowed for the footings to settle, since evidence of weathering and of plant growth on the exposed construction surfaces was recorded. Presumably work transferred to other parts of the project during this phase, perhaps to the superstructure of the Nave for example.

Three external buttresses were recorded on the north wall. The two eastern ones corresponded with internal north–south walls, but the western example seems to have been randomly positioned. They were built against the foundation after it had been laid, but before the superstructure was added. The buttresses probably extended above ground level since the later road ditch was dug around them, which suggests that they not only supported the base of the wall but were also carried up to the eaves to counter the outward thrust of the roof.

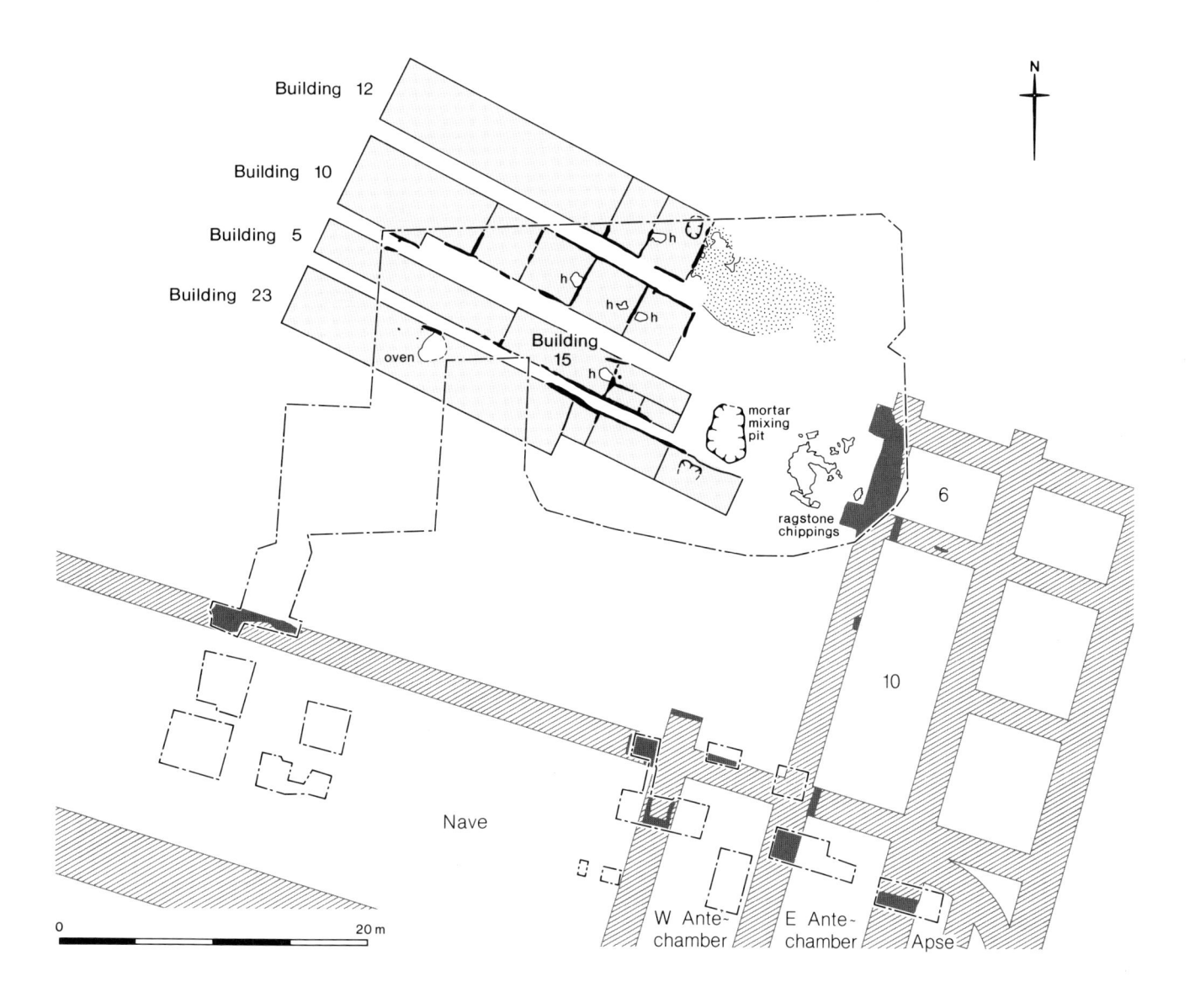

Fig 14 A vast building site, c.AD 100: construction work on the new Basilica has begun. Buildings 5, 10, 12, 15, 20 and 23 may be site huts, stores and canteens used by the building workers. Note mortar mixing pits and spreads of ragstone chippings associated with the laying of the Basilica foundations. Foundations recorded in detail in 1985–6 shown with grey tone; foundations observed or conjectured shown hatched. h = hearth. Scale 1: 400

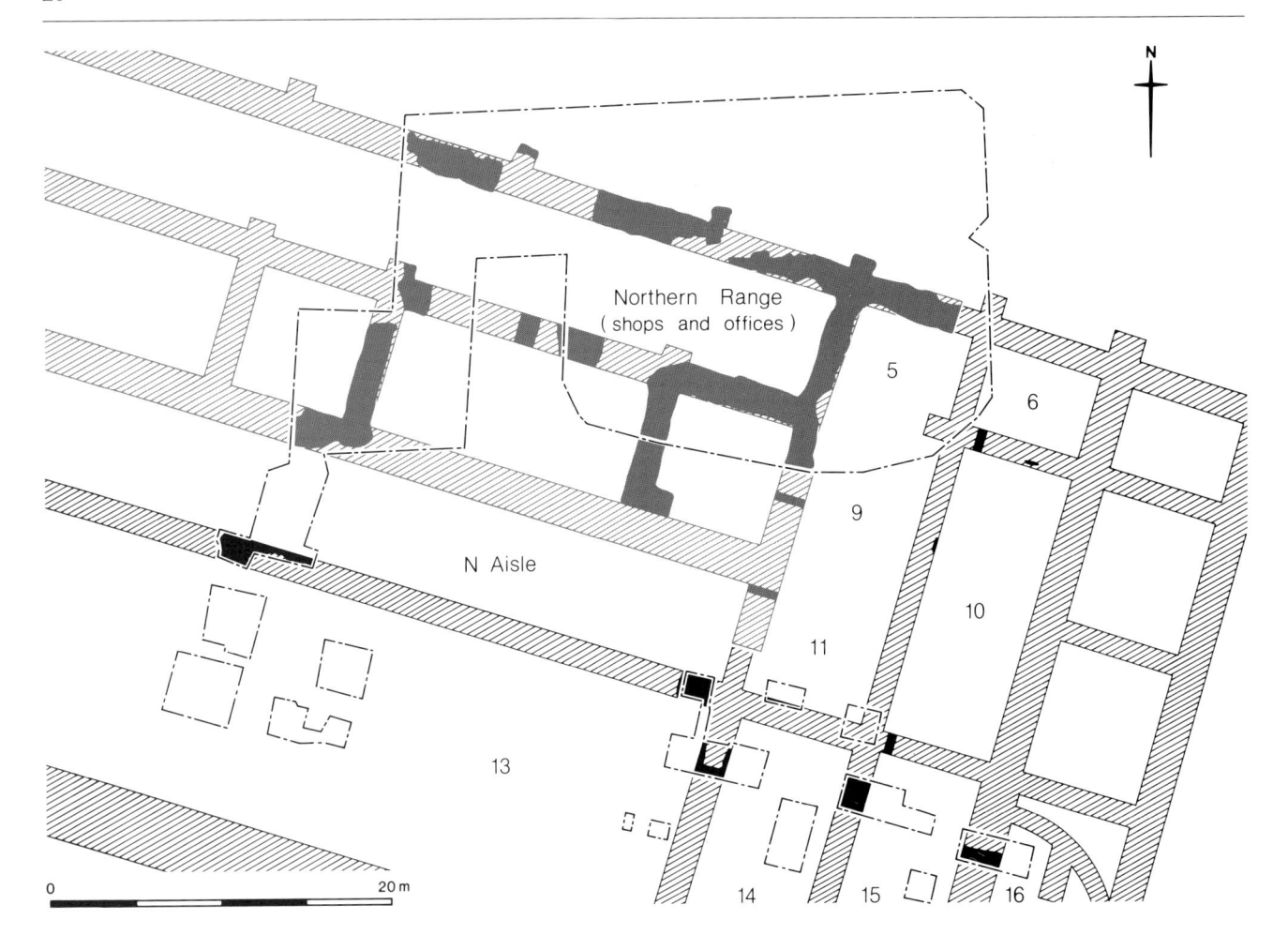

Fig 15 The second phase of Basilica construction saw the foundations of the Northern Range laid: grey tone shows the foundations recorded in detail in 1985–6; foundations observed and conjectured alignments shown with grey hatching. Superstructure of Nave and East Range recorded in detail shown black; superstructure observed and conjectured alignments shown with black hatching. Scale 1: 400

Evidence for the protracted construction sequence recorded in what was to become the North Aisle (Room 11) probably spanned both major phases of construction, starting with the work on the Nave and subsequently coinciding with the setting out of the Northern Range. Towards the end of the long sequence a well was dug, perhaps to provide water for mixing mortar, though a rough channel draining into it implies that it also acted as a sump. Ponding

Pl 9 Unstable foundations: the Northern Range of the Basilica, disturbed by later medieval stone robbers, looking east. Since the foundation trenches cut earlier ditches and quarries which had not been firmly backfilled, the Basilica footings cracked as they settled. Two of these ancient cracks can be seen immediately above the shoulder of the excavator. (Area N)

Pl 10   A muddy building site in the 2nd century AD: these well-preserved hoof prints represent the delivery of the many loads of stone required to build the new Basilica. The noticeable lack of cart ruts suggests that stone was brought in panniers by pack-horses or mules. (Area N)

caused by rainfall may well have caused problems until the Basilica was roofed over, for waterlogged make-up levels and midden-like deposits were also observed south of the Nave. Indeed, similar boggy deposits recorded just beyond the Northern Range had been churned up by hoofed animals, presumably mules, each carrying two panniers filled with 100kg of stone (Landels 1978, 172). The evocative pattern of hoofprints still survived, close to a tip of ragstone representing a delivery area for building materials. A more telling image of the realities involved in attempting to build a new Rome on a rain-soaked muddy field in an outpost of Empire would be hard to find (Pl 10).

Pl 11   Roman mortar mixing-pit: the 2x100mm scale rests on the outline of timber boards (perhaps an old door?) preserved by the mortar which was being prepared on it. (Area W). The feature was cut by several medieval pits

Pl 12 Roman scaffolding: base of a 2nd-century timber scaffold used during the erection of the Basilica walls. Although the wood has decayed, the position of the timbers can be traced. To the south of the 5x100mm scale is the outline of a timber preserved when wet Roman mortar poured over it had set. (Area N)

Before work on the superstructure began, the uneven horizon at which the foundations were laid was levelled up. Several mortar-mixing platforms used in the next phase of activity were recorded. They were usually set adjacent to the walls, and one of the best-preserved examples comprised some 10 planks laid side by side on the floor of a shallow plank-lined cut. Excess mortar had been shovelled to one side, forming a solidified mass around the platform, while the remains of the final mix had been left to set *in situ*, thereby preserving the shape of the planking (Pl 11).

Traces of the framed base of a timber scaffold were recorded just outside the external face of the north wall (Pl 12). The evidence survived as decayed traces of worked timber which were encased within a shell of mortar, showing that the wooden structure was in use when the mortar was still wet. This shows that the structure must have functioned while the construction of the Basilica was progressing. However, since it was sealed by the make-up levels for the new road it would seem that the street cannot have been in use until after the Northern Range was completed. The scaffold base incorporated a 10m length of timbers laid parallel to the north wall but some 0.6m north of it. These were lapped by a series of substantial north–south members laid at intervals of 2m, marking the position of the buttressed standards which would have supported the elevated working platform.

The superstructure, like the foundations, was almost certainly built in two discrete phases. Indeed, work on the public rooms such as the Nave, Antechambers and Apse may well have been completed before construction began on the walls of the Northern Range. In general, four courses of tiles laid over the foundations marked the base of the wall proper, which had offsets on both sides of the footings (Col Pls E and G). The tile courses performed important functions, acting as a datum and as a width guide for the construction of the lower superstructure while compensating for settlement of the foundations. Then seven courses of squared ragstone rubble were laid in a 0.9m lift. No walling survived *in situ* above this height on the recent excavations, but in 1880

Henry Hodge recorded that this level was capped by a single tile course at 14.3m OD, forming the base of the next lift. The wall seems to have been further reduced in width by means of offsets associated with a second tile bonding course four tiles thick, followed by four ragstone and two tile courses with no further offset, in a pattern that was probably repeated to the eaves.

The walls of the Basilica varied in width according to their projected height and load-bearing requirements. Thus in the Northern Range the partition walls were 1.2m wide and the central wall was 1.3m wide, while the north wall of the Northern Aisle was up to 1.5m wide with the north wall of the Nave 1.6m wide. The walls which crossed the Nave and Antechambers had to carry the additional burden of gables and the central roof ridge without the aid of buttresses or flanking walls and were therefore the thickest, varying from 1.7m to a massive 2.4m.

The first mortar surface in the Nave was laid at c.13.3m OD, but was cut by at least two large post pits set 5m apart (Fig 16). These may represent a series of posts supporting a suspended timber floor, further evidence for which is discussed in Chapter 9. By contrast, the first surface in the adjacent Western Antechamber was gravel, later patched with mortar, while the Apse, like the Nave, probably had a raised, suspended floor. The evidence for this comes not from the recent excavations but from observations, made just to the east of our site over 100 years earlier, of a central masonry pier upon which the operative surface may have lain. Within the North Aisle the initial mortar surfaces were partially sealed by layers of weathered midden material, not the type of deposit normally expected within Roman public buildings. This implies that this part of the complex had not been completed: perhaps construction work was still in progress, even though the Nave was now functioning.

The southernmost set of rooms in the Northern Range (Rooms 2, 3/7 and 8) probably functioned as

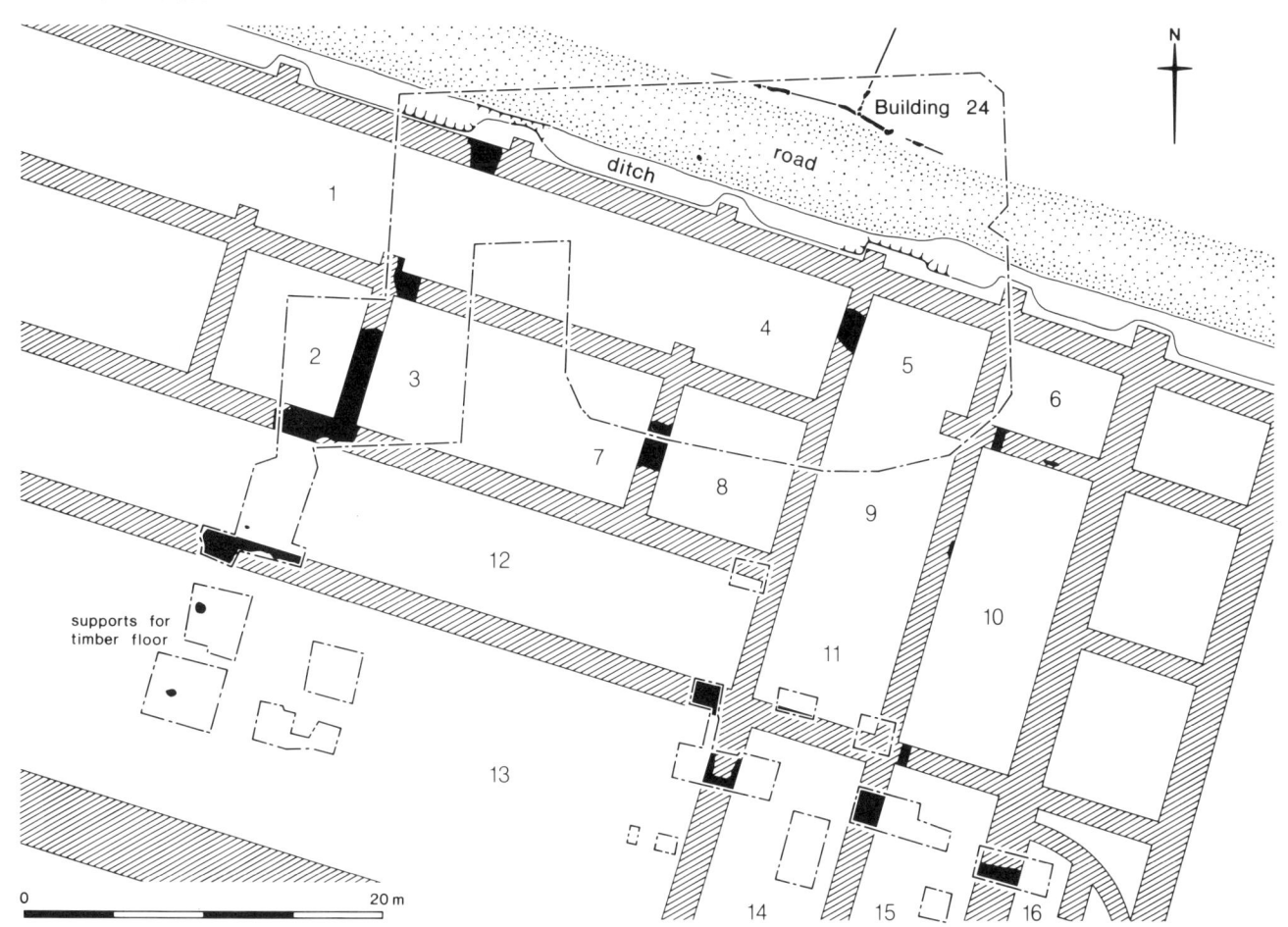

Fig 16 London Basilica, early 2nd century: entire complex now operative. Superstructure recorded in detail shown black; superstructure observed and conjectured alignments shown hatched. Scale 1: 400

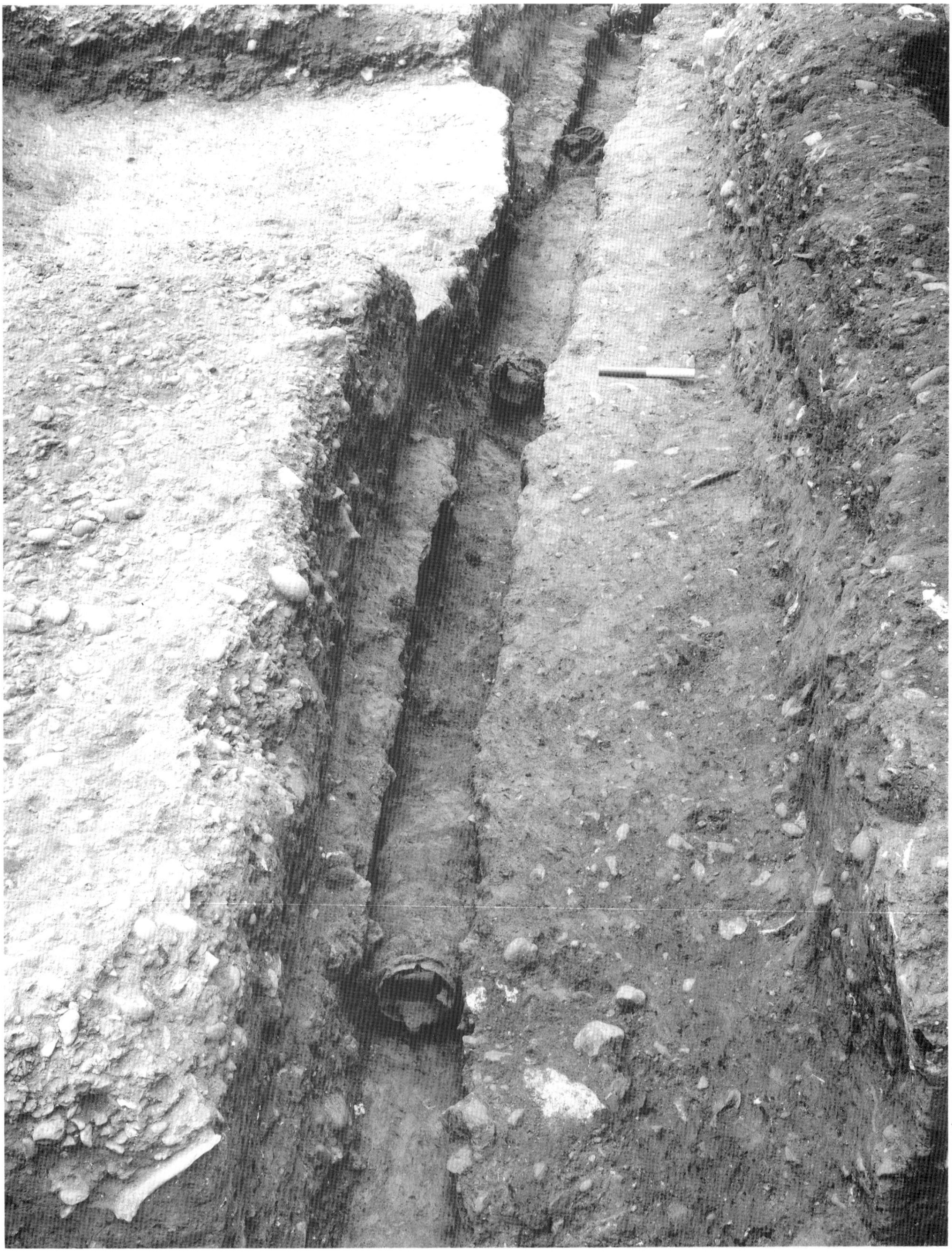

Pl 13 Provision of public utilities: the 2nd-century town centre redevelopment also saw the buildings north of the new road supplied with piped water. Although the hollowed-out wooden pipes have decayed, the iron collars which joined them still survive in this length of pipe trench, next to the 2x100mm scale. (Area N, looking west)

offices, at least in the initial phases of the Basilica's history. The earliest floor in two of these rooms was of mortar laid at the same level as those in the other public rooms, and therefore was presumably designed to function with them. Some dark-coloured wall plaster still adhered to the south wall of Room 2, a unique survival in the complex.

The northernmost set of rooms was quite different, for they fronted the street, and it is thought that access to them was only from the north, rather than from the public rooms. They presumably functioned as commercial premises quite independent of the Basilica itself. This interpretation is further supported by the fact that the floors of these rooms were resurfaced far more frequently than those elsewhere in the complex, and utilised thinner make-up levels and thinner mortar and brickearth floors. Although the masonry walls of Room 1/4 defined an area 4.5m wide and at least 31m long, it is clear that it was regularly subdivided by timber partitions during its life. Scorched areas marked the presence of hearths and braziers, and the remains of features which could represent screens, benches, cupboards or racks were noted. It seems therefore that this part of the building was let out as a series of individual shops directly fronting the street.

To the north of the complex a new gravel road was laid out as an integral part of this major civic centre redevelopment (Fig 16 and Pl 16). The cambered surface was some 5m wide, and was traced for at least 26m across the north end of the site. Along its southern edge was a 1.5m-wide flat-bottomed ditch, passing around the external buttresses on the north wall. This left a berm 1m wide which was consolidated with mortar to reduce erosion. The ditch was presumably designed to carry rain water from the Basilica roofs (a massive catchment area: see Chapter 9) as well as the run-off from the street. The road was subsequently resurfaced eight times, the metalling accumulating to a depth of over 1m, and the storm drain was recut and cleared on numerous occasions while the thoroughfare and Basilica were still in use.

The remains of Building 24 were recorded immediately north of this new road. A 5m length of the southern wall survived, together with part of an internal room division marked by a 'T'-shaped timber-stained slot packed with brickearth. A substantial post hole next to a tile and mortar surface probably represents a door post and its adjacent threshold. Traces of a similar brickearth wall extending some 5m to the east on a similar alignment could be part of the same building. The internal floors were surfaced with brickearth. The general form and construction techniques used in Building 24 seem little different from those of the buildings only recently demolished to make way for the new Basilica. After a period of some 10 to 15 years, the first road was resurfaced and Building 24 was replaced by Building 25, of which only part of the west wall and an internal floor survived. The wall line comprised a series of stake holes representing a wattle wall, west of which were external surfaces. The property pattern established in the first phase does not seem to have been replicated. Along the northern edge of the resurfaced road a trench was dug up to 0.8m wide and 0.8m deep. Into it a series of hollowed-out timbers some 200 × 200mm in cross-section was laid end to end, although only traces of the wood survived in the excavation. The timbers had been joined with metal collars some 6m apart, after which the trench was infilled with clay to keep the pipe watertight (Pl 13).

Thus by the early 2nd century, the area had been transformed with the construction of the Basilica together with the northern range of shops fronting a wide metalled street, beyond which new timber and brickearth buildings were connected to a piped water supply. Here was a rapidly developing town enhanced with a full range of public facilities.

Early or mid-2nd century: Repairs, reconstructions and the first fire
(Fig 17)

The Basilica was built over an area which, as we have seen, had been extensively cut by pits, quarries and ditches in the previous 50 years of occupation. These features had not been solidly infilled, and the loose, organic backfill material used dried out, shrank and compacted. In addition, the raft upon which the Basilica was laid was not of good quality hardcore such as broken brick or tile but was simply the mixed upcast from the digging of the foundation trenches. This material subsequently settled and subsided by different amounts in different areas. Taken together, the poor quality of the raft coupled with the very unstable nature of the underlying horizon were to provide serious problems for the Basilica for the duration of its life.

Subsidence adversely affected many of the floors in the building at an early stage. In some cases, such as Room 8, it was so severe that the room was probably never occupied in the first phase. Further evidence to support this suggestion came from the examination of bones found in one of the grey silt layers within this room. The remains of three field voles and one mole were found close together, and it seems likely that they were derived from a pellet regurgitated by a barn or a shorteared owl. The bones represent the remains of one evening's feeding, after which the owl perched above the finds spot to digest the meal. The presence of owls roosting in the Basilica strongly suggests that at least this part of the complex remained uncompleted and unoccupied for a substantial time. This discovery also highlights the rural aspect of this new town, for the presence of field voles shows that there must have been rough grassland within 200 to 300m of the Basilica. Ultimately the problem of the subsiding surfaces was overcome by filling Room 8 with thick, compensatory dumps.

Even more damaging were the cracks in the foundations, which required patching of the masonry and the addition of a small buttress to the wall between Rooms 13 and 14, for example. Perhaps as a consequence of this repair work, the opportunity was taken to redesign the Nave. This represents a major rebuilding exercise which saw the north wall of the North Aisle razed and replaced by a series of brick piers supporting an arcade which opened directly into the Aisle. The base of one such pier was found in the recent excavations, similar to the substantial pier fragment still surviving in the basement of 90 Gracechurch Street (Col Pls I and J). The Western Antechamber now became an extension to the Nave. Following the demolition of its west wall, the Eastern Antechamber was also opened out, but the Apse

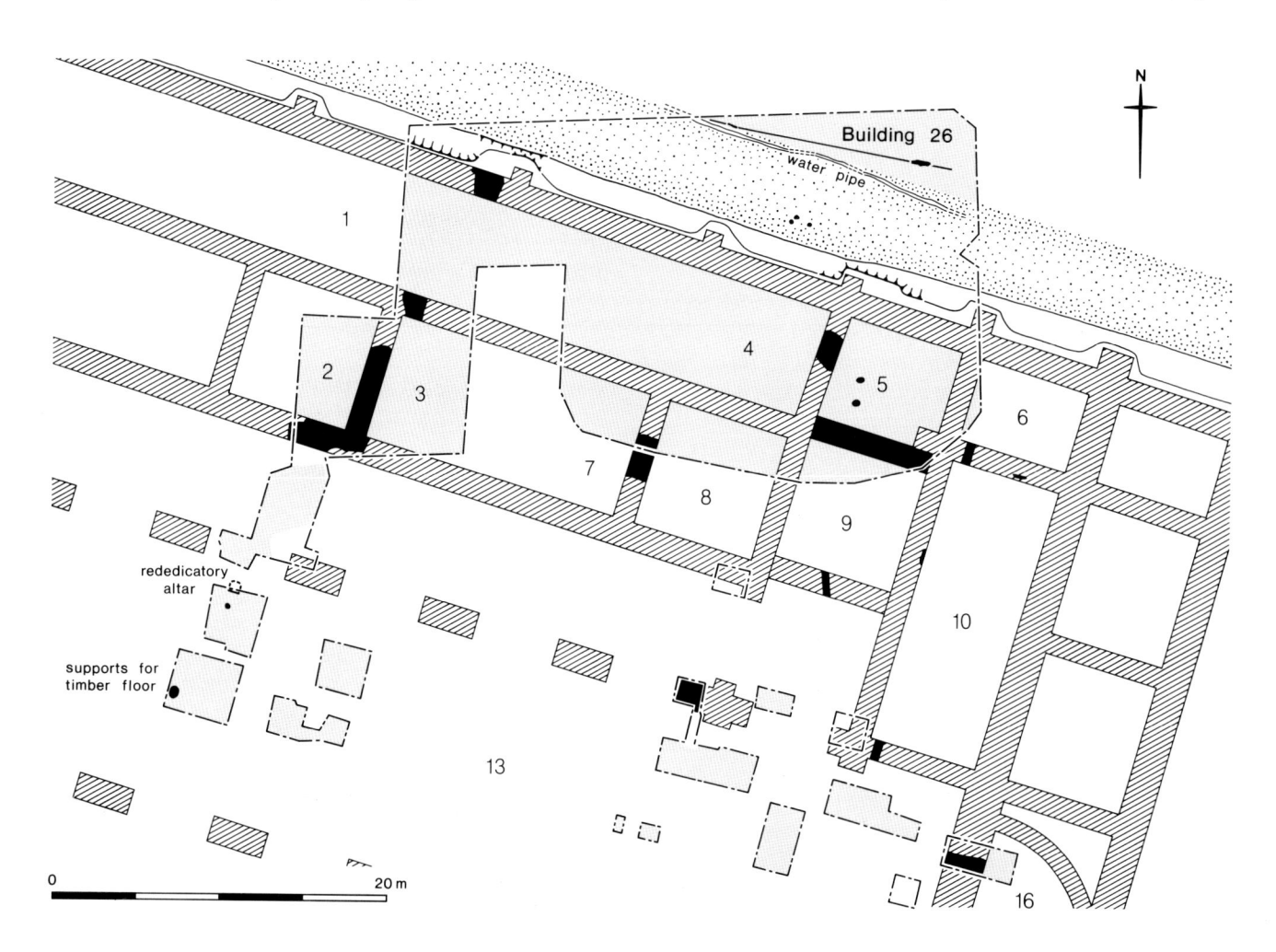

Fig 17 London Basilica, 2nd century: rebuilding and a major fire. The Nave was separated from the North and South Aisles by piers before damaged by fire. Grey tone shows extent of burning recorded in 1985–6; wall symbols as for Fig 16. Scale 1: 400

remained screened off. The internal area of the Basilica was levelled up with a thick raft of demolition debris, after which an extensive area of the public rooms and office range was sealed by a brickearth slab up to 0.7m thick. In the Nave, this was cut by post holes thought to represent support for a suspended timber floor.

No sooner had this major redevelopment been completed than the building was damaged by fire, the imprint of which was clearly marked by the severe and extensive scorching of the brickearth slab in the public rooms. In the Northern Range a timber floor or wall was destroyed and the wooden partitions subdividing Rooms 1/4 and 5 were also burnt. It is not known whether this fire was accidental or deliberate: if it was the latter, then it could represent unrest in the town or a similar calamity. Other evidence for the deliberate destruction of Roman public works comes in the form of the fragments of imperial statuary, such as the severed bronze hands found discarded in the area of the Forum in 1867 and the decapitated head of Hadrian, probably carried from the Forum and hurled into the Thames, from whence it was recovered in the 1830s. Whatever the cause of the 2nd-century fire in the Basilica, it meant that work on its rebuilding had to begin all over again.

Mid-2nd century: Post-fire rebuilding

A small ragstone plinth bearing a plastered niche was recorded on the burnt floor surface of the Nave. Since it was not itself scorched but was sealed by the make-up levels associated with the post-fire rebuilding, it must have been constructed after the fire, but before reconstruction work began. It is therefore just possible that it represents a small rededicatory altar, erected for a ceremony to mark the beginning of the new building programme, presumably in an attempt to persuade the gods to gaze with more beneficence upon the ill-fated Basilica. After major clearance, extensive refurbishment began, marked in the public rooms by the introduction of a non-combustible *opus signinum* floor. Since this replaced a suspended timber floor, the area formerly occupied by the airspace beneath the joists and boards was infilled to ensure that the new floor was at the right level to function with the old doorways and windows. The make-up material used formed an extensive layer of sorted building material, some of it burnt, up to 1m thick. Clearly this was derived from the fire-damaged superstructure of the Basilica and, beneath the Eastern Antechamber, it incorporated large quantities of the painted plaster which had formerly adorned the walls of this room (Chapter 9: Figs 37 and 38; Col Pl N). By contrast, the level of floors in the Northern Range was not raised to such an extent. Here the debris was cleared away and the rooms resurfaced with thin mortar floors.

Evidence of fire-damaged structures was also recorded beyond the street to the north of the Basilica. Contemporary with the third phase of the resurfaced road was a third phase of occupation deposits, most of which seem to represent external surfaces. However, the presence of a slot and a brickearth wall fragment show that there was at least one structure there (Building 26) which differed in position from both Buildings 24 and 25. The occupation horizon was sealed by a dump of redeposited fire debris, including burnt mud bricks and charcoal fragments. This shows that a brickearth and timber building in the vicinity had been burnt down, although no evidence of scorching or *in situ* burning was observed immediately north of the road. A brickearth slab sealed the fire debris, and in that an L-shaped slot was recorded, representing the robbed southern and western walls of Building 27. This was at least 3.5m wide, and had external surfaces to west and south. The building was also burnt down and sealed beneath another horizon of fire debris. Rebuilding did not take place immediately, and it is possible that the property plot remained vacant for some years, even although the road was resurfaced. The building which did eventually occupy this plot (Building 28) had a mortar floor and a hearth, but little trace of wall lines was recorded. The contemporary road was resurfaced yet again, and the waterpipe replaced.

It seems reasonable to assume that one or other of the fires which were recorded to the north of the street was the one which so severely damaged the Basilica. Although both events took place in the 2nd century, neither can be identified with the so-called Hadrianic Fire which, it has been argued, destroyed much of Roman London some time before *c*.AD 125. The reason is simply that the Basilica was barely completed by *c*.AD 125, after which major rebuilding took place, the street was resurfaced at least three times, and Buildings 24, 25, 26 and possibly 27 were all constructed and replaced before the conflagration.

Later 2nd and 3rd centuries: Neglect and refurbishment

Following the fire, the sequence of development recorded in the Nave began with accumulations of grey silt, thin tread layers and patchy mortar or brickearth surfaces overlying parts of the new *opus signinum* floor. This seems to reflect neglect of the refurbished structure, although the silting was less noticeable further east, barely affecting the Apse and former Antechambers, which were therefore presumably better maintained. However, a second *opus signinum* floor laid over the silts in the Nave, this time with a durable surface of broken tile, probably represents a determined attempt to restore the building. Subsequently a series of posts and stakes was set into this surface in the middle of the Nave, of which the two largest were aligned east–west, directly beneath the roof ridge. These may therefore have had a structural function related directly or indirectly with the roof. The other post holes were smaller and seemed randomly placed, representing a number of different activities on different occasions. Whatever their precise functions, they are arguably not what might reasonably be expected in the middle of the Nave if it were still being used as a large meeting hall. However, there is evidence to suggest that the Nave may well have been subdivided towards the end of this period, for Henry Hodge recorded a better quality floor of thin tiles at its eastern end, with a tessellated pavement at a higher level in the Eastern Antechamber. This could imply that the major public functions held in the Basilica were now confined just to the eastern end of the Nave and the Apse, with the rest of the Nave made over to other uses.

Meanwhile, to the north of the Basilica, the road was resurfaced over a raft of east–west timbers, of which only decayed traces survived. On its northern edge, Building 29 was erected. A line of five post pits represented one of the walls of this structure, a different construction technique from that used in the earlier buildings. This building and its associated road were subsequently replaced in turn, but the new structure, Building 30, suffered the same fate as several of its predecessors, for it burned down. All that survived was the east–west robber trench marking the line of its south wall, which was full of fire debris.

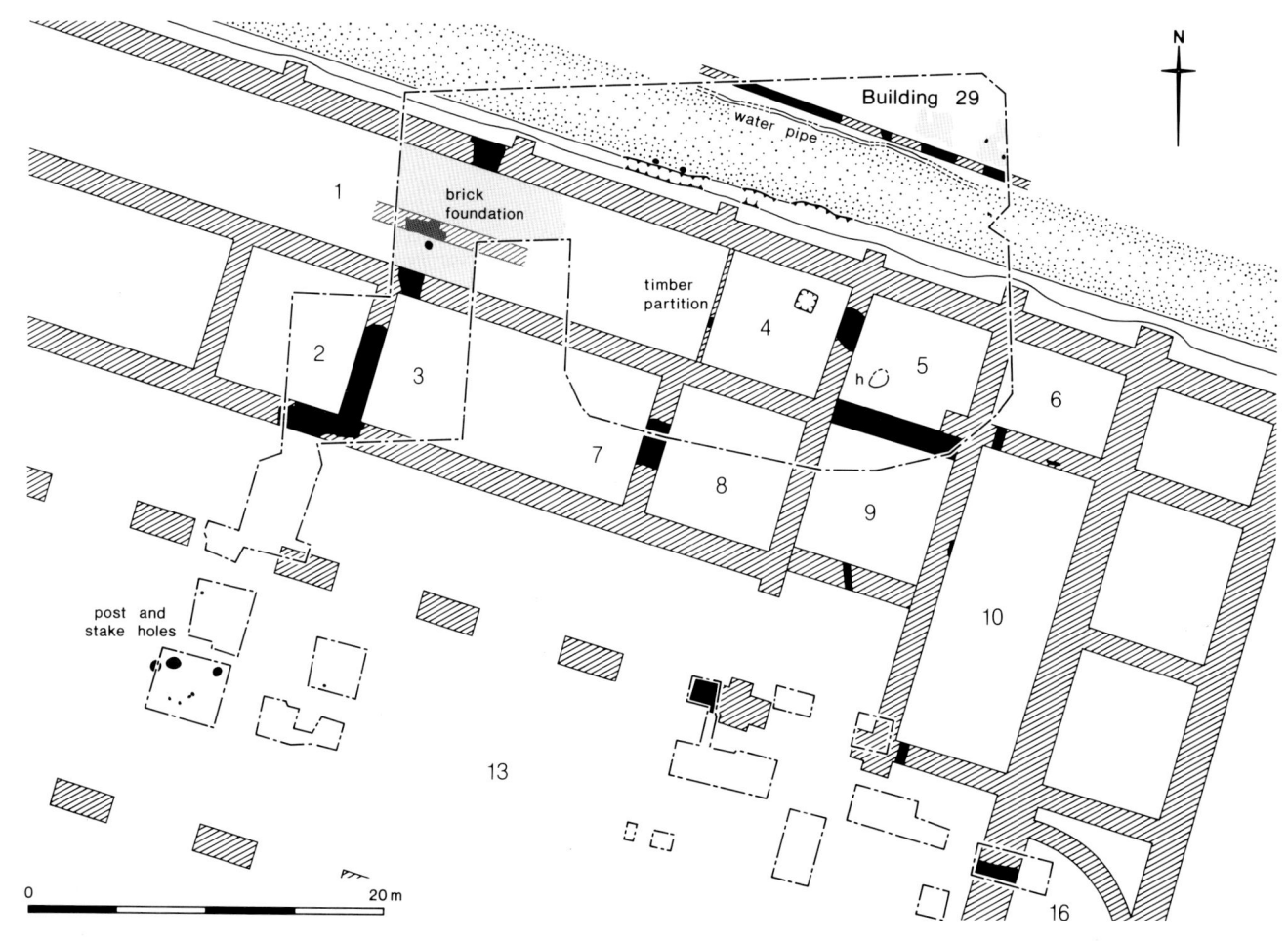

Second fire and reconstruction
(Fig 18)

During this period, fire also damaged the Basilica, but this time it seems that the Northern Range was worst affected, timber partitions burning down and the roof collapsing. Over the spread of burnt tiles in Room 1/4 a new wall foundation comprising reused wall bricks was laid out east–west (Col Pls O and P), suggesting further subdivision of the range following its refurbishment. This was later sealed by a mortar and brickearth surface which had been patched several times, suggesting that this part of the building continued in use for some considerable time after the fire.

There is little evidence to suggest that the Nave or Antechambers were as badly damaged in this fire as in the previous conflagration: the small areas of burnt brickearth slabs which were recorded in that area probably reflect quite separate events. However, the Nave was resurfaced at about this time with a third phase of *opus signinum* floor, which sealed the grey silt accumulations, made good various areas of subsidence, and seems to have extended over the better maintained surfaces at the east end of the Nave and into the Apse itself. Broadly contemporary with these developments were the series of thin surfaces laid in Rooms 5 and 9. Although these included burnt material, this was probably derived from hearths or ovens set in the middle of the room rather than from fire damage. This material seems consistent with a continuing sequence of domestic occupation, and may be contrasted with the thicker *opus signinum* floors of the public rooms.

Late 3rd and early 4th centuries: Demise and demolition
(Fig 19)

With the noticeable exception of the Apse, most of the Basilica was demolished down to the level of the final floor and the site carefully cleared at some time in the early 4th century. The evidence for the demise of the Basilica, the largest public building in the province, is

Fig 18 London Basilica, late 2nd to early 3rd century: another fire and subsequent refurbishments. Extent of burning recorded in 1985–6 shown in grey tone. Note hearth (h) in Room 5. Wall symbols as for Fig 16. Scale 1: 400

as follows. The final floor level in all rooms where the sequence survived intact and unaffected by subsidence was at *c.*14.3m OD. This was sealed by grey silts containing loose building material, which seems to have accumulated before the collapse of the roof, since it was sealed by spreads of roof tile and then by sections of collapsed walling. The presence of the silts beneath the demolition material suggests that the Nave was either no longer fully maintained or had been abandoned before the walls were demolished. By contrast, Hodge records that the final floor in the Eastern Antechamber was directly sealed by rubble, showing that this room had remained in use right up to the end.

The silt horizon was in turn sealed by darker grey silts, and similar deposits have been observed directly overlying the levelled wall stubs at a similar height. There was a noticeable lack of large deposits of building debris comparable to the thick demolition deposits recorded within the Nave after the first fire for example. This is significant, for it demonstrates that the Basilica was demolished and the site systematically cleared of building material (presumably for use elsewhere) before the darker grey silts accumulated over the site (Pls 14 and 15). The building was not left standing as a derelict ruin, like some of the great monastic churches after the Dissolution. Instead soil seems to have formed over the top of it, and the area reverted back to fields. The site of the provincial capital's great Basilica fell beneath the plough as Roman trade, administration and urban life gave way to the rigours of self-sufficiency.

Much of the Basilica walling was subsequently dug up for reuse in the medieval period. As a consequence, the highly disturbed state of the foundations as revealed in the recent excavations give a poor impression of the actual state in which the Romans left the demolished Basilica below the contemporary ground surface. However, careful analysis of all surviving and recorded fragments suggests that the entire masonry carcass was left complete up to a height of *c.*14.3m OD, that is, up to the second tile offset, the level of the final *opus signinum* floor. None of the buried superstructure down to the first tile offset or the lower foundations was robbed out before the 10th or 11th century: the Romans were only responsible for the wholesale demolition and clearance of the above-ground walling. Nevertheless, this task was effected so thoroughly that once silts and soils began developing over the area in the 4th century, the site and plan of the Basilica disappeared first from view and ultimately from memory.

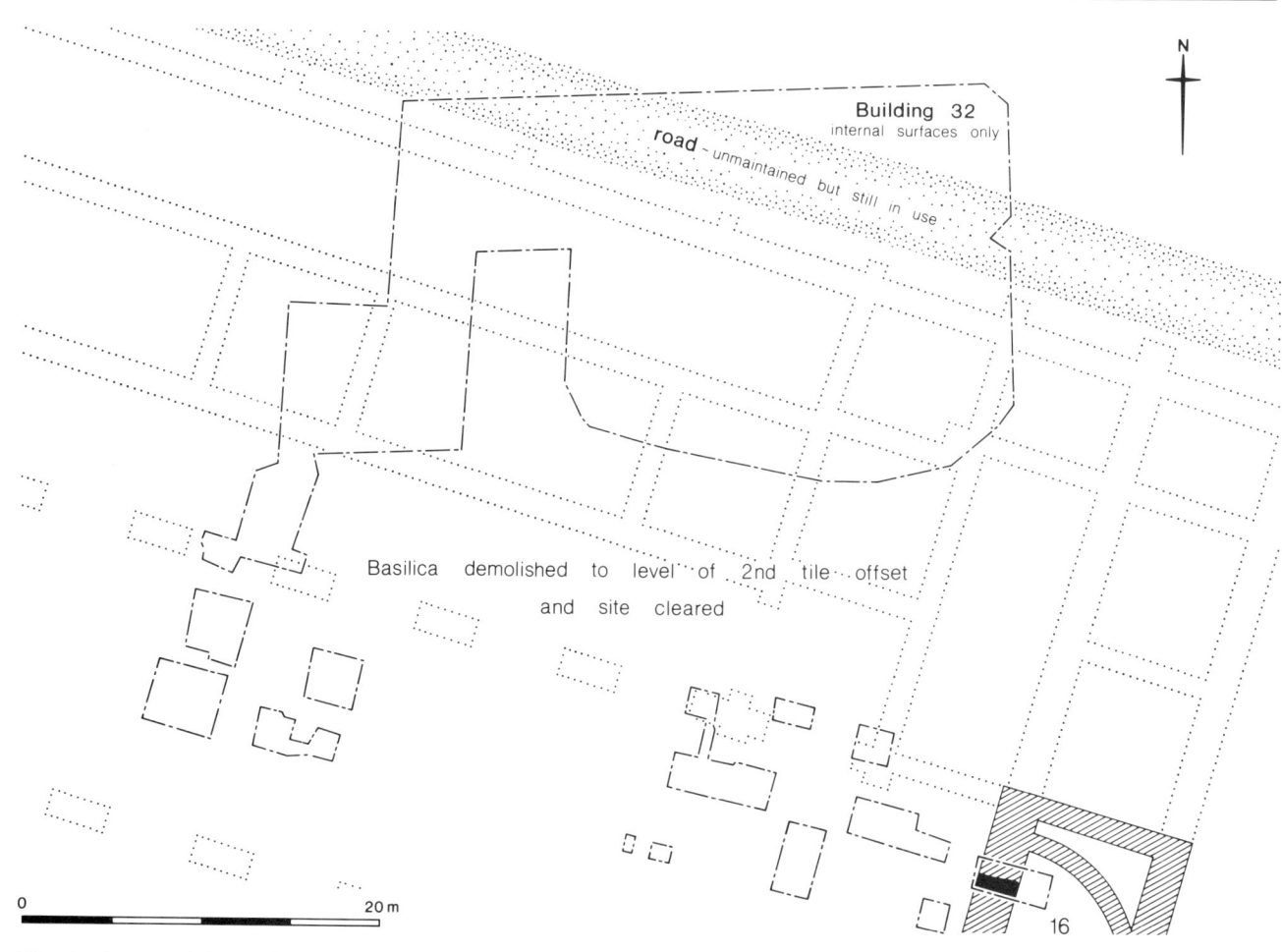

Fig 19 Demise of the London Basilica, c.4th century: all the walls shown with dotted lines were demolished and sealed beneath grey silts, with the exception of the Apse (Room 16). Scale 1: 400

RIGHT
Pl 14 Roman Basilica systematically demolished: subsurface remains of the Basilica as left by the Romans, following the careful demolition of the superstructure, but before the medieval stone robbing took place. The view is westwards over Area S towards Area W, Area N to the north. This is a computer-enhanced image produced by Paul Wootton, working from the image used in Pl 15

OPPOSITE
Pl 15 Foundations of the Basilica unsystematically quarried: remains of the Basilica as found in 1986. The 10x100mm scales rest on the rectilinear skeleton of the walls of the Northern Range, seen here looking west over Area S towards Area W. The massive masonry foundations were much disturbed in the early medieval period, when the stone was quarried for building work elsewhere: cf.Pl 14

From fields to Forum

Pl 16 The streets of London in the 2nd century: the 10x100mm scale rests on the well-prepared surface of the new road: cf.Pl 17. In the foreground are the Northern Range foundations, separated from the road by a wide storm drain into which ran the rain water from the huge Basilica roof. (Area N, looking north)

RIGHT
Pl 17 The streets of London in the late 3rd/early 4th century: the 10x100mm scale rests on the worn and rutted surface of the last of nine road surfaces: cf. Pl 16. Although it ran next to the headquarters of the town's administration responsible for such facilities it was not maintained after c.AD 275. (Area N, looking north-east)

Some of the reasons for the demolition of this most prestigious building are discussed in Chapter 11. All that remains to be considered here is the fate of the Apse, the surviving walls of which were among the few exceptions to the rule outlined above (see Chapter 8). Once again, it was the objective recording of Henry Hodge which provided the evidence, from an area just beyond the 1986 excavations. He showed that the walls of the Apse still survived to a height of up to 15.4m OD in 1880, 1m higher than the general level to which the rest of the Basilica had already been razed in the 4th century. It is therefore possible that the Apse had been deliberately left, forming the nucleus of a structure standing in apparent isolation on the top of the hill.

To the north of the Basilica in the late 3rd century, a new gravel and cobble road surface had been laid out over a substantial raft made up of broken tile and mortar. This proved to be the last time the street was comprehensively resurfaced, and as a consequence it became far more rutted than any of the previous metallings, which had all been regularly replaced at 10 to 15 year intervals. The latest surface was so worn that is thought to have been in use for at least twice as long as the others (cf. Pls 16 and 17). A series of post holes represent the evidence that a structure, Building 31, was built to the north of the road to replace the burnt Building 30, but these may form part of a veranda rather than the main body of the structure. Thereafter a period of decline is apparent, for mud and silts sealed the remains of Building 30 and the street, and filled the roadside ditches. Nevertheless, the road must have still been in use since the mud was cut by ruts from the passage of traffic. The provision of public services, such as the maintenance of roads, was clearly at an end: the town must have been in a period of crisis. However, life continued for at least a short while into the 4th century, since traces of another building were recorded beside this neglected thoroughfare. All that survived of Building 32 was a thin spread of burnt brickearth over a mortar bed. Like so many of the buildings on the Leadenhall Court site, it was finally destroyed by fire; analysis of the associated debris shows that it had been of brickearth and timber construction. This building seems not to have been replaced and marks the end of the direct evidence of Roman occupation in this area. The fire horizon which covered it was in turn sealed by a horizon of grey silts similar to that which ultimately sealed both the road and the Basilica.

Although the field record of the building sequence therefore suggests that occupation of the area terminated in or by the early 4th century, some later Roman material was recovered from the site, although never in association with the obvious remains of buildings. The latest identifiable issues of Roman coins were datable to AD 330–341 for example, while some later 4th-century pottery was found in disturbed contexts such as the backfill of medieval trenches cut to remove stone from the Basilica foundations. The presence of this material on the site shows that activities which resulted in the loss and dispersal of coins and pottery continued in the area at a date up to 50 years later than that assigned to the latest recorded occupation deposits. Possible explanations for this apparent anomaly are that the buildings associated with the final generation of occupation here were truncated or eroded by activity immediately prior to the accumulation of the grey silts, or that worm and root action in the soils which ultimately sealed the final building horizon broke down the brickearth and timber components of those structures (cf. Yule 1990). Whatever the explanation or precise date, the fate of Roman London is clear: public and domestic buildings in this part of the town, in the heart of the civic centre, were ultimately abandoned – urban life did not survive here into the medieval period.

3 New towns

SAXON DEVELOPMENTS AT LEADENHALL AD 450–1195

Gustav Milne

With the departure of the Roman garrison, the administration and defence of the province of Britannia passed directly into the hands of reluctant native British officials by the end of the 5th century. In the event they proved no match for the Saxons who ultimately took over the country, reallocating the rural estates amongst their own followers. This effectively isolated the Roman townships and destroyed the administrative and economic system upon which they depended: the first major attempt at urbanisation in Britain came to an end after a period of some 400 years.

By the beginning of the 6th century then, the site of Roman London was all but deserted: only the City wall survived, perhaps enclosing little more than fields, just as the walls of Silchester or Verulamium do to this day. The period of time which separates the demise of the Roman civilisation from the documented development of medieval life was once termed the Dark Ages: appropriately enough, on archaeological sites in London where occupation horizons of both the late Roman as well as the late Saxon town are found, the two are separated by a layer of dark grey silts (Pl 18). No clearer evidence for discontinuity could be sought: the first London had flourished and failed.

AD 450–890: From Londinium to Lundenwic

On the Leadenhall Court site, the levelled remains of Londinium lay beneath the horizon of dark grey silts, but the earliest datable material from levels above it represented activity in the 10th or 11th centuries. Recent archaeological research has shown that the Leadenhall area, and indeed much of the City, lay open and relatively undeveloped for several centuries. On the face of it, such a long hiatus in the development of London is hard to reconcile with the surviving documentary evidence of the town which includes, for example, an early 8th-century description of London as a 'mart of many nations resorting to it by sea and land' (Stevens 1970, 68).

This crucial question was only resolved as late as 1984–5, when it was finally realised that, although there was most certainly a mid-Saxon successor to Londinium from c.AD 600 to c.900, it did not lie within the Roman town walls at all. Instead, a completely fresh site was chosen to the west of the City along the Strand, between the River Fleet and Westminster (Vince 1990). This remarkable change of site serves to show that the form town life took, as it re-emerged in England in the 7th-century, was not along the once familiar Roman lines but was based on quite new concepts of urbanism developed by the Saxons themselves.

This new town was known as Lundenwic, 'wic' meaning market town. It seems to have prospered and, as an unfortunate consequence, attracted the unwelcome attentions of Viking raiders. In the late 9th century, the Londoners were forced to retreat within the Roman walled area, a more readily defensible site. Lundenwic, like Londinium before it, was abandoned and its site became known as the Old Market Town, or Ald-wych.

34

New towns

Pl 18 Dark-Age fields and a medieval market: the 10x100mm and 5x100mm scales rest on dark grey silts (perhaps representing an early medieval field) sealing the demolished Basilica. To the right (north), are four chalk foundations which supported piers of the 15th-century Garner's northern range. (Area N, looking west)

AD 890–1195: From Lundenwic to London Town *(Fig 20)*

A settlement was therefore established at the end of the 9th century, in the reign of Alfred the Great, on the site of Londinium. However, it held little in common with the earlier Roman town, save for the City wall and the position of its gates. This late Saxon town was laid out over an area in which few Roman walls survived above ground to influence the alignment of the new medieval streets. Initially, the major settlement seems to have been confined at most to a rectangular area bounded by the Thames to the south, Cheapside to the north, St Pauls to the west and Billingsgate to the east (Milne 1990). As the population grew, so the settlement expanded over the areas inside the walls which had formerly been left open.

These processes were clearly observed on the Leadenhall Court excavations. The medieval street system which developed in the area around the site included the road now known as Cornhill and

Leadenhall Street: this ran diagonally over the levelled remains of what was once the largest building in Londinium, cutting directly across the grain of the Roman layout. The difference in the street pattern provides further evidence for the discontinuity of occupation within the walled area. It also demonstrates that the demolition and clearance of the Basilica must have been thorough, since there was clearly no trace of the Roman civic centre substantial enough to dictate the course of subsequent streets.

Although the buildings of the new Londoners were truncated by deeply cut modern basements, evidence for the reoccupation of the general area was nevertheless plentiful (Fig 20). The location of the yards to the rear of the buildings was marked, characteristically, by the presence of pits and wells. Finds included a range of early medieval pottery vessels, a pattern-welded knife, several bone casket plates, a loom weight, crucible fragments and some gold thread. Some of the pits were square or rectangular in plan, and it was noticeable that these did not respect the north-east/south-west Roman alignment, but were dug parallel to the Leadenhall Street or Gracechurch Street frontages. This showed

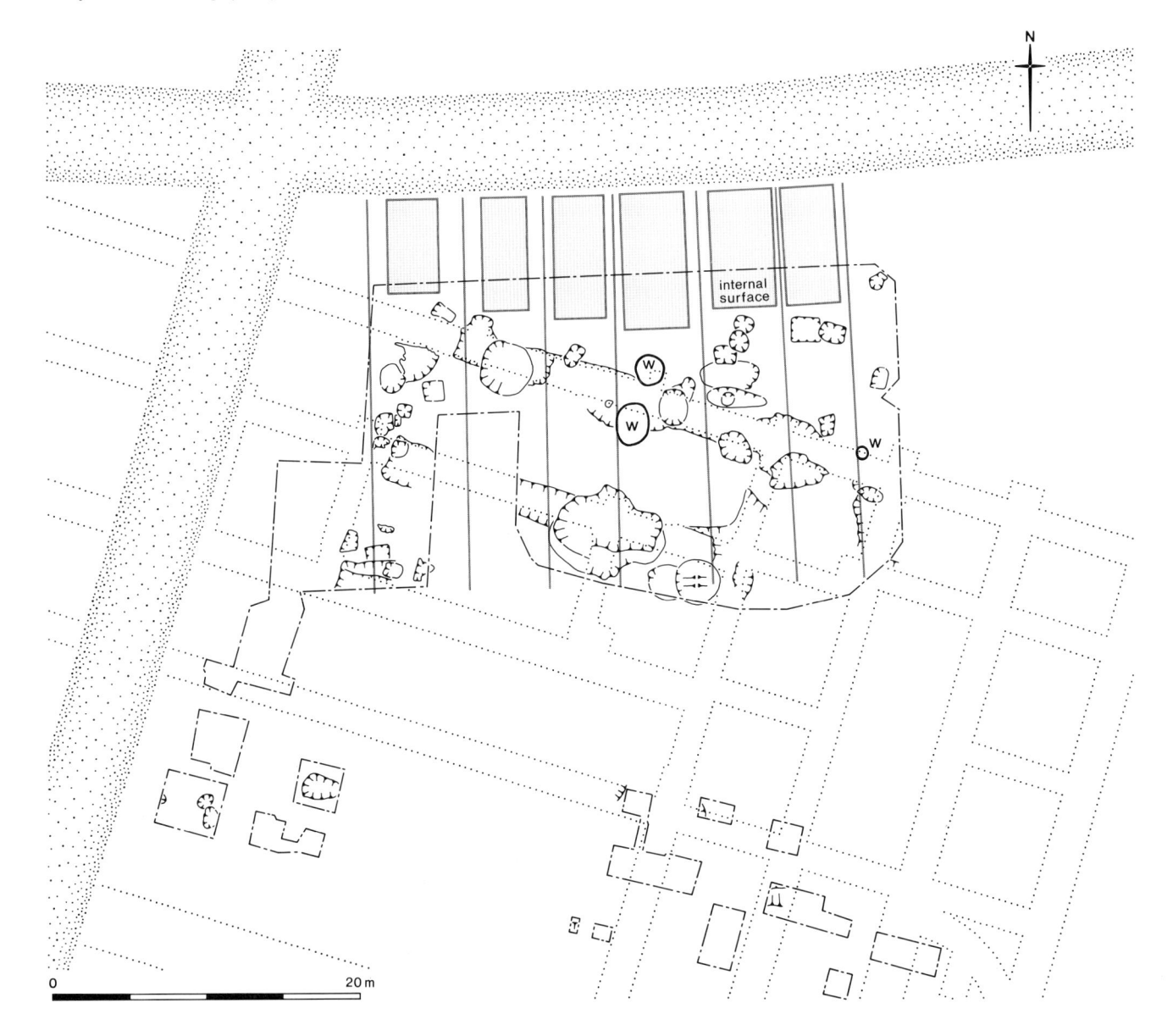

Fig 20 A new town plan: the conjectured outline of Saxo-Norman buildings set within burgage plots fronting the street (now called Leadenhall Street) to north: cf. Roman property plots shown in Fig 9. The medieval houses would have occupied the unpitted zone against the new street frontage, with pits and wells in the backyards to south. The digging of these Saxo-Norman pits fortuitously exposed the walls of the Basilica, resulting in the unsystematic robbing of the foundations shown here. Scale 1: 400

that new Saxon properties were laid out in an insula bounded by those streets. Further study of the distribution and contents of the pits established when the area was reoccupied and suggested the orientation and width of the burgage plots laid out in the new development, as will now be shown.

Although the majority of deposits which accumulated on the site in the 5th to 12th centuries had been destroyed when later cellars were dug through them, some of that material survived in the backfill of trenches cut to quarry Roman masonry foundations. The trenches contained much dark grey silt interspersed with layers of brickearth and mortar. Examination of the coins and pottery from these levels showed that the mortar deposits represented disturbed early Roman material, whereas the grey silts were derived from the horizon which sealed the demolished Basilica and contained mainly 4th-century material, but with some 11th- or 12th-century pottery mixed in. Significantly, this range of pottery does not contain any 5th-to 9th-century wares, and thus there is strong negative evidence showing that there was no significant occupation of the area in that period.

There is, however, positive evidence to date the reoccupation of the site. One set of pits contained material which need not be later than AD 950–1000. This suggests that the Saxon settlement had expanded northwards from the initial nucleus in the Eastcheap–Billingsgate area, where occupation seems to have begun just a generation or so earlier, c.900–950 (Horsman et al. 1988, 112; Milne 1990). By contrast, just to the north of the Gracechurch Street–Leadenhall Street junction, the development of the Bishopsgate frontage may be a generation later (Milne et al. 1984). Another group of pits on the Leadenhall Court site was associated with material in the date range 1050–1150, while pottery dated from 1150–1250 was found in the third group. These show that the same properties continued in use for a period of 200 years or more before the area was subjected to major redevelopment.

During this period, sections of the buried Basilica foundations were exposed and quarried for building stone. The manner in which the stone robbing took place demonstrates that no part of the Basilica was visible above ground and that no memory of the plan of that huge structure survived. Some of the pits from the earliest Saxon phase on the Leadenhall Court site partially cut into the Basilica foundations seemingly by accident since half the cut lay over and half beyond the line of the wall. Having thus discovered that substantial masonry remains survived in the backyard areas, later trenches were deliberately dug at various times to remove the stone, but always in an unsystematic, piecemeal manner. This contrasts with other sites where all usable stone was quarried at one time from neatly-cut robber trenches, the alignment of which thoroughly and effectively conforms to the plan of the masonry building. At Leadenhall, the markedly differing quality of survival of the Basilica remains across the site clearly shows that not all the land was open and available for stone robbing but had been parcelled out into discrete property plots before the existence of the Roman building was established. These robber trenches were rarely more than 5 to 10m long, and probably therefore reflect the width of the long narrow burgage plots which stretched south from the Leadenhall Street frontage or eastwards from Gracechurch Street.

In contrast with other recent excavations (e.g. Horsman et al. 1988), little direct evidence was recovered from Leadenhall Court of the buildings associated with these new Londoners. However it is possible to suggest that those houses were probably laid out on the new street frontage, rather than set back in the middle or rear of the property plots. The evidence to support this suggestion is the distribution of the pits, very few of which encroached upon an area which ran parallel to the new street frontages and was some 5 to 10m wide. It is argued that it was over this unpitted zone that the Saxon inhabitants erected their buildings, although the contemporary ground surface has subsequently been truncated. Support for this suggestion comes from similar studies elsewhere in London (Horsman et al. 1988, 12) as well as from the Leadenhall Court site itself. In the northern part of the excavation, fragments of a sequence of internal brickearth floors were recorded slumped into the base of an earlier pit, the fills of which had compacted and subsided. This shows that at least one Saxon building had been built up against the Leadenhall Street frontage.

An orderly arrangement of long, narrow burgage plots therefore characterised this part of the City in the 11th and 12th centuries. The pattern was similar in character (but not orientation) to that noted in AD 80–90, swept away by the extensive redevelopment of the civic centre in AD 100. A similar fate befell part of the early medieval pattern of property holdings by the early 13th century, when the digging and filling of pits in the backyard stopped abruptly. This suggests that the yards were no longer occupied or accessible. The reason for this change in the townscape was probably the superimposition of a much larger complex on to the Leadenhall site, the eponymous hall itself, and this will be described in the following chapter.

This concludes the summary of the evidence of the demise of Londinium and the subsequent rebirth of the town in the Saxon period, in as much as it was represented by the archaeological records made on the Leadenhall Court site. The next chapter takes the story forward, but this time making use of new classes of evidence, in particular documentary data, the like of which has not survived to illuminate the first 1000 years of Leadenhall's history. Thus the archaeological material summarised in this and the previous chapter reveals crucial episodes in the development of the City which are otherwise unrecorded. Quite apart from establishing the character and chronology of urban redevelopments in different periods, such archaeological evidence provides a new perspective on London's history. It shows that the story is not one of continuous expansion from a sound Roman foundation, for there have been substantial reversals in fortune. Indeed, one of the longest chapters, a period of 500 years from the 5th to the late 10th century, marks the time when town life had collapsed completely, after which fields and farms may have been laid out and worked within the Roman town walls. For part of this period the new town of Lundenwic prospered to the west of Londinium, but this too failed, presumably as a consequence of Viking raids. The Late Saxon settlement which gradually grew to fill out the Roman walled area was therefore a new foundation, an English and not a classical town. When the Department of Urban Archaeology began its comprehensive programme of archaeological research in 1973, it was thought that the City had been continuously occupied from the Roman period for 2,000 years (Biddle et al. 1973, 9). As a direct consequence of our work, we have been forced to revise that figure to a mere 1,100 years, fundamentally rewriting the City's history in the process. London is no longer seen as the oldest surviving town in Britain, for that title is now bestowed on Ipswich.

4 The 'Ledene Hall' and medieval market

MEDIEVAL AND MODERN LEADENHALL 1195–1990

Mark Samuel and Gustav Milne

From this point onwards our understanding of the site's development is increasingly enhanced by such documentary records as survive coupled with study of maps and plans from the 16th century onwards. Nevertheless, the archaeological evidence is still able to illuminate this period, most notably in the case of the 15th-century Garner (Samuel 1989). As for the building which it replaced, the original 13th-century Leadenhall, few documentary references survive and regrettably the archaeological evidence recovered was at best meagre. This chapter opens with an attempt to reconcile insubstantial fragments of archaeological and documentary data, from which a provisional plan of the first Leadenhall is compiled which locates its site for the first time. It then goes on to summarise what is known of the history of the later medieval market and its fate. An assessment of the archaeological evidence for this unique building is presented in Chapter 11.

1195–1455: The 'Ledene Hall'
(Fig 21)

In 1195 the site was acquired by the Nevilles, an aristocratic family from Essex, who built a great hall and domestic complex there to serve as their town house. The 13th-century hall must have been a building of some consequence, since its name 'Ledene Hall', which is first mentioned in 1296 (Thomas 1923, 6), was subsequently given to the adjacent street. Fig 21 is an attempt to show the layout of this urban aristocratic estate and is based on the archaeological evidence of its foundations, direct and indirect documentary references, and on analogy with contemporary buildings. The Leadenhall apparently lay on the northern side of a courtyard which was flanked by ranges of ancillary buildings with gatehouses to north and east.

Recent research suggests that the precise site of this building may have been located, but much of the evidence which supports this suggestion is indirect, and comes from assessments of the later levels on the Leadenhall Court site. Documentary evidence suggests that the Leadenhall initially survived the completion of the 15th-century Garner (Thomas 1923, 20). This assumption is indirectly supported by the archaeological observations: had the entire Leadenhall been demolished in advance, then reused stone would surely have been utilised in quantity for the Garner foundations and walls, but this was clearly not the case as the field records show. This implies that the hall stood within the area enclosed by the later Garner (Samuel 1989, 144), and thus the courtyard of the 15th-century building should reflect the outline and position of the 13th-century hall.

Significantly, the recent excavations revealed several square truncated foundations in that area: three are aligned on Leadenhall Street (Fig 21 and Pl 19), while two follow the line of Gracechurch Street in the west. Foundations on a similar alignment were recorded to the east in the 1880s, and it is tempting to interpret the two groups as the eastern and western ends of the hall. The western foundations therefore probably mark the boundary between the hall and a small garden opposite the choir of St Peter Cornhill, recorded as adjoining the Leadenhall in 1320 (Cal LB E, 119). (This north–south boundary is of some note,

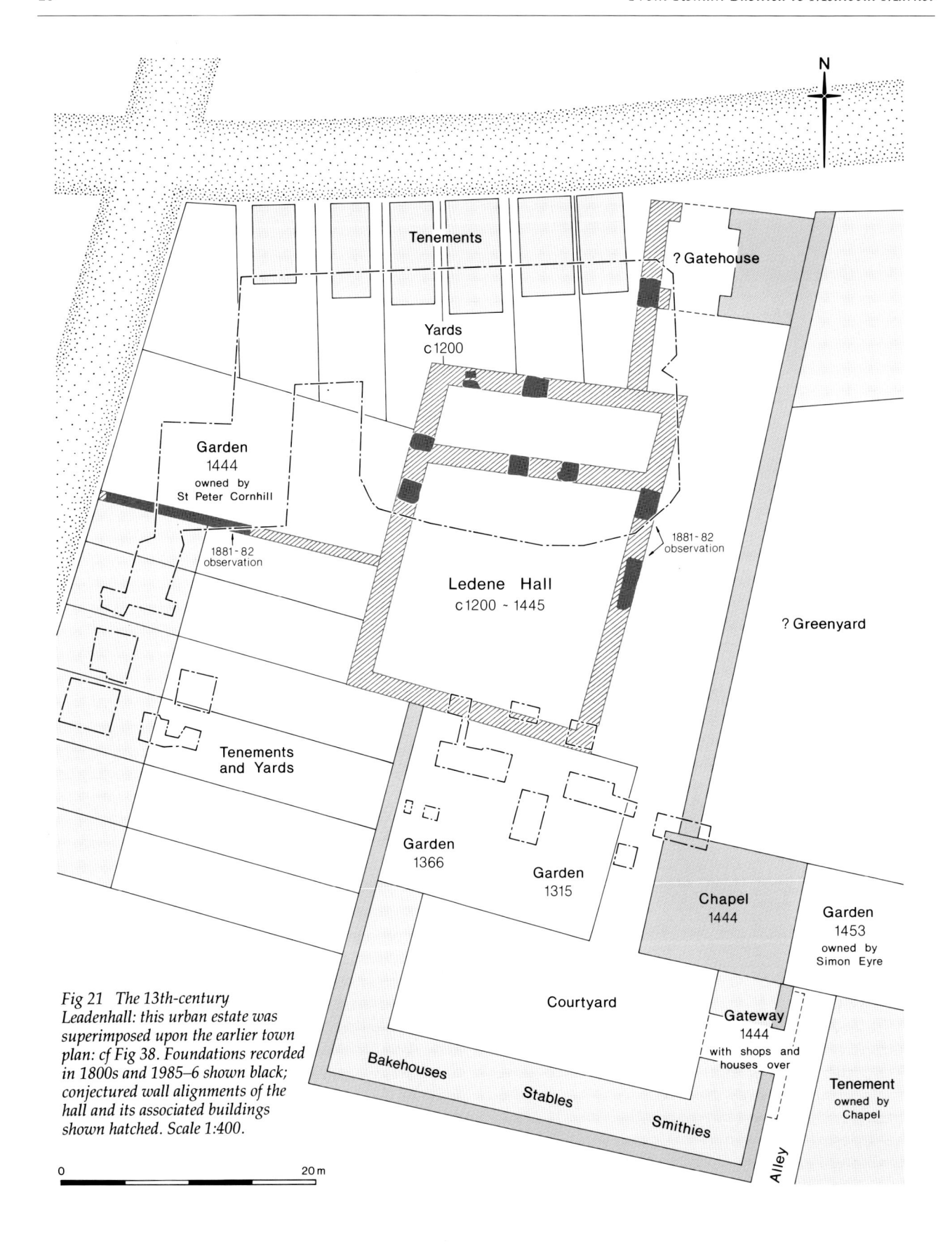

Fig 21 The 13th-century Leadenhall: this urban estate was superimposed upon the earlier town plan: cf Fig 38. Foundations recorded in 1800s and 1985–6 shown black; conjectured wall alignments of the hall and its associated buildings shown hatched. Scale 1:400.

Pl 19 Building on the past: square foundation of the 15th-century Garner laid over demolished remains of an earlier building (with 5x100mm scale), presumably part of the 13th-century Leadenhall complex. (Area N, looking east)

for it was common to all the properties on the eastern side of Gracechurch Street. The City subsequently had to buy up this entire frontage to build the western range of the 15th-century Garner.)

These foundations are interpreted as stanchions upon which foundation arches rested, a technique known to date back to at least 1220. A fine waterleaf capital and part of an arch voussoir were recovered from these foundations, and these must have been derived from the demolition of a Norman building of late 12th-century date. The building represented by the stanchions must therefore have been built after that date, possibly in the early to mid-13th century. A provisional assessment of a small group of pottery from its destruction levels which includes Cheam ware manufactured after 1380 is consistent with a demolition date in the mid-15th century (Samuel 1989, 144, note 62). Although it cannot be proved that the foundations certainly supported the Nevilles' Leadenhall, the foundations do indicate the presence of a substantial masonry building on its most probable site.

The Leadenhall was essentially similar to other contemporary town houses such as Ely Place, Holborn and Arundel House on the Strand, known from old prints and drawings (Schofield 1984, 65, 87). Documentary evidence suggests that it would have had a series of lesser service buildings in addition to the hall itself. A triple doorway at one end would have led to a buttery, kitchen passage and pantry, with a spiral stair at the opposite end leading to the solar. There would certainly have been a private chapel, and other buildings ranged around a yard such as bakehouses, stables and the servants' quarters. A gatehouse presumably projected northwards to Leadenhall Street (beneath the northern range of the later Garner), and would have been dominated by the great lead roof of the hall behind it. Another gatehouse, which led towards Lime Street is mentioned in the land transactions.

The interior of the great hall at Penshurst Place, Kent, gives some idea of how the Leadenhall may have looked in its heyday. The aisled hall would have been heated by a central hearth, the smoke rising to a louvre at the centre of the high pitched timber roof. The Lord of the Nevilles feasted in the company of his household and guests. Together with his family and the important guests, he sat at the centre of a long table raised at one end of the hall, where he could be seen by all at the other tables ranged along the length of the hall. Close by him were the 'cup boards', boards on trestles upon which gold and silver cups and plates were ostentatiously displayed. The more gently bred household officers sat at the steward's table, while others were supervised by the marshal of the hall, clerk of the kitchen or other yeomen household officers (Girouard 1980). The architecture and layout therefore expressed the strength and unity of the household as well as the hospitality of its lord. But what happened to this vision of chivalric splendour?

In the 14th century it became unfashionable for the lord and lady to eat in hall, and by 1400 the day of the Great Hall set in the heart of the City had passed. Although the Nevilles continued to live in the complex, it seems that they now leased the spacious hall to guilds that lacked chambers for their meetings (Williams 1963, 267), while a court of justice was occasionally held there in the 1320s (Cal LB E 119). An additional source of income came from using the large courtyard as a market, for it is known that country poulterers set up their stalls here by 1321 (Thomas 1923, 1).

The City administration now took over the running of this market, one of the few places in which non-freemen could trade in London. For example, in 1377 country cheesemongers were ordered to bring their wares here (Thomas 1923, 8). Taxes paid by such country stall-holders went towards the upkeep of the town wall, so that it was worth the City's while to maintain the courtyard for their use. Expenses were recovered by the rents on a garden annexed to the hall and owned by the City. The old courtyard therefore became a market which was centrally situated but, unlike most of its contemporaries, was not held in the street, and thus did not obstruct the traffic in the main thoroughfare: as such, its potential was soon recognised. With the death of Alice Neville in 1394, the Neville connection ceased, and in 1411 the Leadenhall passed to the City (Thomas 1923, 14). The elderly mayor, Richard Whittington, doubtless thought that the City might as well own the market which it had administered for so long. The stage was set for the next major development in the area's history.

1440–1455: The building of the Garner
(Figs 22, 23)

After repeated shortages of grain in the early 15th century, the City decided to build a granary at Leadenhall and on 30 March 1440 two Aldermen and two Commoners were appointed to organise the work. General taxes were not usually imposed for

Fig 22 Plan of the present-day City showing position of 15th-century Garner, market and chapel at Leadenhall in relation to Old London Bridge and medieval markets held at The Shambles, Cheapside and the Stocks. Scale 1: 20,000

public works, for legacies and donations were preferred. Such gifts were seen as pious acts: this was an age when religion was intimately interwoven with everyday life. However, all was not peaceful in London in that year. A group of Tailors was imprisoned for trying to shout down proceedings when a Draper was elected Mayor in the newly-completed Guildhall. Under the terms of their royal charter awarded in 1423, the Drapers now had exclusive rights to determine the quality of the cloth they dealt with: the Tailors were fearful for their rights. Another prosperous draper and prospective mayor, one Simon Eyre, observed the goings-on with alarm. He must have appreciated that if the power and prestige of the mayoralty were to be extended, it must not seem to be motivated by self-interest.

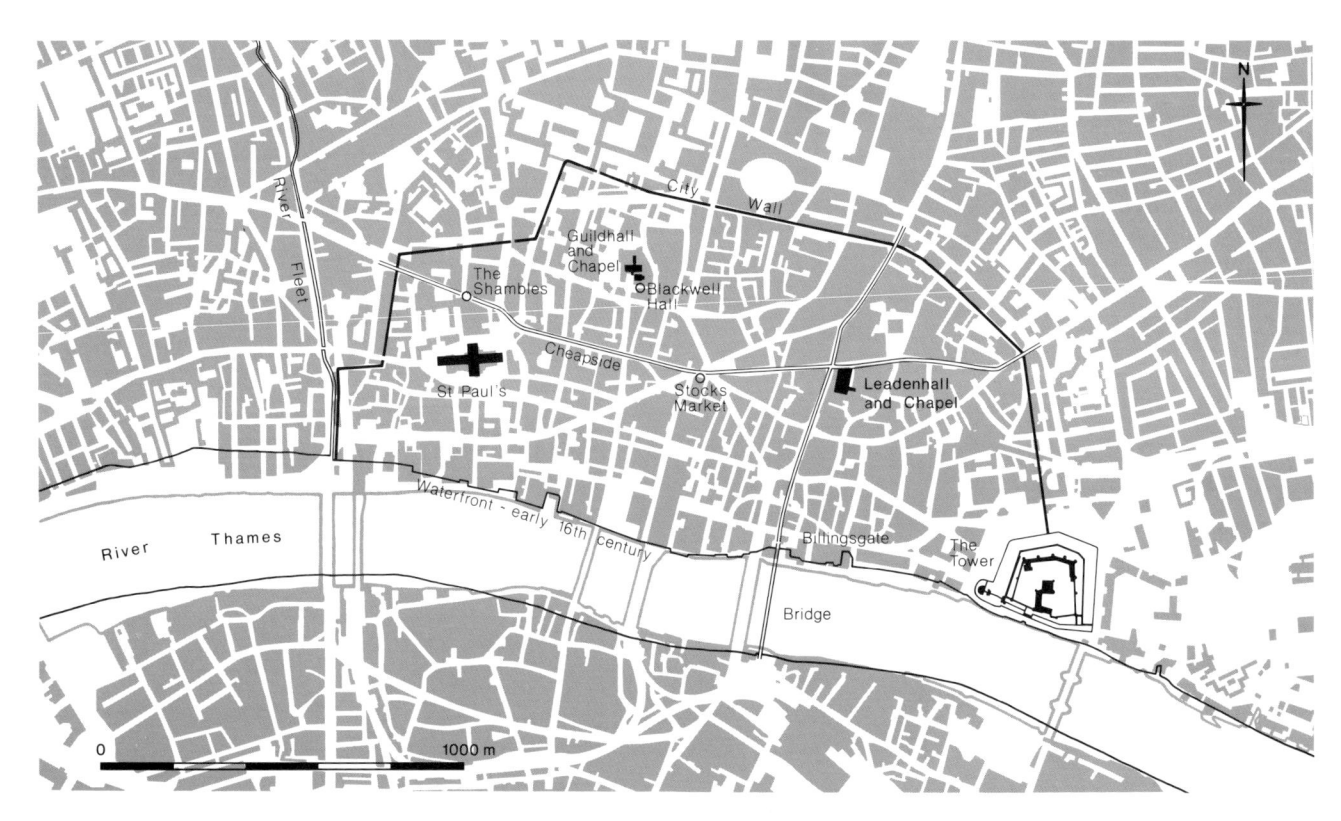

Perhaps it was this thought which prompted him to promote the construction of the Garner so ardently, for here was a project which, by preventing a shortage of bread, would remove a major source of discontent. Such a scheme also strengthened the City at the expense of the Crown, for London was dependent upon royal licence for the import and export of grain. Because such a licence could be withheld, the City was obliged to remain on good terms with the king, especially during the periods of shortage which occurred in the early 15th century. By maintaining its own stocks of grain, the City's independence would be notably enhanced. Simon Eyre therefore bore all the expenses of the Garner's construction for seven years, with the City paying for the complex pattern of necessary land purchases.

Work began slowly, for the sites of the east and west ranges were still in private hands in December 1442. The foundations for the northern and southern ranges seem to have been completed first, after which the work came to a halt and the mason, John Croxtone, returned to his work on the Guildhall Chapel in 1443. In May the following year, the Lime Street approach frontage was bought, and this incorporated an 'ancient gate', presumably the eastern gatehouse of the Leadenhall. Thereafter work could start on the eastern range. It seems that another gatehouse survived until the 1440s since its foundations were reused in the footings of the new Garner. The election of Simon Eyre as Mayor in 1445 ensured speedier progress for the project, and once all the new land had been acquired, buildings cleared and the rest of the foundations laid, the walls rose quickly.

The foundations of this building were recorded in 1986, and those archaeological records enabled the position of the medieval market to be plotted in relation to the modern street frontage for the first time. In addition, an upstanding fragment of the west wall was discovered encased within a 19th-century office block, from which it proved possible to calculate the height of the building, while study of 177 moulded stones derived from doors, arches and windows facilitated the reconstruction of the 15th-century facade. These noteworthy archaeological contributions to the documented history of this unique medieval market are discussed in detail in Chapter 11 (see also Samuel 1989; Samuel in preparation).

1455–1666: The Garner before the Great Fire (Fig 23, Pl 20)

By 1455, the building was substantially complete, ready to serve its dual purpose as both a garner and a market. On 27 March, the Common Council resolved that the market for poultry, victuals, grain, eggs, butter and cheese held previously at the Old Leadenhall should now be held within the newly-built Garner on the 'common soil of the Commonalty' (Thomas 1923, 20). This implies that the market continued to be housed in the old hall, which must have remained standing during the construction programme. This in turn supports the probability that the Leadenhall lay within the courtyard of the 15th-century Garner. Like the 1st-century forum before it, it remained in use while a larger building was built around it, and was only demolished once work on its replacement was complete (cf. Fig 31). However, at least one prestigious building in the vicinity must have been demolished before the Garner was built, since fragments of Caen stone were found reused in its west wall.

The new Garner at Leadenhall comprised four ranges around the central courtyard: the arcaded ground floor functioned as part of the common market (Fig 23). These public or common markets were retail markets at which country folk from the surrounding districts could sell their produce on a particular day of the week at a particular place directly to the townspeople, and stood in contrast to the City's own shopkeepers, who were able to sell to citizens six days a week from their own shops. The arcade was the 'seld' mentioned in documents.

There is also evidence that a grammar school and a chapel were built at the same time as the Garner, the chapel being built on the site of the Leadenhall's domestic chapel and retaining its square crypt. Although paid for by Simon Eyre, it was meant to serve the market people, and the City therefore bought the land it stood on, making it common soil. It was intended to house the choristers trained in the adjoining school.

To the north of the chapel was the school, traces of which were uncovered on the Whittington Avenue excavations (Appendix A). A row of masonry foundations was recorded, similar to those associated with the Garner on the Leadenhall Court site, and this is thought to represent the line of one wall of the 15th-century school. An L-shaped robber trench and further foundations to the west are probably associated. Together they define part of a large rectangular building which was probably arcaded along its southern edge and ran eastwards from the Garner. A watching brief trench on the Leadenhall Court site located a mass of chalk foundation material, probably representing the junction between the two buildings. The structure was so wide that its floors would have required intermediate support, but evidence for such internal walls lay outside the excavation trenches.

No mention is made of this building in the City's records, suggesting that Simon Eyre purchased the land privately, such information as there is for the school coming exclusively from his will. This document records that he obtained land for 'three schools and chambers with all the void ground and a little garden lying eastwards from the said schools', which were to have 'convenient and open lights, free entry and issue to and fro, by and through the new works, there late edified by me, the said Simon.' The

college's substantial staff, whom Eyre endowed with the enormous sum of 3,000 marks to pay for the buildings after his death, were already accommodated in 'chambers and other housing newly made for them'. As well as a team of secular priests, clerks and choristers 'to sing divine service by note' in the chapel, there were also three schools for masters of

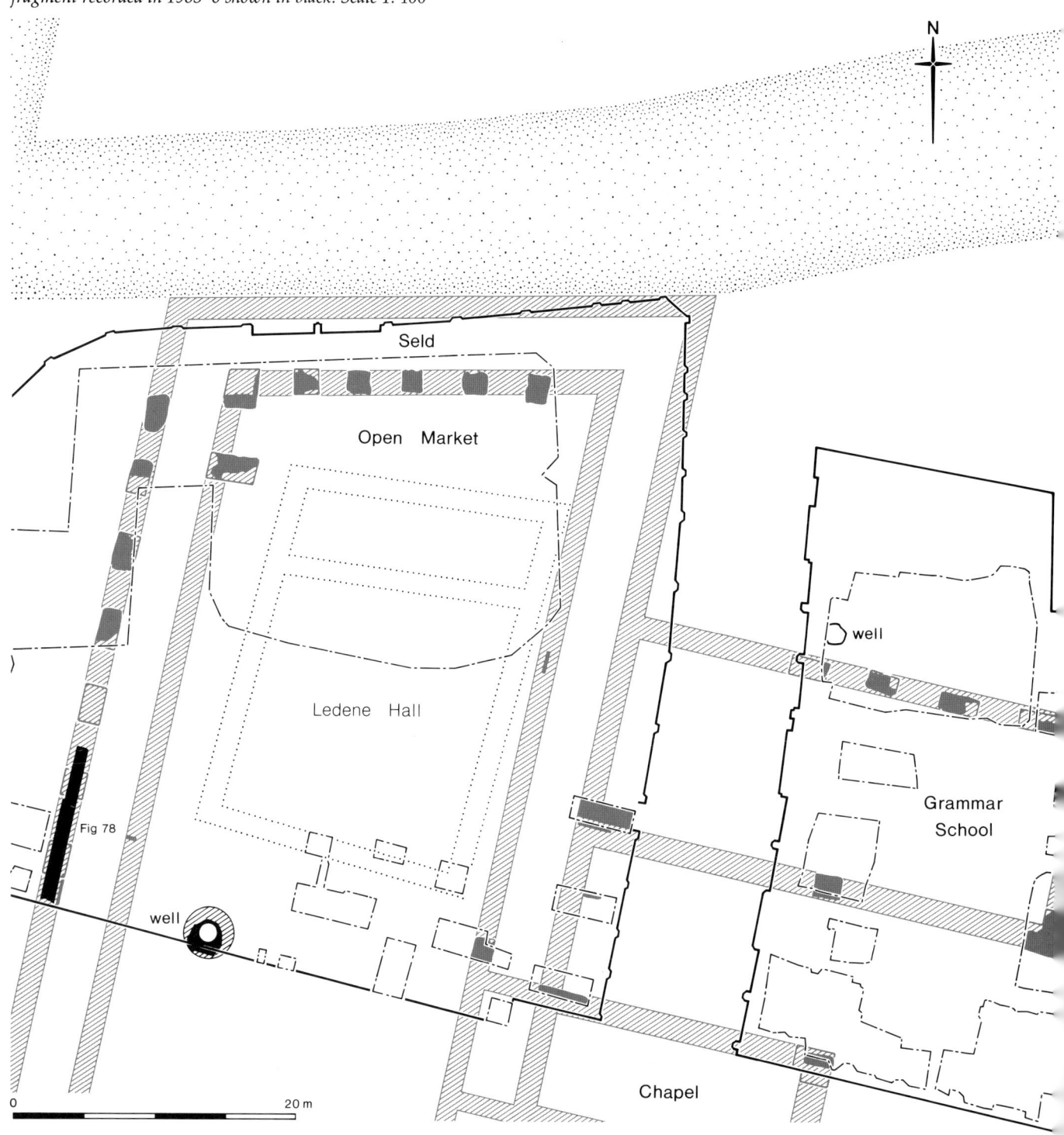

Fig 23 Plan showing part of the 15th-century market, chapel and school built at Leadenhall for mayor Simon Eyre in the 1440s. Foundations recorded in 1985–6 and 1988–9 shown in grey tone; conjectured elements shown hatched; line of upstanding west wall fragment recorded in 1985–6 shown in black. Scale 1: 400

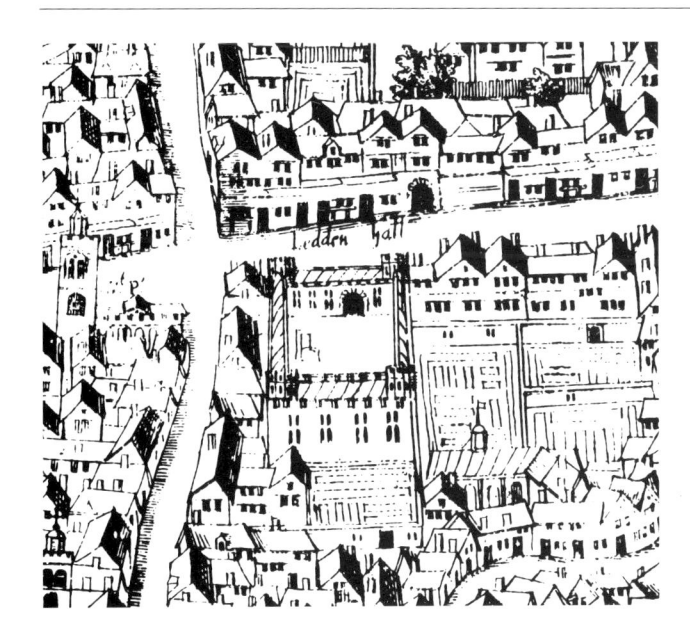

Pl 20 Elizabethan Leadenhall: a view of the Garner from the south, showing corner towers, entrance in northern range, and well in the courtyard. From the 'Copperplate' Map, dated to the 1550s

grammar, writing and song with ushers (PCC Stockton, 13).

Since there was a right of way from the schools to the Garner, the college buildings cannot have extended south of the chapel. It seems that the three schools and the housing all fitted within a single block which, like the Garner, must have been three-storeyed, as the substantial nature of the excavated foundations show. The school was probably arcaded at ground level, and between it and the chapel was a small court, perhaps closed off on its eastern side by a narrower range. This grouping of buildings may be identified with properties represented on the Ogilby and Morgan survey of 1676 (Fig 24a). A court surrounded by school buildings and a chapel is similar to the contemporary plan of Eton College, built in 1442.

The Leadenhall school was typical of its time, bearing little relationship to a school in the modern sense. There was no division between the religious and the secular, and Eyre was as concerned with training choristers as with teaching literacy, wanting the highest standards of singing for divine service in his chapel. It was only with the Reformation that song schools were suppressed as superstitious. The endowment of schools kept by a chantry priest was fashionable in the 15th century (Bannister-Fletcher 1943, 426): the City of London School of 1442 has the same origins for example. However, although Eyre was largely concerned with the standard of singing in his chapel, it seems that he also tried to provide a wider educational service, which was to be administered by the Drapers. Since the students were probably taught to write Latin they would have been teenagers rather than children. The Leadenhall School would therefore fall into a category between school and university (C Barron, pers comm). The schoolroom building may have resembled Archbishop Chichele's school at Higham Ferrers, Northamptonshire, in which case it would have looked very similar to the chapel to the south. Housing for the staff may have been sited on the third (eastern) side of the school-yard.

In addition to the common market, college and chapel, this remarkable 15th-century complex also incorporated a Garner. The two upper floors of the main ranges over the arcade were long, uninterrupted galleries, purpose-built as a granary. It was used as such at some stages in its history, as for example in 1512 when Mayor Roger Acheley was storing grain here during an acute shortage, but this instance is almost the exception which proves the rule. Although Mayor Simon Eyre envisaged the maintenance of permanent stockpiles of grain to be sold to the citizens at normal prices when shortages occurred, the will to give over large areas of valuable storage space solely to the common good was evidently lacking after his death. His successors devised ways of making the building pay for itself. For example, to ease the collection of duties, the storage and marketing of some imported goods was restricted to the new, self-contained building, which proved eminently suitable for this purpose. As early as 1463 lead nails and the 'cloth called Worsteds' were ordered to be stored and sold there, and before the end of the century it was decreed that the weighing and selling of wool as well as the searching, sealing and selling of tanned leather brought into the City should only be conducted at Leadenhall. In the 16th century, some parts of the building were used as a repository for arms and ammunition, and others for the materials for the pageants used in the Midsummer Watch (Wheatley 1956, 144; Masters 1974). The intentions of Simon Eyre were therefore not fully realised: indeed, his executors, the Drapers, even failed to administer his school and chapel, although, as we have seen, Eyre had left 3,000 marks in his will for that very purpose.

In 1618 the Merchants of the Staple leased all the storage space on the eastern and southern sides of the court as well as the chapel and the weigh-house, while the newly-formed East India Company leased much of the space in the western and northern ranges. By 1658 the central role played by Leadenhall in London's textile trade is recorded in a contemporary lease. This shows that virtually all three levels of warehousing were leased to Christ's Hospital for the 'stowadge, keepings and sellings therein of all Suffolke Cloth, Coventry Cloth and Suffolke and Essex Bayes' (Masters 1974, 21). However, the East India Company continued to rent some accommodation there, presumably in the two 'Tackle Houses' recorded on Leybourn's plan of 1677 (Masters 1974, pl VII). Contemporary records show that material was being stored on three levels, and this can only mean that the ground floor which had originally been built as an open arcade for use on market days had been enclosed and subdivided into separate storage rooms. This process can be traced back to at least 1519, and may have begun even earlier. As a consequence, the covered market was now contained within a range of single-storey lean-to buildings built around the edge of the central courtyard and encroaching over it. The markets held here and in the Greenyard to the east of the Garner (the site of the garden belonging to the original Leadenhall) included both a beef market on three days in the week, and a white market, that is one in which other meats such as mutton, lamb, pork, veal and poultry were sold, as the records for 1631 show.

1666: The Great Fire and its aftermath
(Fig 24a)

The Great Fire of London destroyed much of the ancient City in five days in September 1666. However, the otherwise all-conquering conflagration was unable to make any impression on the windowless bulk of the Garner's western and southern ranges: 'a check it had at Leadenhall, by that great building...', as an eye-witness observed (Vincent 1667; Milne 1986, 64). Thirteen thousand houses were destroyed together with most of the public markets, but the City moved swiftly to impose some order on the ensuing chaos once the flames had been extinguished. The Garner at Leadenhall now became the principal focus for the City's markets, in this, its darkest hour. By the end of September, the City butchers (whose shops had all been destroyed) were installed in the central courtyard. The country butchers set up to the east of the Garner in the Little Greenyard, with the Fishmongers in the Old Greenyard, while a white market was established in Leadenhall Street to the north. This pattern continued until London had recovered sufficiently to reorganise itself, for the Great Rebuilding programme was soon under way. By 1668, the fishmongers moved to different premises and the beef market now held in the Leadenhall courtyard and in the Greenyard alternated with a leather and hide market on different days of the week. Ten years after the fire, work on erecting a covered piazza and some 100 stalls around the edge of the courtyard was well advanced as Leybourn's plans show (Masters 1974). In a separate development, a new herb market for the sale of fruit, vegetables and dairy products was established to the south-west of the Leadenhall building. The three storeys of the 15th-century Garner itself continued to be used for storage, Christ's Hospital renewing their lease on the warehouse space in 1738. However, the East India Company withdrew from Leadenhall at that date to their own custom-built buildings elsewhere in the City, and their Tackle Houses were converted into leather warehouses.

1793–1812: The Garner contracts
(Figs 24b, c)

On 9 February 1793 letters patent were granted for enclosing the right of way through the northern range. As a consequence, this range was demolished the following year and replaced by a Georgian terrace. Some of the cellars of these new buildings were built from stones from the old market and were recovered in the 1985–6 excavations (see Chapter 11). The northern sections of the east and west wings were pulled down at the same time, so that the only access to the contracted market was through the Green Market entrance.

Less than 20 years later, in May 1812, the next major redevelopment saw the remainder of the east wing and the chapel demolished, as were most of the southern and western ranges. However, the outer walls of these two wings were retained, against which large sheds were now erected to house the Hide and Horn Markets (Fig 24c).

Fig 24 Protracted demolition of Leadenhall Garner revealed by study of maps: a) 1676: the market after the Great Fire (Ogilby and Morgan); b) 1799: northern range demolished and replaced by houses (Horwood); c) 1878: market buildings demolished, but sections survive in south and west as party walls (OS); d) 1983: fragments of those walls survive major redevelopments in the 1880s, but west wall demolished in 1986 (see fig 42)

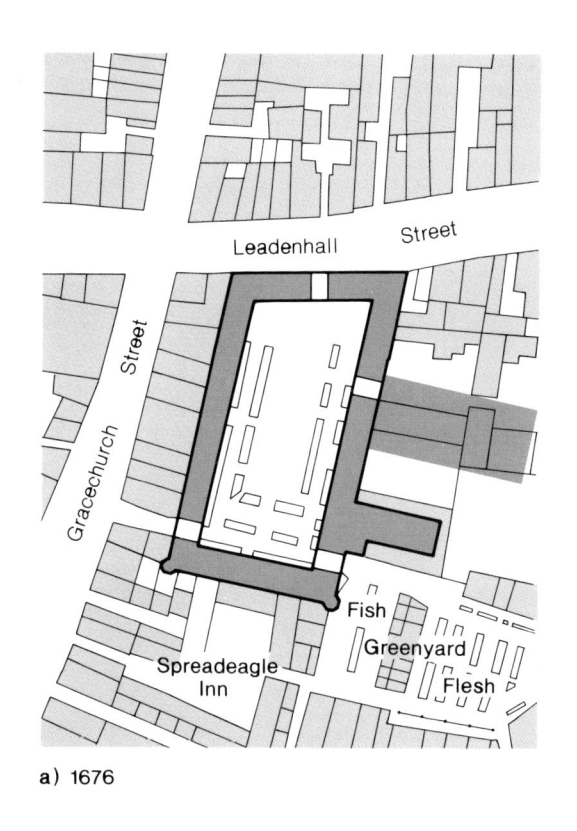

The 'Ledene Hall' and medieval market   47

a) 1676

b) 1799

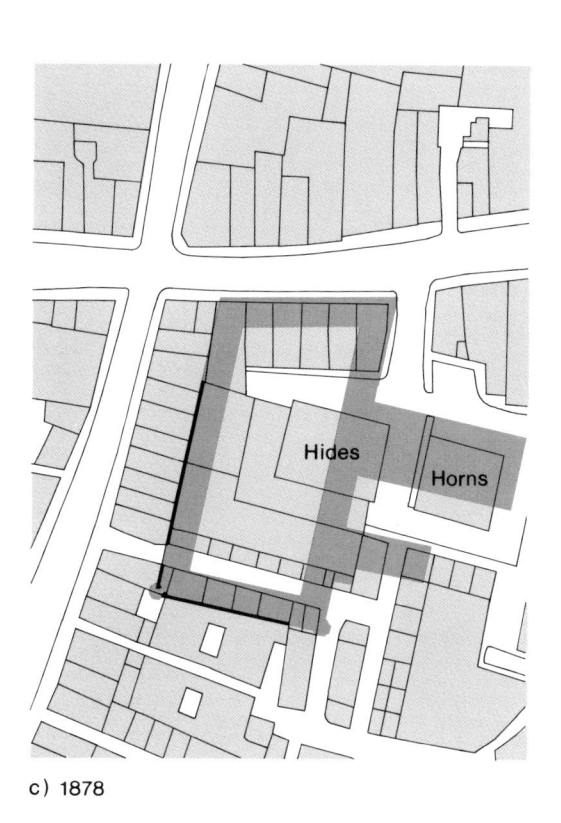

c) 1878

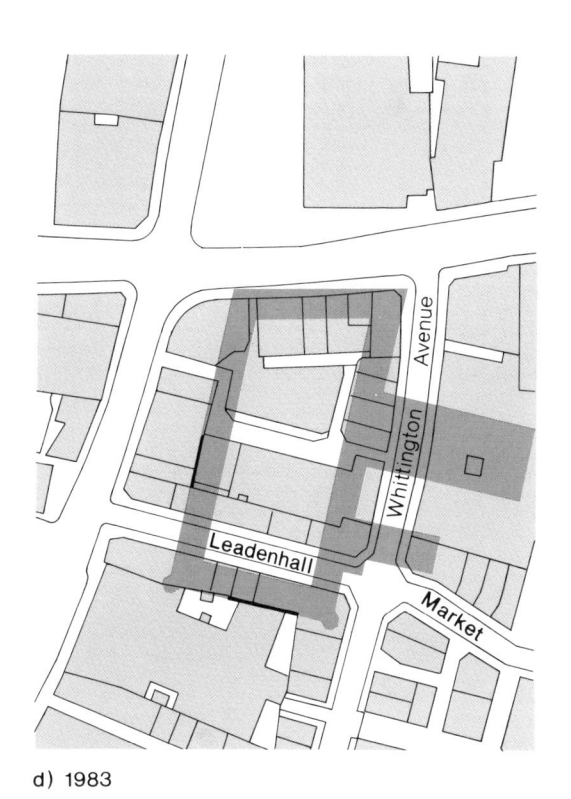

d) 1983

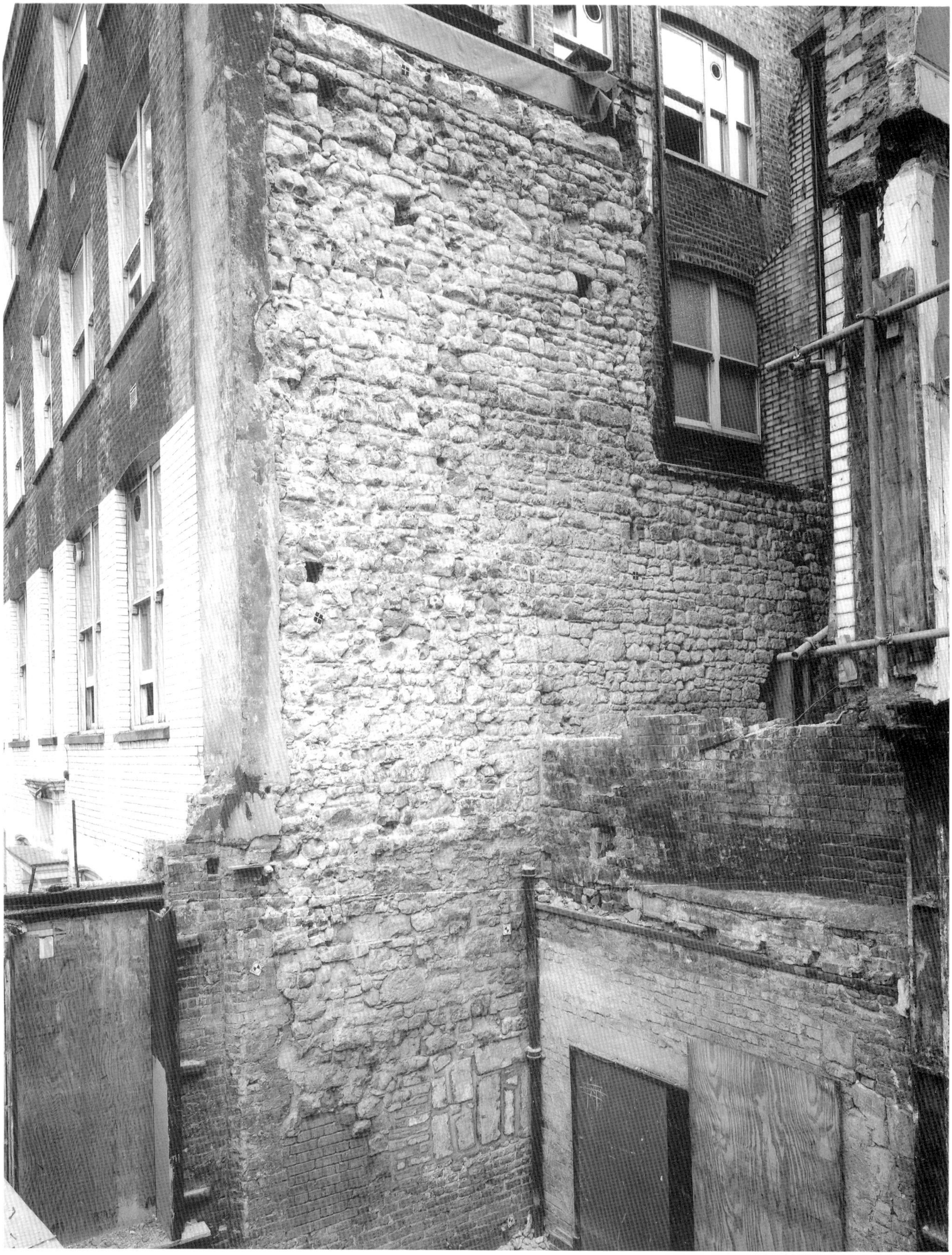

The 'Ledene Hall' and medieval market

OPPOSITE
Pl 21 Stone-walling: this remarkable fragment of the 15th-century Garner survived the Great Fire of 1666, demolition of the rest of the medieval market in the 19th century, and the Blitz in the 1940s. The western (external) face of the west range, as exposed in September 1986, survived to its full height encased within a complex of 19th-century offices: cf. Pl 22 and Fig 42

ABOVE
Pl 22 Last view of east (internal) face of the Garner wall, as exposed in November 1986, just prior to demolition. Note arched chalk foundations below ground floor and dressed ashlar facing used in granary on upper storey: cf. Pl 21 and Fig 42

1880: The new Leadenhall Market
(Fig 24d)

Leadenhall began life as a general food market, and played a central role in the everyday life of London, including its folk lore: it was for example from Leadenhall Market that Scrooge ordered the Christmas turkey for the Cratchits. But in 1880–1 the elegant purpose-built market now known as Leadenhall Market was built to replace the other markets. It comprised a series of shops opening out onto narrow streets covered by a glass roof supported on iron columns. The architect responsible for this much-loved complex was Horace Jones who, like John Croxtone in the 15th century, had also worked on several major public buildings for the Corporation. In his distinguished career he designed Smithfield Market (1867), the old Guildhall Library in Basinghall Street (1873), Billingsgate Fish Market (1875), the old Guildhall School of Music in John Carpenter Street (1887), in addition to that most famous of all London landmarks, Tower Bridge (1894). Leadenhall Market remains a building that is both functional and decorative, exuding an air of spaciousness even though it has been squeezed on to a cramped if charmingly asymmetrical site. But the Market, like the City, has seen great change over the last 10 years for the 'Big Bang' has brought coffee, croissants and champagne into the arcade. The poultry hooks still survive, although most of the fish, fowl and vegetables are now but a memory of Christmas past.

The construction of this covered market and other contemporary developments saw the demolition of the remaining parts of the 15th-century Garner, with the exception of two fragments. Although the late 19th-century Metal Exchange Building was erected over the site of the Hide and Horn Market, the western wall abutted two 17th-century houses which had themselves been built directly on to the outer wall of the medieval Garner. As a result, an 11m stretch of the Garner was fortuitously preserved as a party wall, surviving the demolition of the 17th-century houses shortly after. Part of the Garner's southern wall survived for similar reasons, encapsulated within subsequent developments, and still remains behind 16–19 Leadenhall Market. The lower section of the wall was sketched by Henry Hodge in 1882 (Marsden 1987. pl 9) and clearly marked 'this wall remains'. Fifty years later, its footings were observed by archaeologist Frank Cottrill while working for the Guildhall Museum on the adjacent site in 1934, although the full significance of the observation was not realised at the time. Unfortunately the western wall fragment, having survived the Great Fire of 1666, all the 18th- and 19th-century demolition programmes and the Blitz in the 1940s, was ignominiously demolished in December 1986 during the construction of Leadenhall Court. However, the opportunity was taken to record the remarkable fragment of Simon Eyre's Garner in the detail it unquestionably deserved (Pls 21 and 22; see also Chapter 11).

1986: Leadenhall Court

The present building on the site is the seven-storey Leadenhall Court, a £40 million development incorporating Marks and Spencer at ground level, with 93,000 sq ft of office accommodation on the upper floors. Construction work began in December 1986, the shell was completed in a topping-out ceremony on 21 March 1988, and the building was ready for occupation just one year later. The total construction programme lasted less than two and a half years, which may be compared with the 15 years taken to build the 15th-century Garner and the 30 years needed for the Roman Basilica. But what of the future? Archaeologists viewing the present redevelopment have the benefit of an objectively long perspective: the new Leadenhall Court replaced a number of smaller discrete properties built at various dates and housing a variety of shops and offices. As such this latest development echoes previous phases of the site's long history, for the Roman Basilica, the 'Ledene Hall', and the medieval Garner were all grand designs imposed upon a more diverse pattern of urban ownership. Each one of the grand designs then experienced periods of subdivision and contraction, followed ultimately by demolition. This is the cyclic nature of urban development, a lesson so clearly expressed in our study of Leadenhall's long history, a story which is in essence the story of London itself.

5 The archaeologist as alchemist

TURNING MUD INTO HISTORY

Gustav Milne

The excavator turns mud and stones into paper records: the archaeologist turns those records into history. How is such alchemy achieved? Many methods have been tried and hotly debated: at one end of the spectrum are those who believe in intuition and subjectivity (not necessarily the same thing), at the other end of the spectrum are those who preach objectivity and hold unshakeable faith in computers. In practice, the Leadenhall Court project needed a little of everything to reach the conclusions presented here: whether these results and their interpretations represent 'The Truth' is quite another matter. In this and the following chapter an attempt is made to show how a chronological framework was imposed upon the field record, that is to say how a sequence of historical events was reconstructed by examining a mountain of plans and A4 record sheets. Once **what** happened was known, **when** was established, then reasons **why** were advanced. But first some basic principles concerning our methodology must be clarified.

Records, reports and publications

There are three quite separate stages in the search for an understanding of the past as represented by the layers at Leadenhall. First is the gathering of the evidence, second, the assessment of that data, and finally the interpretation of that assessment. These three stages are broadly represented by the field record, the archive report, and this book respectively. Although discrete entities all are interrelated. There can be no meaningful publication unless a thorough assessment has been made of the field record, while the true worth of the most meticulously compiled field record will never be realised until the site is discussed in print. A site cannot be preserved just by the act of recording it, any more than a work of art can be preserved by making notes on how many colours were used, before throwing it under a mechanical excavator. The field record must be assessed, and the results published if the sites are to be understood, i.e. 'saved' for posterity. This is not to say that a published report has more worth than the dirty, dog-eared field records; quite the contrary. The better the field record, the better the publication might be, for no amount of PhDs can ever overcome basic omissions in the data collected on site. Archaeological publication is, therefore, an obligation, but one which depends wholly upon a thorough assessment of a sound field record. There can be no substitute for that. As St Paul might have said if he were writing an archaeological manual for the Corinthians: 'There are then, these three things, the field record, the archive report and the publication: but the greatest of them is the field record.'

Collecting raw data

To begin at the beginning: there were on Leadenhall Court, as on other deeply stratified urban sites, the remains of many phases of Roman occupation. They comprised a sequence of overlying layers and intercutting features forming a horizon of deposits over

2m thick. To excavate this site in plan, the basement slabs were drilled out and the modern make-up levels beneath removed. Grid points for planning and bench marks for levelling were established and effective ways of shifting spoil devised. Then each trench was scraped back with shovels, hoes or trowels (or occasionally with mechanical excavators) and full archaeological recording began, one layer or feature at a time. The extent of each and every layer was methodically revealed and recorded before it was removed to expose whatever features lay directly beneath it (Pl 3). The field record for each layer comprised a **plan** just of that layer drawn at 1:20 related to the trench grid (and ultimately the National Grid), with levels related to Ordnance Datum (OD). A standard written description was also compiled on pro-forma **context sheets**, and a possible interpretation suggested. The same context number was used for the plan, context sheet and for the labels in the bag for the finds recovered from that layer. A **field matrix** was also compiled, a table which shows which features were stratigraphically earlier and later than each context number: the importance of this table is considered later.

When the investigation of a particular trench reached and recorded the natural Brickearth or gravel deposits and all evidence of human activity had been examined, the excavations concluded. At that stage all that remained of the thick horizon of ancient deposits were the bags of finds, the photographs, context sheets, plans, and the matrix tables. These records had been checked on site to ensure that basic information had been correctly compiled and that the relationships shown on the matrix tables were consistent with those marked on the field records. Inconsistencies discovered in a field record which was not checked as the excavation progressed often cannot be resolved later, which could mean that little reliance can be placed on the associated sequence.

Establishing a sequence of events

One of the prime tasks of the archaeological team at Leadenhall was to impose order upon the apparent chaos of layers which initially confronted them. In the past, the drawing of earth sections was traditionally used to establish the sequence of events represented on archaeological sites but this methodology has been shown to be unreliable. Many layers, while clear in plan, did not appear in section, and so could not contribute to the site's history, while other layers that loomed large in the baulk were simply distorted features. The section line itself would be determined before excavation began and could well prove to be in an atypical or inconvenient position as work progressed. Worst of all, if sections were to be used to control the site sequence, then the excavation would be constricted by many closely spaced baulks. Since the 1950s and 1960s it has been appreciated that open area excavation (Barker 1977, 12–26) is a far more satisfactory and effective way of recording deeply stratified occupation sequences. The emphasis has shifted from section drawing by rote to the production of a comprehensive series of plans. As excavation methodologies developed to record larger open sites, archaeologists working with complex deeply stratified urban material realised that they needed a more satisfactory system of imposing a sequential framework on the field record than that provided by section-drawing.

The matrix table was the solution which liberated the excavator from the tyranny of the section (Harris 1989). A small part of the Leadenhall matrix is illustrated in Table 1, where the stratigraphic relationships of just under 100 contexts representing the road and buildings north of the Basilica are displayed: the complete matrix table just for Area N has some 2,000 context numbers on it. Such a table represents the stratigraphic connections between layers and features by lines running above or below the context numbers. Given that every context number is on the table, and given that the correct relationships are shown, then that single piece of paper encapsulates the stratigraphic sequence recorded on that site. That having been established, a firm basis is provided from which ancient events might subsequently be deduced. But does the stratigraphic succession thus tabulated directly represent a sequence of historical events? How simple is the move from stratigraphy to chronology?

Earth, water, fire and air

If all our layers were well behaved, then all would be well, for our matrix might indeed represent the sequence of events. However, although we assume that we are recording evidence for the activity of Man, Nature insists on making her presence felt. As a consequence, layers do not keep still after deposition however much we may wish it otherwise. Indeed, whole sequences are subject to post-depositional deformation, such as compaction and slumping. Organic deposits and the foundations of timber buildings dry out and disappear. As soils form within the archaeological sequence such as the dark grey silts (Table 1, N46) which sealed the road and building north of the Basilica (Fig 18), worm and root action breaks down the underlying organic material, perhaps removing whole periods of occupation in the process (cf. Yule 1990). Slumping can also cause many stratigraphic headaches as well as providing some useful additions: in one of the truncated Basilica robber trenches disjointed fragments of an otherwise unrepresented late Roman occupation sequence were recorded, sometimes on edge, sometimes upside down. Such redeposited material can only be shown on the matrix table in its secondary position (i.e. as the fill of the robber trench), while the evidence for these 'missing' events can only be added to the report after the stratigraphic assessment of the matrix has been completed. Water is another problem: for example, water-laid deposits actually percolated into airspaces beneath the north wall of the Basilica after construction, an occurrence quite contrary to the basic laws of stratigraphy.

Leaching, staining and scorching also bring their problems, for excavators are trained to identify layers by looking for changes in texture or colour. However, layers exposed in the sides of pits and ditches can be stained, posthumously as it were, by the later fills of those features. Again the scorching effects of one of the major fires which were identified on the site were recorded on brickearth layers which were sealed at the time of the conflagration. A more extreme example of this phenomenon was noted on a site to the south, destroyed in the Great Fire of 1666: here, burning pitch had percolated through a brick floor and severely discoloured an earlier, medieval floor surface.

From this handful of examples it can be seen that the sequence as recorded is not necessarily the sequence as laid. Further complications are provided by major and minor truncations or erosion horizons which physically remove parts of the sequence, resulting in some layers being physically overlain by others substantially younger than them. Taken all in all, it can be seen that the sequence displayed on the matrix at Leadenhall was no more than a guide, albeit an indispensable one, from which a provisional sequence of events was deduced: our table provided an essential starting point. Its compilation on site served as a check and a control of our excavation procedure, and its subsequent examination formed the basis for the primary archive assessment of the site's development, while providing the means whereby separate trench sequences might be amalgamated. At all stages of the study, the matrix helped to highlight problems which were then resolved by reinterpreting the field records or by the application of reason, intuition and guesswork. To conclude: the matrix is not itself a direct representation of a sequence of events but is merely a sequential ordering of material produced by a series of events yet to be determined. Its study is a means to an end, and not an end in itself. Nevertheless it provided a framework upon which a long sequence of activity was suggested during the compilation of the archive report.

On groups and phasing
(Tables 1–4)

Our excavation therefore saw the site dissected into its smallest component parts, recorded as some 6,000 contexts, which were set within a provisional stratigraphic sequence tabulated on the field matrix. This mass of data was then converted into a more digestible sequence of 325 larger units, called simply **groups**, which were then amalgamated into some 30 calendar-dated **phases** of activity.The conversion process was the compilation of the **archive report,** which may be defined as an ordered summary of the field record which ultimately presents a phased assessment of the activity represented on the site. The structure and content of this report serves two ends. First of all, its structure is the means whereby the supervisor attempts to understand the sequence, while secondly the format is designed to provide a convenient *entrée* for anyone wishing to check or challenge the conclusions reached. It is not seen as a substitute for the field records which, as argued above, are the true representatives of the excavated sequence and must always be consulted in the event of detailed disputation.

The Leadenhall Court report involved several distinct stages of study. The sequence in each one of the trenches was considered separately in the first instance as 19 discrete reports were compiled. These reports examined the trench sequences, building up stratigraphically related groups of varying size, each one representing a building, a series of pits, a floor sequence within the Basilica Nave, a resurfacing of the Roman road or whatever. Table 1 shows a small

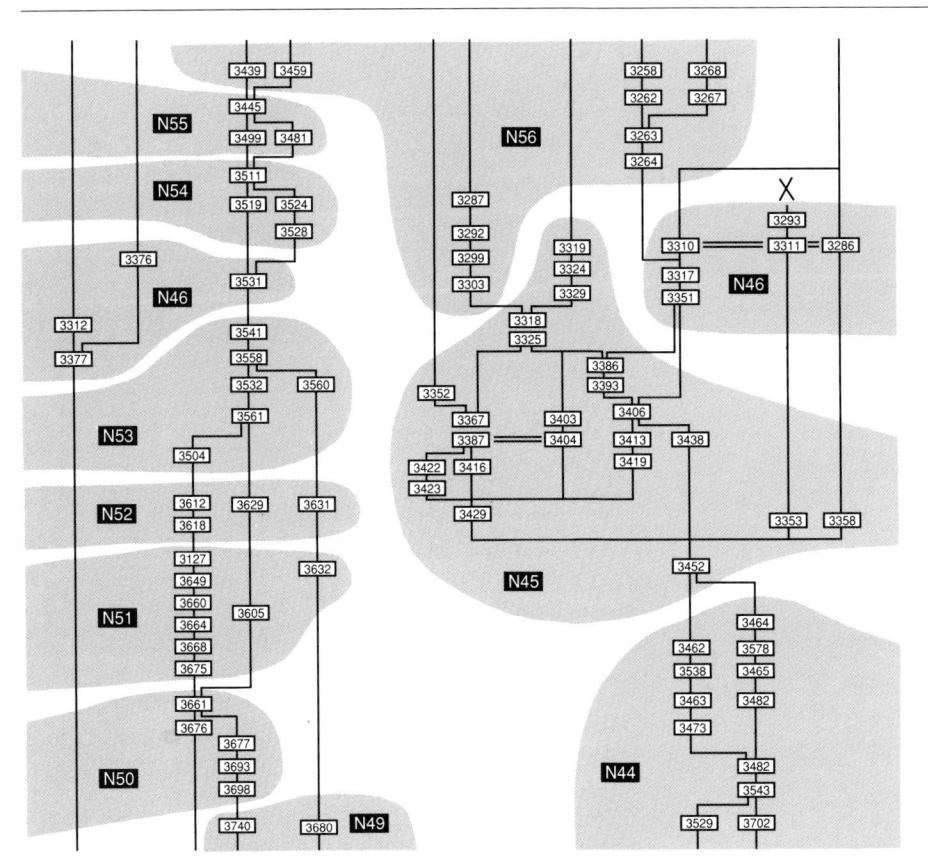

Table 1 Part of the Field matrix from the Leadenhall Court site, Area N (see Fig 4), showing stratigraphic relationships of various archaeological features, represented by the context numbers. Blocks of stratigraphically related contexts have been selected, and are shown shaded with the appropriate Group number, N44, N45, etc

BELOW
Table 2 Grouping the contexts: part of a table showing the stratigraphic relationship of 25 context Groups, N33 to N57. This table concisely summarises the stratigraphic relationships of 687 individual contexts from Leadenhall Court site, Area N

section of the Area N matrix after a number of groups had been identified, while part of the Area N Group sequence is drawn on Table 2 (cf. Table 3): a summary of each group may be found in Table 4. In the archive report, every group was drawn up at 1:20 on one of a series of multi-context plans, together with a list of contexts used, and a brief written description and discussion. The field records had now been converted into 325 groups each with its own plan, arranged into 19 discrete sequences.

Then work on the crucial second stage could begin: the linking of these group sequences (e.g. Table 2) into a master sequence for the site as a whole (Table 3). For this, all the 1:20 group plans were digitised using an AutoCad package. This ensured that there was a security copy of the archive plans on computer and one which could be endlessly reproduced should the need arise. But the more immediate benefit was that all the plans could now be accurately rescaled at the touch of a button, a feature of some consequence on a site as large as Leadenhall Court. Our plans were then plotted out at the smaller scale of 1:100: the entire site could now fit on to the top of a drawing board. Transparent drafting film was used so that each one of the plans could be overlain and relationships between features easily checked visually. Then

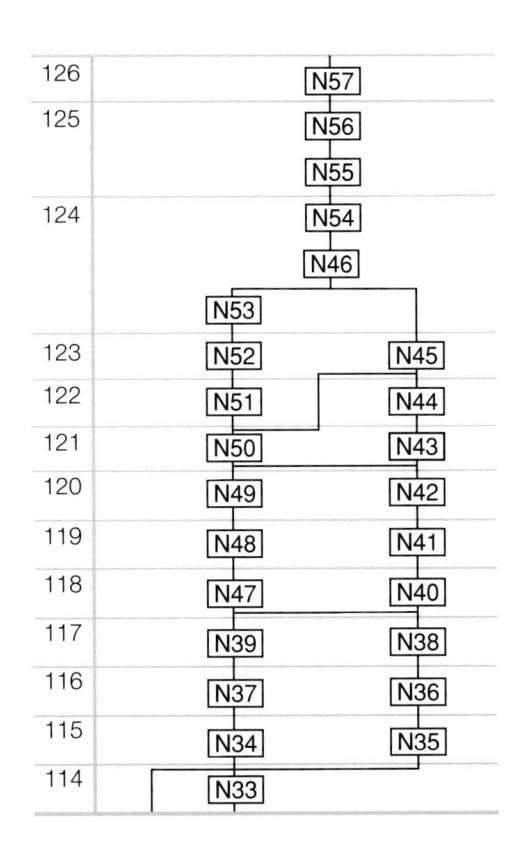

The archaeologist as alchemist 55

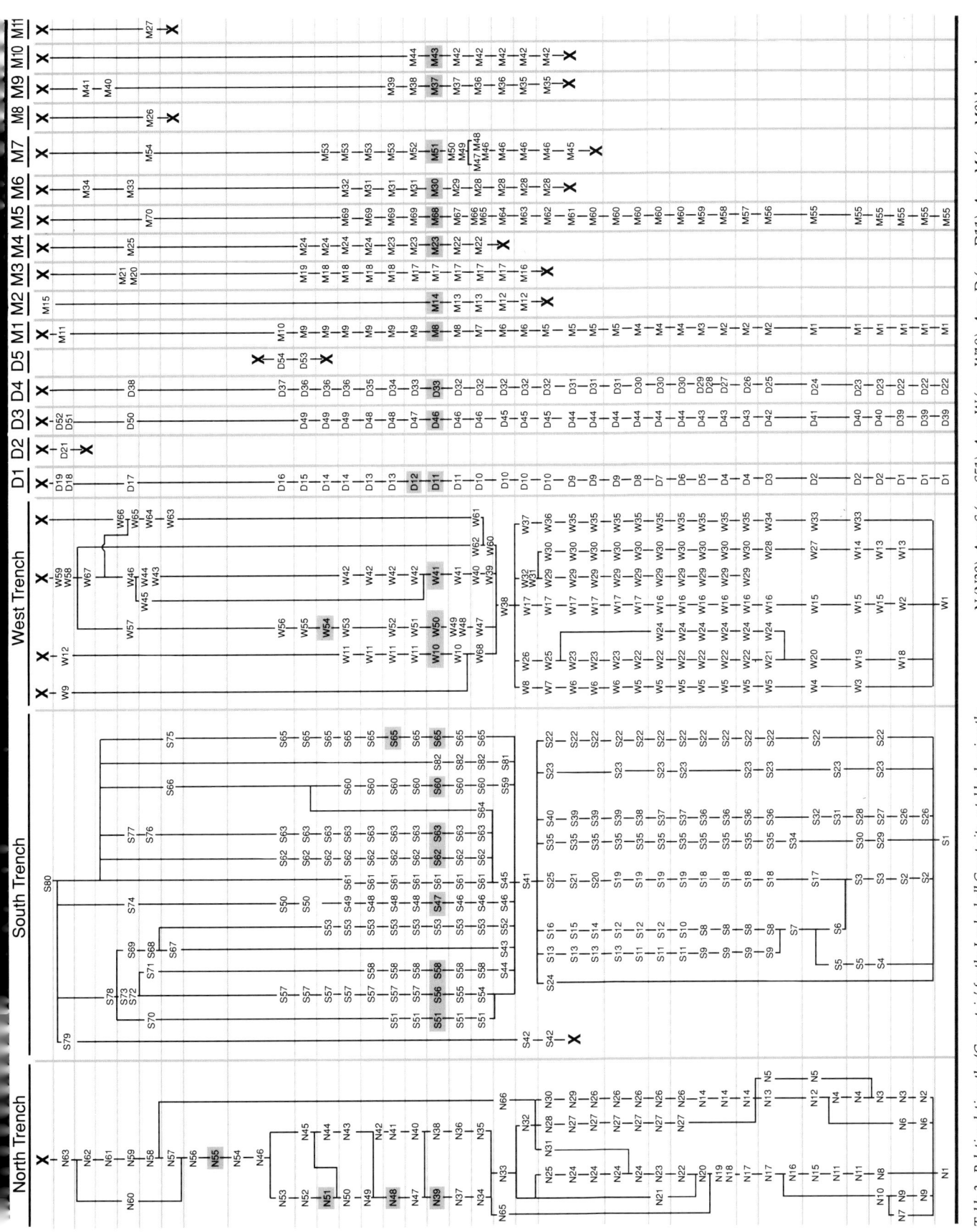

Table 3 Relative dating: the 'Grouptrix' for the Leadenhall Court site, a table showing the stratigraphic relationships of the Groups in each Area and trench (see Fig 4). The horizontal ranking represents the phasing of the site sequence: for example, the fire levels (shown tinted) recorded in Area N (N39), Area S (e.g. S51), Area W (e.g. W10), Area D (e.g. D11), Area M (e.g. M8) have been interpreted as part of the same contemporary horizon on this table. (Table compiled by Chrissie Milne and Paul Wootton)

phasing of the site started by compiling several overlying site-wide 'jigsaws' laid over an outline base plan. This was a slow process which began by attempting to relate group sequences from adjacent areas, and checking the results by matching the group plans together. Correlations between sequences might be established by the identification of a feature such as a wall or fire horizon common to both sequences; different surfaces in different areas sealed, cut by or overlying a common feature; different surfaces in different areas laid at the same level. In addition, a scatter of pits or other features which contained the same range of pottery could be considered to be contemporary, if there was no more direct stratigraphic reason for concluding otherwise.

The first attempt produced 35 site-wide phases of relatively dated activity. Further assessment together with consideration of the datable artefacts found in association with the groups saw that total refined to some 30 calendar-dated phases: these are represented in tabular form by the 30 horizontal lines of groups shown in Table 3, and by the site plans reproduced in Chapters 2 and 3. Once this preferred site-sequence was established, then the dating material from one trench could be used to suggest the date for the same phase in another area from which no finds were recovered. For example, the dating for the major fire horizon shown toned in Table 3 can be determined by considering all the material recovered from groups in that horizon: thus pottery dated to AD 120–140 from Group N39 can be used to suggest a date for the fire identified in Group S65, from which there were no finds (Table 4).

However, it must be stressed that the site sequence as presented in Table 3 can be reinterpreted simply by moving the groups into later or earlier phases, or by creating additional phases. The sequence discussed in this report is not based on **the** interpretation but on **an** interpretation of the phasing.

It may come as a surprise to some readers that our site phasing was only established some years after the excavation finished, for that must imply that the site was not dug 'in phase', as the jargon has it. That observation is absolutely correct however, for each trench was constrained by its own deadlines: no two trenches were started on the same day. The site was not dug 'in phase' although each area was excavated in the correct reverse stratigraphic order, in so far as we could determine it. The phase plans illustrating this report therefore show a series of horizons which, while representing features thought to be contemporary, were never exposed simultaneously during the excavation itself.

The archive assessment used at Leadenhall therefore worked from groups, which are stratigraphic units, into phases, the chronological divisions. This system seemed appropriate for the particular complexities of this project, but it should be stressed that a different system is in use for other excavations currently being studied by the Museum. On these, a more complex subgroup and group system has been developed.

It is also worth mentioning why this system of 'Groups and Phases' was used on the Leadenhall project in preference to the more traditional 'Periods and Phases' so beloved by other archaeologists. One problem is that the word 'period' has many meanings. It can refer to an historic period such as Roman, Saxon or medieval, defined by calendar dates and applicable throughout the country. It may refer to ceramic periods, defined by the presence or absence of particular wares, and only applicable to a particular region. Then there is the archaeological period, in which 'major' events such as the building of a house (= period) are arbitrarily distinguished from 'minor' events (= phases) such as the addition of an extra room. That division would only be applicable on that particular site. Again there are now (for want of a better phrase) stratigraphic periods in which phases of activity are identified sandwiched between site-wide horizons such as major fire levels. Such a system is obviously only applicable for sites which are obliging enough to provide features covering the majority of the area, usually the less complex excavations.

However defined, a 'Periods and Phases' system was seen as too rigid a structure for this archive report since it obscured the difference between stratigraphy and chronology, and would have made both minor and major reinterpretation inconvenient. It is argued here that the groups-first/phasing-second method used for Leadenhall Court represents a far more flexible approach, in which an infinite number of discrete trench sequences can be assessed up to an appropriate level of interpretation, after which phasing can begin involving as few or as many of those separate sequences as required.

This chapter presents a summary of the methodology whereby the contexts from Leadenhall Court were converted into a sequence of events: how that sequence was dated and thereby turned into history is discussed in the following chapter.

The archaeologist as alchemist

Group		Pottery	Stamp	Coin
AREA N				
N1	Natural	40-70	-	-
N2	Slot	70-100	-	-
N3	Quarry: cremations	50-70	-	-
N4	External dumps	70-100	70-100	-
N5	Buildings 4 & 9	-	-	-
N6	Post holes	-	-	-
N7	Ditch	50-70	-	-
N8	Ditch	60-80	-	-
N9	Post holes	40-70	-	-
N10	Pit	55-70	-	-
N11	External dumps	60-80	-	-
N12	External surfaces	70-100	-	-
N13	Buildings 9 & 11	70-100	-	-
N14	Building 10	70-100	-	-
N15	Alley: midden: well	70-100	70-85	Sestertius
N16	External surfaces	70-100	-	1-E3
N17	Yard: pit	70-100	50-75	?64-66
N18	Yard: midden	70-100	65-90	-
N19	Pit	70-100	70-85	69-79
N20	Building 12	70-100	60-75	1st
N21	Building 20	70-100	-	-
N22	Building 12	70-100	70-90	-
N23	Building 12	70-100	55-100	-
N24	Building 12	70-100	65-90	71-73
N25	Midden	80-120	70-100	-
N26	Building 12	70-100	-	-
N27	Building 12	70-100	45-60	-
N28	Building 10	100-120	-	?64-66: 69-79
N29	Building 10	85-100	-	85: L1-2
N30	Building 12: demolition	80-120	70-95	L1-2
N31	Midden	100-120	70-95	-
N32	Bas construction: N Range	100-120	65-90	41-64
N33	Make-up Road 1: Bas: N Range	100-120	70-120	69-79: 86: M1-2
N34	Building 24	100-120+	-	-
N35	Road 1	100-120	55-70	-
N36	Road 2	120-140	65-90	-
N37	Building 25	120-140	-	-
N38	Road 3	120-140+	-	-
N39	Building 26: fire debris	120-140	80-110	69-79
N40	Road 4	120-140	-	-
N41	Road 5	140-160	-	-
N42	Road 6	140-160	-	98-117: 119-138
N43	Road 7	140-180	-	-
N44	Road 8	140-200	140-200	-
N45	Road 9	200-400	-	-
N46	Silts over Road 9	250-300/400	-	-
N47	Building 27	120-160	70-120	L1
N48	Building 27: fire debris	120-160	55-80	-
N49	Building 28	140-180	140-165	-
N50	?Building 29	140-180	-	-
N51	Building 30: fire debris	180-230	-	-
N52	Building 31	180-230	-	-
N53	Activity N of Road 9	230/250-300	-	-
N54	Building 32	250-300/400	-	-
N55	Fire debris	250-300	-	-
N56	Cuts in road silts	350/400	-	270-280(vi)
N57	Bas robbing	1000-1150	-	-
N58	Bas robbing	1130-1180	160-190	270-280: 330-335: 330-337: 346-361
N59	Pits	1150-1200	60-90	69-79: 222-235:270-280: 342: M3-L3
N60	Building 33	-	-	-
N61	Leadenhall	1250-1350	-	-
N62	Garner	1250-1500	-	270-280
N63	Cellar	1760-1900	-	-
N64	Roman occupation	50-100	-	-
N65	External dumps	+/- 120	70-85	86
N66	Bas construction: N Range	+/- 120	-	-

Group		Pottery	Stamp	Coin
AREA S				
S1	Natural	-	-	-
S2	Ditch	50-80	-	-
S3	Slab: post holes: quarry	60/65-80	60-75	M1
S4	External dumps	60/65-80	-	-
S5	Building 4	-	-	-
S6	Building 4	65-80	-	-
S7	External dumps	70-100	55-65	69-79
S8	Building 6	70-100	-	-
S9	Building 6	70-100	-	-
S10	Building 6	70-100	60-90	-
S11	Building 6	70-100	-	-
S12	Alley	70-100	70-90	M1
S13	Midden	70-100	-	-
S14	Buildings 15 & 23	70-100	55-80	250-150 BC
S15	Buildings 15 & 23	70-100	-	-
S16	Buildings 15 & 23	70-100	-	-
S17	Buildings 9 & 14	70-100	65-90	64-66
S18	Building 10	70-100	-	-
S19	Building 10	70-100	-	-
S20	Building 10	70-100	-	-
S21	Building 10	70-100	65-85	-
S22	Roman occupation	70-100	55-80	-
S23	Roman occupation	60/65-80	-	M1
S24	Pit and posthole	70-100	55-70	-
S25	External activity: mortar mixing	70-100	55-80	-
S26	Post holes	-	-	-
S27	Ditches	40-100	-	-
S28	Building 2	55-70	-	-
S29	Ditches	40-70	-	-
S30	Building 1	-	-	-
S31	External dumps	65-80	65-95	-
S32	Building 14	65-80	65-85	-
S33	Post & stake holes	-	-	-
S34	Building 14	70-100	70-85	-
S35	Building 16	70-100	70-85	-
S36	Building 16	80-100	80-100	69-79(ii): M1
S37	Building 21	80-100	-	-
S38	Midden	80-100	65-90	69-79
S39	Building 22	80-100	65-95	-
S40	Building 21: demolition	-	-	-
S41	Truncation level	-	-	-
S42	Bas construction	70-120	55-80	41-64: 72
S43	Bas construction	80-100+	-	-
S44	Bas construction	80-100+	-	-
S45	Bas construction: Room 5	80-100+	55-70	-
S46	Bas construction	80-100+	70-80	-
S47	Bas: Room 8: fire	100-120	55-70	71: 87
S48	Bas: Room 8	100-120+	-	-
S49	Bas: Room 8	-	-	-
S50	Bas: Room 8: last floor	200-300/400	-	-
S51	Bas: Room 4: fire	80-100+	-	-
S52	Bas: Room 4	80-100+	-	77-78
S53	Bas: Room 4: fire	70-120	-	-
S54	Bas: Room 4	80-120+	-	69-79: 72-79
S55	Bas: Room 4	80-100+	-	-
S56	Bas: Room 4: fire	80-120	-	-
S57	Bas: Room 4	120-200/250	-	-
S58	Roads 1-6	140-180	80-110	-
S59	Bas: Room 5/9	80-100+	-	-
S60	Bas: Room 5/9: fire	70-150	-	-
S61	Bas: Room 5	120-200/250	-	-
S62	Bas: Room 5	70-120	-	73-79
S63	Bas: Room 5: fire	250-400	-	-
S64	Bas: Room 5	-	-	-
S65	Bas: Room 6: fire	-	-	-
S66	Bas robbing: 5/9	1000-1150	-	-
S67	Bas robbing buttress: Room 7	950+	-	-
S68	Bas robbing: 4/7	1050-1150	-	-
S69	Bas robbing: 4/7/8	1050-1250	-	330-335
S70	Bas robbing: 4/8; 5/9	1050-1250	-	268-270
S71	Pits	250-400	-	-
S72	Bas robbing	1150-1250	-	270-280
S73	Pits	1150-1250	-	268-270

ABOVE AND FOLLOWING TWO PAGES
Table 4 Towards absolute dating: Group Dating Table for Leadenhall Court site. This reference table lists every context group, Area by Area, with a summary of the datable material recovered from the associated contexts. When used in conjunction with Table 3 calendar dates may be suggested for the phases represented. (Table compiled by Chrissie Milne and Paul Wootton)

Group		Pottery	Stamp	Coin
S74	Pits	1050-1150	-	-
S75	Bas robbing: 6/10	-	-	-
S76	Bas robbing: 5	300-400	65-90	-
S77	Well	1150-1200	-	270-280: 330-341: L3: M4-L4
S78	Med foundations	1380-1550	-	-
S79	Cellar	1600-1750	-	-
S80	Machine clearance	1600-1750	40-100	-
S81	Bas construction: Room 11	-	-	-
S82	Bas: Room 11	-	-	-

AREA W

Group		Pottery	Stamp	Coin
W1	Natural	-	-	-
W2	Tree holes	50-70	-	64-66
W3	Building 3	40-70	-	-
W4	External dumps	60-80	-	-
W5	Building 6	70-100	40-70	-
W6	External activity	70-100	65-85	69-79 (ii)
W7	Bas construction	70-100	-	-
W8	External dumps	70-100	-	-
W9	Pit: well	1850	-	-
W10	Bas: Room 2: fire	70-100	-	-
W11	Bas: Room 2	-	-	-
W12	Pits: drains	-	-	-
W13	External dumps	40-70	-	-
W14	Pit	60-80	-	-
W15	External dumps	60-80	60-90	41-64
W16	Building 6	60-80	-	69-79
W17	Building 6: demolition	70-100	65-90	71
W18	Quarry	40-100	-	-
W19	External dumps	55-80	-	-
W20	External dumps	55-80	-	-
W21	Building 6	60/65-80	-	-
W22	Building 6	60/65-80+	-	-
W23	External activity	70-100	65-90	69-71
W24	External surface	60-80	-	-
W25	Building 23	70-100	55-100	-
W26	Bas construction	70-100/120	55-80	-
W27	External dumps	70-100	-	M1-L2
W28	Buildings 5 & 9	70-100	-	-
W29	Building 10	70-100	65-90	-
W30	Buildings 5 & 10	70-100	40-70	-
W31	External surfaces	70-100	75-100	64-66
W32	Bas construction	70-100	65-90	-
W33	Midden	55-70	-	-
W34	Building 5	55-70+	-	-
W35	Building 5	70-100	70-100	-
W36	Buildings 5 & 15	70-100	65-85	-
W37	Bas construction	70-100	-	-
W38	Bas foundations: N wall Room 1	70-100	-	-
W39	Bas construction	70-100	70-100	64-66
W40	Bas construction: Room 3	70-100	-	M1-M2
W41	Bas: Room 3: fire	70-100	-	-
W42	Bas: Room 3	120-140/60	-	98-117
W43	Pit	1050-1250	-	-
W44	Bas robbing	1150-1250	100-140	-
W45	Bas robbing	1050-1150	-	270-280 (ii): 330-335
W46	Bas robbing	1400-1500	-	-
W47	Bas: Room 1	70-100+	55-80	77-78
W48	Bas: Room 1	100-120	-	-
W49	Bas: Room 1	100-120	70-85	-
W50	Bas: Room 1: fire	100-120	-	-
W51	Bas: Room 1	100-120+	-	-
W52	Bas: Room 1	100-120+	-	-
W53	Bas: Room 1	120-300	-	-
W54	Bas: Room 1: fire	-	-	-
W55	Bas: Room 1	-	-	193-211
W56	Bas: Room 1	40-400	-	-
W57	Pits	1150-1200	-	-
W58	Cellar	1150-1200	140-200	-
W59	Cess pit	-	-	-
W60	Bas construction	100-120	65-80	-
W61	Roadside ditch	120-160	-	-
W62	Make-up and Road 1	100-120+	-	-
W63	Pits	950+	-	-
W64	Bas robbing	1050-1150	-	270-280
W65	Pits	1050-1200	-	-
W66	Pit	1100-1200	-	-
W67	?Garner	1600-1650	-	-
W68	Bas: Room 2	-	-	-

AREA D

Group		Pottery	Stamp	Coin
D1	Pit	-	-	-
D2	External activity: midden	55-70	40-65	-
D3	External activity	65-80	65-90	-
D4	Building 8	-	-	-
D5	External dumps	65-80+	-	L1-E2
D6	External dumps	-	-	-
D7	Pit	70-100	-	-
D8	Bas construction	70-100	-	69-79
D9	Bas construction	70-100+	-	-
D10	Bas construction: Nave	70-100+	-	-
D11	Bas: Nave: fire	70-100+	-	-
D12	Bas: Nave: fire	-	-	-
D13	Bas: Nave	-	-	-
D14	Bas: Nave	120-200/250	-	-
D15	Bas: Nave	-	-	-
D16	Bas: Nave: demolition	1050-1150	-	-
D17	Pits	1050-1500	-	-
D18	Cess pit	-	-	-
D19	Well	1650-1800	-	-
D20	Well infill	1820-1900	-	-
D21	Cellar infill	1800-1900	-	-
D22	Natural	-	-	-
D23	Midden	70-100	-	-
D24	External activity	70-100+	-	-
D25	Building 8	70-100+	-	-
D26	Building 8	70-100	-	69-79
D27	Building 8: demolition	70-100+	-	-
D28	External dumps	70-100+	-	-
D29	Building 17	70-100+	-	-
D30	Building 17	70-100	-	-
D31	Building 17: demolition	70-100	-	-
D32	Bas construction: Nave	+/- 120	-	-
D33	Bas: Nave: fire	-	-	-
D34	Bas: Nave	-	-	-
D35	Bas: Nave	-	-	-
D36	Bas: Nave: last floor	250-400	-	-
D37	Bas: demolition	-	-	-
D38	Pit	1050+	-	-
D39	Natural: quarry	-	-	-
D40	External dumps	55-70+	-	-
D41	Midden	70-100	-	-
D42	External dumps	70-100+	-	-
D43	External surface	70-100+	-	-
D44	Midden	70-100+	-	-
D45	Bas construction	70-100+	-	-
D46	Bas: Nave: fire	-	-	-
D47	Bas: Nave	120-200/250	-	-
D48	Bas: Nave	-	-	-
D49	Bas: Nave: last floor	250-400	-	-
D50	Dark earth: pits	1150-1250	-	-
D51	External dumps	1050-1500	-	-
D52	Cellar	1820-1900	-	-
D53	Bas: Nave: last floor	-	-	-
D54	Bas demolition	-	-	73-78

AREA M

Group		Pottery	Stamp	Coin
M1	Natural	-	-	-
M2	Building 13	-	-	-
M3	Building 19	70-100	-	-
M4	Building 19	70-100+	-	-
M5	Bas construction	70-100+	-	-
M6	Bas construction	70-100	55-65	-
M7	Bas: Room 14	70-100+	-	-
M8	Bas: Room 14: fire	70-100	-	-
M9	Bas: Room 14: last floor	120-160	-	-
M10	Bas: Room 14: demolition	-	-	-
M11	Pit	70-120	-	-
M12	Bas construction	-	-	-
M13	Bas: Nave	-	-	-
M14	Bas: Nave: fire	70-120	-	-
M15	Modern make-up	-	-	-
M16	External dunps	-	-	-
M17	Bas: Room 15	-	-	-
M18	Bas: Room 15	-	-	-
M19	Bas: Room 15	-	-	-
M20	Pits	-	-	-
M21	External dumps	-	-	-
M22	Bas: Nave	-	-	-
M23	Bas: Nave	-	-	-
M24	Bas: Nave	-	-	-
M25	Pits	-	-	-
M26	Pit	-	-	-
M27	Bas robbing	-	-	-
M28	Bas construction	40-100	-	-

The archaeologist as alchemist

Group	Pottery	Stamp	Coin
M29 Bas: Room 15	70-120	-	-
M30 Bas: Room 15: fire	70-120+	-	-
M31 Bas: Room 15	120-200	-	-
M32 Bas demolition	120-200+	-	-
M33 Pits	1000-1150	-	-
M34 Garner	40-150	-	-
M35 Bas construction	-	-	-
M36 Bas: Room 16	55-100	-	-
M37 Bas: Room 16: fire	-	-	-
M38 Bas: Room 16:	55-100+	-	-
M39 External dumps	-	-	-
M40 Pits	1150-1350	-	-
M41 Garner	-	-	-
M42 Bas: Room 11	-	-	-
M43 Bas: Room 11: fire	-	-	-
M44 Bas: Room 11	-	-	-
M45 Bas construction	55-100	-	-
M46 Bas construction: Room 13/14	60-80	-	-
M47 Bas construction: Room 13/14	-	-	-
M48 Bas: Room 13/14	60-80+	-	-

Group	Pottery	Stamp	Coin
M49 Bas: Room 13/14	70-120	-	-
M50 Bas: Room 13/14	70-120	60-90	41-50
M51 Bas: Room 13/14: fire	-	-	-
M52 Bas: Room 13/14	120-200	120-160	-
M53 Bas: Room 13/14	120-200+	-	-
M54 Pits	1050-1150	-	-
M55 Natural	-	-	-
M56 Building 7	65-80	-	-
M57 Building 7	65-80	-	-
M58 Building 7: demolition	70-100	65-85	77-78
M59 Building 18	70-100+	-	-
M60 Building 18: demolition	70-100+	70-85	64-66
M61 Bas construction	70-100+	-	-
M62 Bas construction	70-100+	-	30-42: 68-69
M63 Bas construction	70-100+	40-70	-
M64 Bas: Room 12	100-200	80-100	-
M65 Bas: Room 12	100-120	-	-
M66 Bas: Room 12	100-120	-	-
M67 Bas: Room 12	100-120+	-	-
M68 Bas: Room 12: fire	100-120+	-	-
M69 Bas: Room 12	100-120+	-	-
M70 Pits	1000-1150	-	-

6 An absolute chronology

Barbara Davies with Jenny Hall and Gustav Milne

The act of recording an ancient structure is not itself enough: it needs to be dated before it can be understood and before implications for its social context can be drawn. To excavate a church is one thing: to date it to the 4th or to the 14th century quite another. Absolute (or calendar) dating also provides the means whereby buildings, finds, features and sites can be sensibly compared one with another. This is certainly true of the Roman Basilica, which was first uncovered in 1880: meaningful discussion of its function and changes in its use could only begin after the broad calendar dates for its construction, use and demise had been established as a result of the 1985–6 excavations. How that building related to the contemporary townscape and how it compared with fora elsewhere in the province could also be considered for the first time. At an even more basic level, the questions of precisely when it was erected, how long it served its primary function, and whether it was demolished before or after the Roman administration withdrew from the province c.AD 400 could finally be resolved. Even the most recent study of the Forum compiled in 1985 could find 'absolutely no archaeological evidence to date the period when the complex ceased to be used' (Marsden 1987, 76). Archaeologists need to know when a building was built before they can ask the reason why.

Having established a comprehensive framework of relatively dated events and features representing activity on the Leadenhall Court site (see Chapter 5), the field archaeologists now turned to their specialist 'finds' colleagues to see if they could impose a series of broad calendar dates upon part or all of that relative sequence. The results are summarised in this chapter, and focus on the Roman levels in particular.

Many methodologies are currently used on sites in Britain, such as dendrochronology, radio-carbon dating, the examination of inscriptions, ceramics, coins and other artefacts. However, on many sites the pottery evidence provides a broad date range for the occupation represented, while the coins are used to refine that picture. On the Leadenhall Court site, the situation was reversed, for it was the study of the pottery in association with the stratigraphic analysis which provided the closer dating.

Clearly no attempt to date a site should rely on the study of just one class of artefact, but must consider the evidence from all quarters. Most important of all, such studies must be related to the stratigraphic analysis, and the conclusions drawn must take into account the contradictions and inconsistencies which will inevitably arise.

Old money
(Table 5)

Since most official Roman coins carry the head of an emperor and a legend, it is normally possible to deduce the year in which a given example was minted (Mattingly et al., 1923–1967): thus, unlike most other objects found on archaeological sites, coins are intrinsically datable. There are drawbacks to their use however. Coins are much rarer finds than potsherds: only 62 out of the 325 groups shown on Table 4 contained identifiable coins. Of the 119 Roman coins found during the excavations, virtually all showed signs of wear. Many were in a corroded condition, unfortunately a fate shared by most of the metal objects from the site. However, 91 coins are identifiable, and these are summarised in Table 5.

There are 29 coins in column A, which represents the pre-Basilica levels. These were found with 14 others, unidentifiable beyond the fact that they are 1st-century types. The time span of the coins is wide: the earliest is a very worn Republican as of c.250–150 BC (such coins are known to have remained in circulation for some time), while the latest is a coin of Titus (AD 77–8).

The second group (B in Table 5), which represents the construction of the Basilica, has 10 coins, the earliest of which are three copies of mid-1st-century Claudian asses. There is also a gold aureus of Galba, dated to AD 68–9. This is most unusual, since Roman gold coins are rarely found on City sites and coins of Galba are not abundant. The latest closely dated coin from the group, an as of Domitian of AD 86 could indicate that the construction was completed by the end of the 1st century. However, the coins in columns A and B cover a similar date range. Since the aes coinage of Claudius and Nero remained in circulation for some time, and as the bulk of coins are late 1st-century in date, it would be safe to assume that the construction of the Basilica began during that period, but study of the coins on their own does not provide a firm date for the completion of the building.

Only 10 coins were recovered from levels within the Basilica itself (column C in Table 5). Eight of these are 1st-century in date, while the latest coin is a possible silver-washed denarius of Septimius Severus (AD 193–211), indicating that the Basilica remained in use for at least 100 years. Regrettably, few coins are lost in a building which was in use and regularly swept clean. Only 4% of the total identifiable coins from Leadenhall Court can be associated with the life of that public building, a figure which may be compared to that for the underlying levels, where a generation of domestic occupation produced over 30% of the coins and over 60% of the pottery from the site.

The coins from the post-Basilica levels (column E in Table 5) show that the Basilica ceased to be in use some time after the early 3rd century. Of the 29 identifiable coins from this group, the earliest securely datable one is a denarius of Julia Mamaea of AD 222–35. The rest are antoniniani, including 17 late 3rd-century radiate copies, a common find on City sites. There are also six early to mid-4th-century coins, the latest being a copy of a 'fallen horseman' type dated to AD 348–61. As on many other London sites, there are none of the later Roman coins which are found elsewhere in Britain.

Periods 1 to 14		A	B	C	D	E	F	Totals	%
1	up to AD 41	1						1	1
2	AD 41 - 68	10	4	1			3	18	20
3	AD 69 - 96	17	6	7	1	2		33	36
4	AD 96 - 117	1		1	1		1	4	5
5	AD 118 - 138					1		1	1
6	AD 139 - 161								
7	AD 162 - 180								
8	AD 180 - 192								
9	AD 193 - 222			1		1		2	2
10	AD 222 - 278					20	3	23	25
11	AD 279 - 294								
12	AD 294 - 330						1	1	1
13	AD 331 - 348				1	5	1	7	8
14	AD 349 - 402					1		1	1
Totals		29	10	10	4	29	9	91	
Periods	%	32	11	11	4	32	10		

Table 5 Coin histogram: table showing distribution of identifiable coins from the Leadenhall Court site: A = pre-Basilican levels; B = construction of Basilica; C = Basilica in use; D = road and buildings to north of Basilica; E = post-Basilican levels; F = unstratified (site clearance levels, etc)

Taking the stratigraphic assessment and the coin evidence together, it is clear that work on the Basilica began after AD 78, was completed sometime after 86, and that the building fell out of use sometime after 211. Given that all these coins were worn, the dates cited here only represent the earliest date after which those events must have happened. However, the discovery of 3rd- and 4th-century coins in levels stratigraphically later than the Basilica do not on their own provide a clear indication of when the complex was demolished, since worn coins could have remained in circulation for an unknown period. Nevertheless, the coins from Leadenhall Court provided a broad framework upon which to build the chronology of the site's development in the Roman period.

'Computer dating'
(Tables 6–8)

The introduction of computer technology in the Museum of London towards the end of 1981 has had a major impact on the dating of London sites. Basic site data ranging from context descriptions to a record of all the materials excavated from each layer can now be entered on computer at speed. The sorting and retrieval of such information allows study of the datable elements to proceed rapidly: thus it is possible

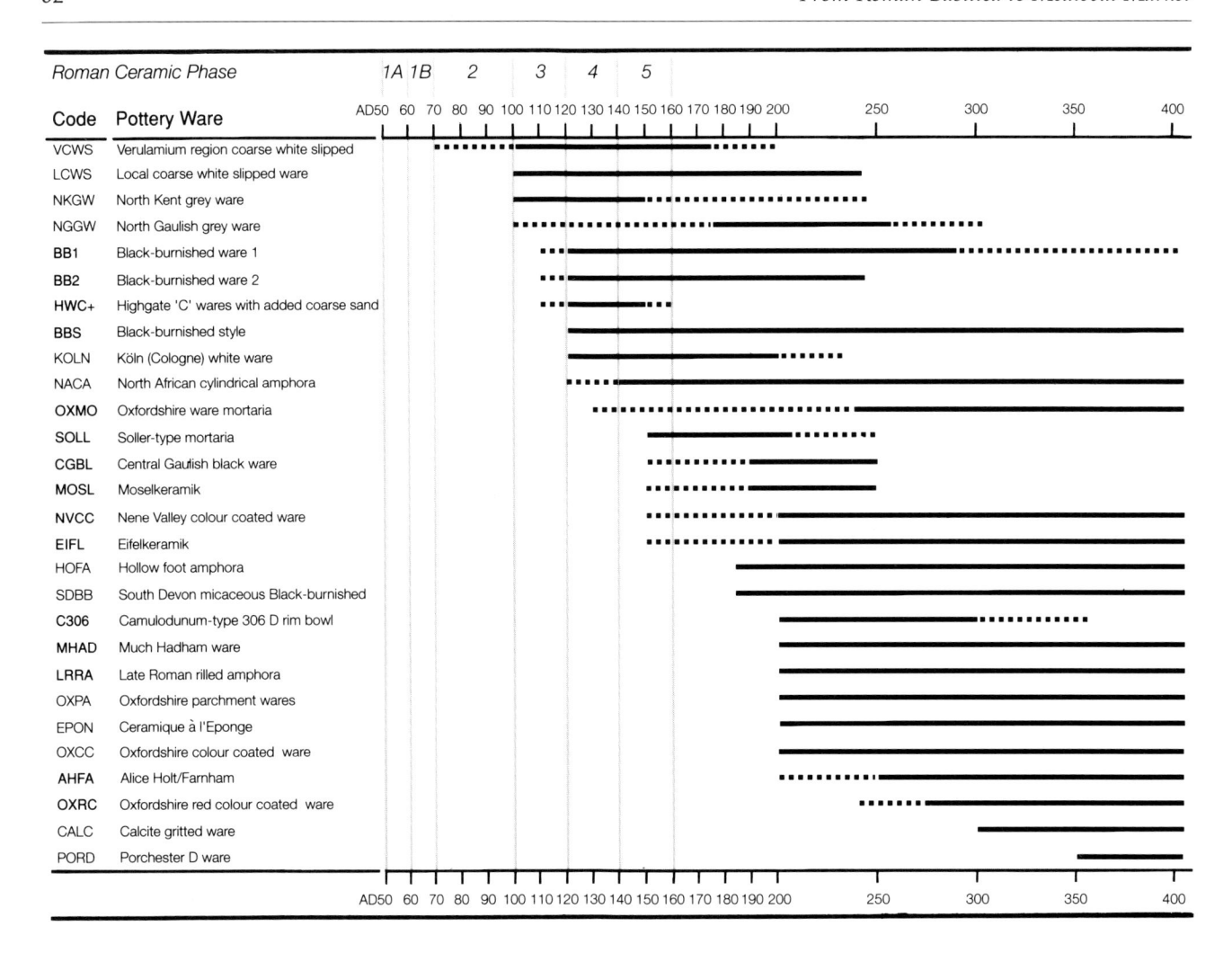

Roman Ceramic Phase		
Code	Pottery Ware	Date range
VCWS	Verulamium region coarse white slipped	
LCWS	Local coarse white slipped ware	
NKGW	North Kent grey ware	
NGGW	North Gaulish grey ware	
BB1	Black-burnished ware 1	
BB2	Black-burnished ware 2	
HWC+	Highgate 'C' wares with added coarse sand	
BBS	Black-burnished style	
KOLN	Köln (Cologne) white ware	
NACA	North African cylindrical amphora	
OXMO	Oxfordshire ware mortaria	
SOLL	Soller-type mortaria	
CGBL	Central Gaulish black ware	
MOSL	Moselkeramik	
NVCC	Nene Valley colour coated ware	
EIFL	Eifelkeramik	
HOFA	Hollow foot amphora	
SDBB	South Devon micaceous Black-burnished	
C306	Camulodunum-type 306 D rim bowl	
MHAD	Much Hadham ware	
LRRA	Late Roman rilled amphora	
OXPA	Oxfordshire parchment wares	
EPON	Ceramique à l'Eponge	
OXCC	Oxfordshire colour coated ware	
AHFA	Alice Holt/Farnham	
OXRC	Oxfordshire red colour coated ware	
CALC	Calcite gritted ware	
PORD	Porchester D ware	

Table 6 Main types of pottery found on the Leadenhall Court sites with approximate date ranges (see also Davies & Richardson forthcoming)

to see at a glance how coins or inscriptions correlate with the relative sequence defined by stratigraphic analysis as well as with material dated by ceramic stamps or by methodologies such as dendrochronology.

Computerisation has also revolutionised the study of Roman pottery (Tyers & Vince 1983). Before 1981, provisional pottery dating was established after the physical examination of an assemblage and recorded as a brief summary of the number of sherds, together with a suggested date range, all of which was laboriously plotted by hand. New technology has transformed this process into a series of more detailed records using a system of codes which list the size (small, medium or large) and condition of every context assemblage from a site, the presence of every pottery fabric and form within that context, and its earliest and latest date. A 'spot date' can now be established for any context or group of contexts simply by examining these computer lists. The speed at which such data can be collected and assimilated means that pottery from current sites can be processed during or immediately after excavation, and past sites can be reassessed with ease.

Detailed information of this kind is now readily available for over 250 sites within the City and the computer can produce lists of all finds (not just pottery) from those sites sorted by stratigraphic phase. As a site can produce from several hundred to over 10,000 contexts, the resulting archive is vast. Analysis of this data base has shown that similar patterns of ceramics consistently appear in groups of a similar date.

These hypotheses were then tested by comparing the relative quantities of different pottery types from a well-stratified site. Almost one metric tonne of pottery from the Newgate Street site (GPO75; Perring & Roskams 1991) formed the basis for this study

An absolute chronology

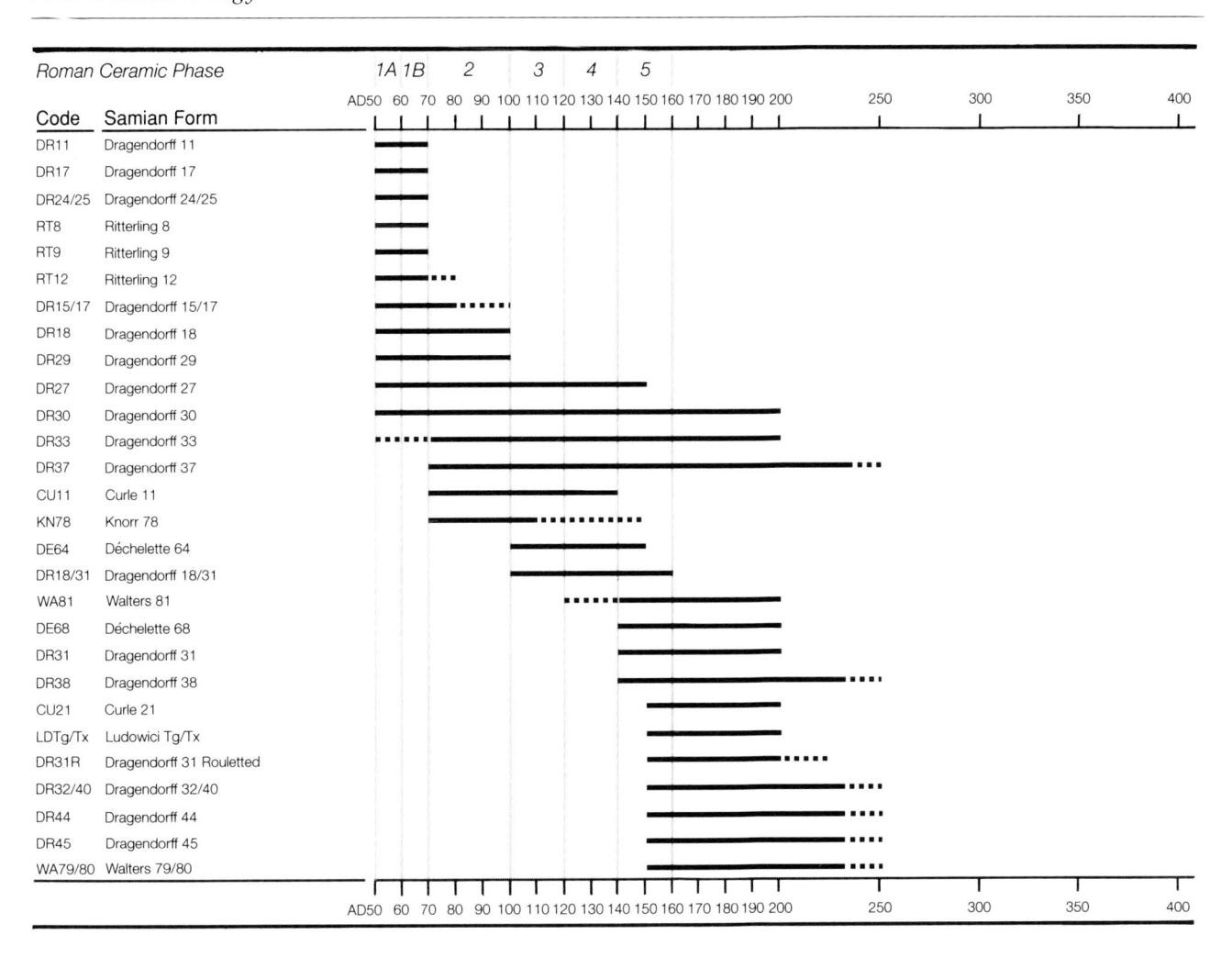

Code	Samian Form
DR11	Dragendorff 11
DR17	Dragendorff 17
DR24/25	Dragendorff 24/25
RT8	Ritterling 8
RT9	Ritterling 9
RT12	Ritterling 12
DR15/17	Dragendorff 15/17
DR18	Dragendorff 18
DR29	Dragendorff 29
DR27	Dragendorff 27
DR30	Dragendorff 30
DR33	Dragendorff 33
DR37	Dragendorff 37
CU11	Curle 11
KN78	Knorr 78
DE64	Déchelette 64
DR18/31	Dragendorff 18/31
WA81	Walters 81
DE68	Déchelette 68
DR31	Dragendorff 31
DR38	Dragendorff 38
CU21	Curle 21
LDTg/Tx	Ludowici Tg/Tx
DR31R	Dragendorff 31 Rouletted
DR32/40	Dragendorff 32/40
DR44	Dragendorff 44
DR45	Dragendorff 45
WA79/80	Walters 79/80

Table 7 Date range of Samian pottery forms from Leadenhall Court site. Compare the relatively precise date ranges shown for some of these forms with the wider ranges given for much of the pottery in Tables 6 and 8.

(Davies & Richardson forthcoming: for archive reports see Bibliography). The main Roman sequence spanned the period from AD 50 to 150, within which two major fire destruction levels formed clear datable horizons, a phenomenon noted on many other sites within the City. The earlier of these levels seems to be the result of the sacking of the town by Boudicca c.AD 60, while the other represents a conflagration in the early 2nd century which has been dated by Geoff Marsh on the basis of externally datable material to the early 120s (Dunning 1945; Marsh 1981). Within these parameters the sequence consisted of a series of discrete structural developments for which an absolute chronology was suggested, based on the intrinsically dated evidence of coins and independently datable material such as Samian stamps and other imported pottery. The fabric and form of each sherd of pottery was identified, weighed and the surviving rims measured (Tyers & Vince 1984). This data was then correlated with the stratigraphic sequence, thereby plotting the rise and fall of each pottery industry and its products within specific periods of time. The dating of the Newgate Street site pottery was then checked and refined with the examination of other well-stratified sites in the western half of the City, together with deposits on sites in the Walbrook valley (Maloney & de Moulins 1990), near the waterfront (Milne 1985), and more recently, in the eastern half of the City (Williams forthcoming).

By using this information with care, it has proved possible to construct models of the principal ceramic components for particular periods of time – a series of **ceramic phases** (Davies & Richardson forthcoming). The period AD 50 to 150 is one of dramatic growth in London matched by a rapid evolution in ceramics, as illustrated by the chronologies of Samian vessel forms

64 — From Roman Basilica to Medieval Market

Roman Ceramic Phase		1A	1B	2	3	4	5

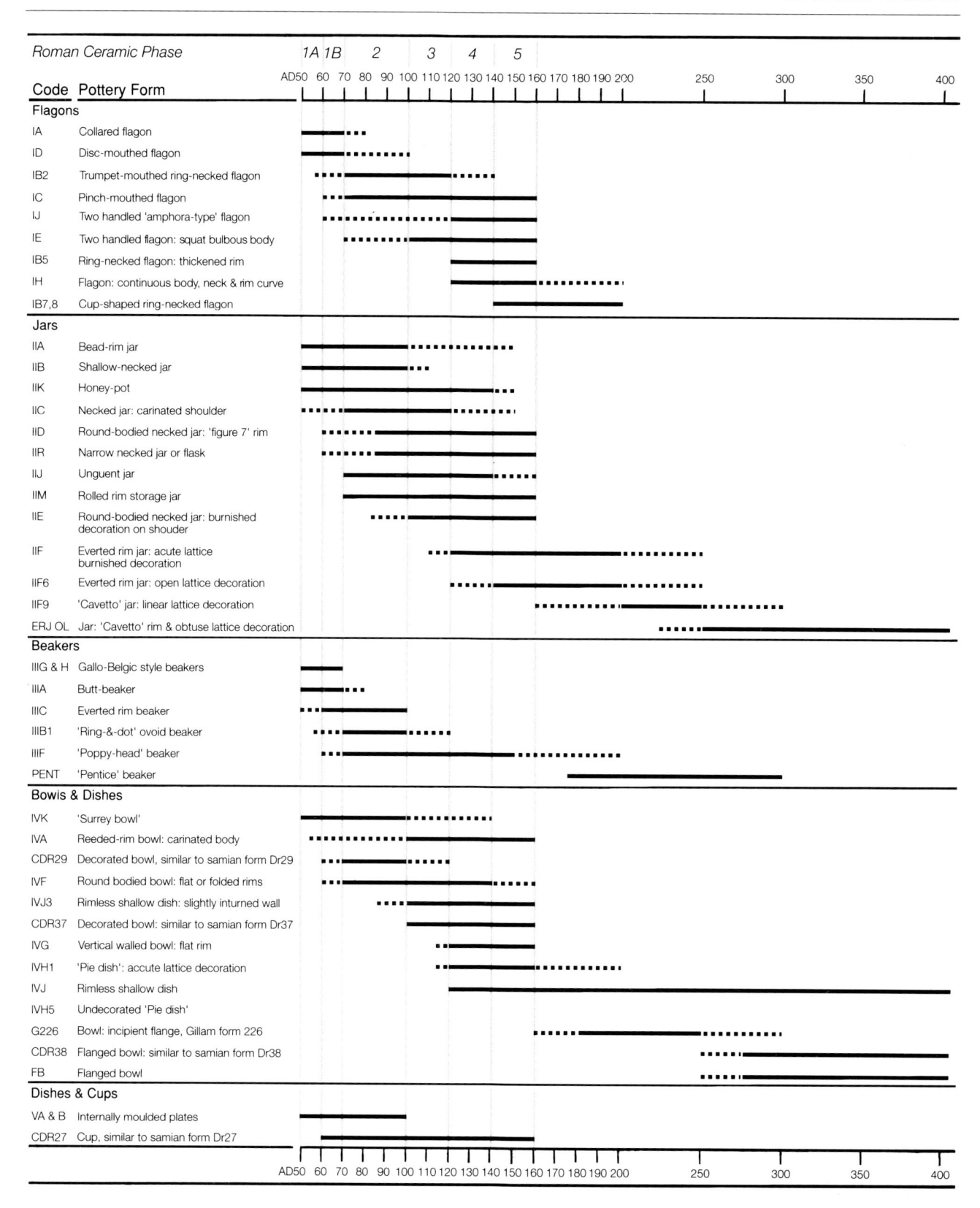

Code	Pottery Form
Flagons	
IA	Collared flagon
ID	Disc-mouthed flagon
IB2	Trumpet-mouthed ring-necked flagon
IC	Pinch-mouthed flagon
IJ	Two handled 'amphora-type' flagon
IE	Two handled flagon: squat bulbous body
IB5	Ring-necked flagon: thickened rim
IH	Flagon: continuous body, neck & rim curve
IB7,8	Cup-shaped ring-necked flagon
Jars	
IIA	Bead-rim jar
IIB	Shallow-necked jar
IIK	Honey-pot
IIC	Necked jar: carinated shoulder
IID	Round-bodied necked jar: 'figure 7' rim
IIR	Narrow necked jar or flask
IIJ	Unguent jar
IIM	Rolled rim storage jar
IIE	Round-bodied necked jar: burnished decoration on shoulder
IIF	Everted rim jar: acute lattice burnished decoration
IIF6	Everted rim jar: open lattice decoration
IIF9	'Cavetto' jar: linear lattice decoration
ERJ OL	Jar: 'Cavetto' rim & obtuse lattice decoration
Beakers	
IIIG & H	Gallo-Belgic style beakers
IIIA	Butt-beaker
IIIC	Everted rim beaker
IIIB1	'Ring-&-dot' ovoid beaker
IIIF	'Poppy-head' beaker
PENT	'Pentice' beaker
Bowls & Dishes	
IVK	'Surrey bowl'
IVA	Reeded-rim bowl: carinated body
CDR29	Decorated bowl, similar to samian form Dr29
IVF	Round bodied bowl: flat or folded rims
IVJ3	Rimless shallow dish: slightly inturned wall
CDR37	Decorated bowl: similar to samian form Dr37
IVG	Vertical walled bowl: flat rim
IVH1	'Pie dish': accute lattice decoration
IVJ	Rimless shallow dish
IVH5	Undecorated 'Pie dish'
G226	Bowl: incipient flange, Gillam form 226
CDR38	Flanged bowl: similar to samian form Dr38
FB	Flanged bowl
Dishes & Cups	
VA & B	Internally moulded plates
CDR27	Cup, similar to samian form Dr27

ABOVE AND OPPOSITE
Table 8 Date range of pottery forms from Leadenhall Court site

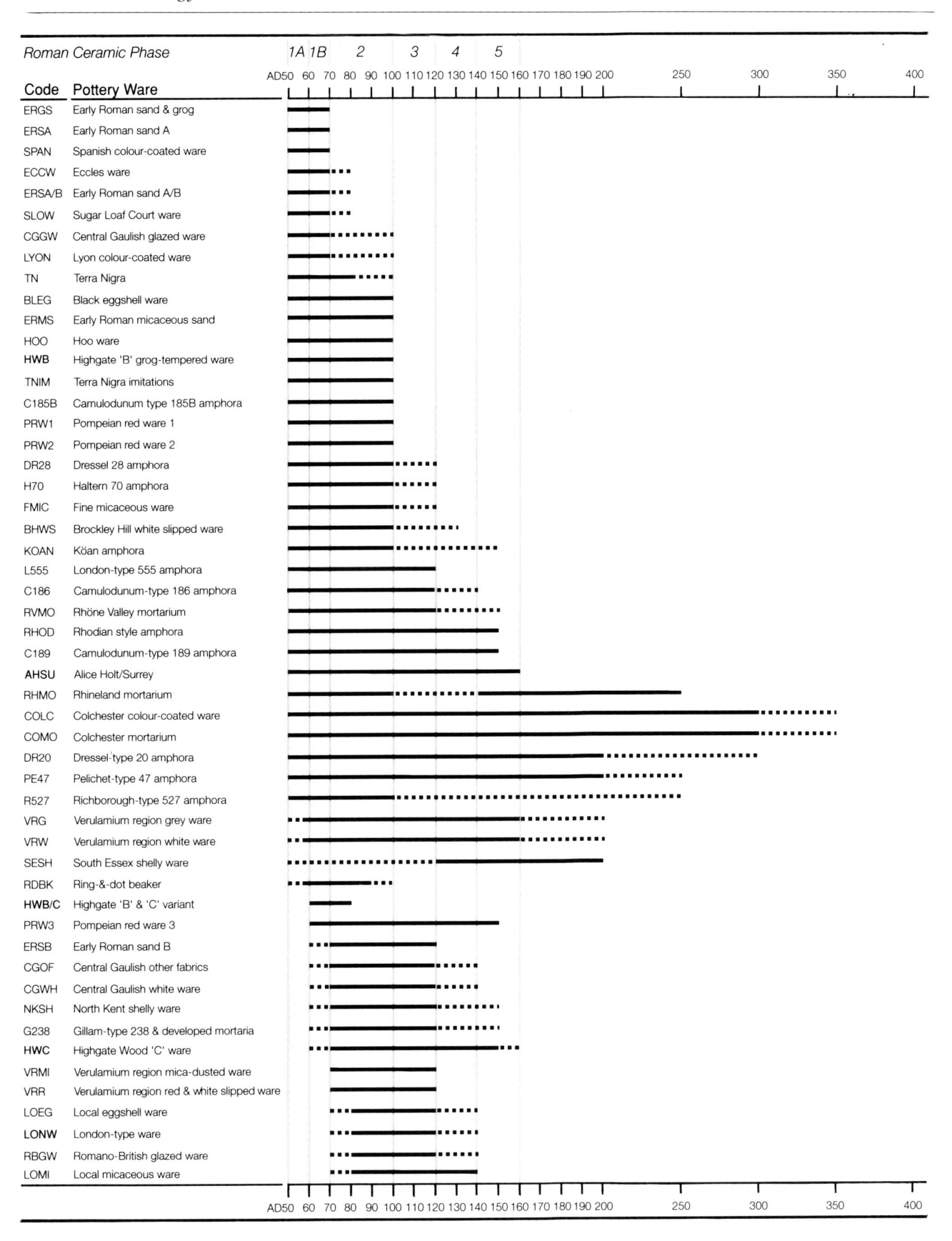

An absolute chronology

Roman Ceramic Phase		1A	1B	2	3	4	5				
Code	Pottery Ware	AD50–70	80–100	110–130	140–160	170–200	250	300	350	400	

Code	Pottery Ware
ERGS	Early Roman sand & grog
ERSA	Early Roman sand A
SPAN	Spanish colour-coated ware
ECCW	Eccles ware
ERSA/B	Early Roman sand A/B
SLOW	Sugar Loaf Court ware
CGGW	Central Gaulish glazed ware
LYON	Lyon colour-coated ware
TN	Terra Nigra
BLEG	Black eggshell ware
ERMS	Early Roman micaceous sand
HOO	Hoo ware
HWB	Highgate 'B' grog-tempered ware
TNIM	Terra Nigra imitations
C185B	Camulodunum type 185B amphora
PRW1	Pompeian red ware 1
PRW2	Pompeian red ware 2
DR28	Dressel 28 amphora
H70	Haltern 70 amphora
FMIC	Fine micaceous ware
BHWS	Brockley Hill white slipped ware
KOAN	Köan amphora
L555	London-type 555 amphora
C186	Camulodunum-type 186 amphora
RVMO	Rhône Valley mortarium
RHOD	Rhodian style amphora
C189	Camulodunum-type 189 amphora
AHSU	Alice Holt/Surrey
RHMO	Rhineland mortarium
COLC	Colchester colour-coated ware
COMO	Colchester mortarium
DR20	Dressel-type 20 amphora
PE47	Pelichet-type 47 amphora
R527	Richborough-type 527 amphora
VRG	Verulamium region grey ware
VRW	Verulamium region white ware
SESH	South Essex shelly ware
RDBK	Ring-&-dot beaker
HWB/C	Highgate 'B' & 'C' variant
PRW3	Pompeian red ware 3
ERSB	Early Roman sand B
CGOF	Central Gaulish other fabrics
CGWH	Central Gaulish white ware
NKSH	North Kent shelly ware
G238	Gillam-type 238 & developed mortaria
HWC	Highgate Wood 'C' ware
VRMI	Verulamium region mica-dusted ware
VRR	Verulamium region red & white slipped ware
LOEG	Local eggshell ware
LONW	London-type ware
RBGW	Romano-British glazed ware
LOMI	Local micaceous ware

65

(Table 7) and in the transition from imported to locally made fabrics and from native to Romanised vessel forms. The combination of all these factors within well-dated sequences has led to the identification of six Roman Ceramic Phases (hereafter RCP) for this period. Each is defined by the presence, absence or, in some cases, quantity of fabrics and forms within the proposed phases (Table 6). Fabrics are considered in relation to each other but individual vessel types can provide quite precise dates (Table 8). As a consequence, coarse wares, the most common pottery type recovered, have proved to be a most useful dating tool. The suggested dating for these phases is:

> RCP1A: *c.*AD 50–60/1
> RCP1B: *c.*AD 60/1–70/75
> RCP2: *c.*AD 70/75–100
> RCP3: *c.*AD 100–120
> RCP4: *c.*AD 120–140
> RCP5: *c.*AD 140–160

The assemblage from Leadenhall Court also enhanced our understanding of early Roman pottery in London through the abundance of externally datable material recovered from the many well-stratified phases covering the period AD 70–100. Researchers may soon be able to distinguish between assemblages at the beginning and those at the end of this period.

The study of London's later Roman pottery is less well advanced, with the notable exception of the large early 3rd-century group from the waterfront on the St Magnus House site (Richardson 1986). Many of the late Roman deposits from the City are unsuitable for developing a corpus of wares and forms, but there are important sites where a rapidly changing sequence extends to the end of the 4th century (Milne 1985): a study of such sequences is in progress. In the meantime the dating of later Roman deposits on current sites relies on associated coins and on types of pottery which have already been studied outside the London region, such as the Alice Holt/Farnham, Nene Valley and Oxfordshire wares. Research on London's Roman pottery is therefore continuing.

Leadenhall Court: dating the developments

Since over 80% of the features excavated on the Leadenhall Court site were of Roman date, this study will concentrate on the Roman sequence.

Initial activity: *c.*AD 50–65 *(Figs 5, 6)*
In common with most other sites in the City, the Leadenhall Court site produced little evidence of pre-Roman occupation. The absence of a Boudiccan fire horizon (*c.*AD 60) and the paucity of early Roman material from the site is in marked contrast to sites excavated to the south of the Forum, as at 5–12 Fenchurch Street (FEN 83) for example.

The earliest material from the Leadenhall Court excavations consists of very small groups of pottery (Table 4, N6, N9, S2, S26), which are broadly assigned to the period AD 50–70/75 (RCP1). Although it is therefore possible that occupation began here in the AD 50s, the absence of later wares may simply be attributed to the small size of the assemblages. Verulamium region grey and white wares were present in the fills of one of the earliest features, a ditch in Area S (S2). Since the kilns which produced this pottery began production in the AD 50s (Castle 1973), it is possible that occupation of this part of the site may have begun at a similar time.

More substantial evidence for pre-AD 60 activity is provided by a small group of cremation urns from the abandoned floor of a brickearth quarry (N3). Unfortunately the top of the only urn to survive *in situ* had been broken off in antiquity (Pl 8). This type of shallow necked jar (Table 8, type IIB) in early Roman micaceous sandy ware is found in levels sealed by Boudiccan fire debris on some London sites, but the form and fabric continued until the end of the 1st century (Table 6). However, since the small cemetery was superseded by a phase of activity associated with a coin of AD 64, a broad date range of AD 50–60 may be suggested for the cremations.

Early activity on the site is also attested by the presence of early pottery in later features, in particular from a large and a medium assemblage from the extreme south-west corner of the site (D2 D40), and a smaller one from Building 3 (WS). The majority of these wares are commonly associated with RCP1A (AD 50–60), in particular the collared flagons (Table 8, type IA), wares from the kilns at Eccles in Kent which ceased production shortly after AD 60. In conclusion, although there are no buildings identified on the site which can be dated with certainty to this phase, the presence of cremations and of residual pottery demonstrates that there was some activity in the vicinity in the period AD 50–60.

Buildings 1–4: *c.*AD 65–70/75 *(Figs 7, 8)*
The earliest stratified coin recovered from the site was an as of Nero, dated to AD 64–6. It was found in the backfill of a hole dug to remove a tree (W2), part of

Col Pl A Living room: the 10x100mm scale rests on the earth floor of a 1st-century artisan dwelling (Building 12) defined by stubs of mud-brick walls. To the south (right) of the hearth in the foreground are tile supports for a cupboard. Beyond that, a doorway opens out on to a narrow alley parallel to Building 10. To the east, cut by a medieval well, midden material is piled up against the rear wall. (Area N)

Col Pl B Vernacular architecture in 1st-century London: the outline of two brickearth - walled buildings can be traced beneath the modern steel struts, cut by medieval pits and by the masonry foundations of the later Basilica. The 10x100mm scale lies in a room within Building 12 (foreground), separated from Building 10 by a narrow alley. Note the narrow walls and small room size. (Area N)

Col Pl C Interior decoration: the 2x100mm scale rests in the corner of a room in Building 6. The walls comprise brickearth daubed over a wattle core, with a plaster rendering on the internal face. (Area W)

Col Pl D 1st-century fitted kitchen: a domestic hearth built against an internal wall, with brickearth surround and tile apron. The 5x100mm scale rests on ash and charcoal raked out of the fire. To the west (right), the broken pottery and tile probably represent the position of a kitchen cupboard. (Area M)

Col Pl E (above) Inside the 2nd-century Basilica: the 5x100mm scale rests on the mortar floor (cut by pits) of a room in the Northern Range defined by masonry walls rising above a quadruple tile course. (Area W)

Col Pl F Foundation level: general view of the Basilica foundations looking west. (Area S)

Col Pl G (above) 2nd-century Basilica: masonry walls with brick corners. Part of the Northern Range showing the much-disturbed junction of two internal walls (10x100mm scale). The site has been excavated below the level of the operative floor surface, exposing the offset foundations. Note remains of internal tile buttress, cut by modern concrete on western edge of excavation (right) projecting into Room 1. (Area W, looking south)

Col Pl H The eastern portico: cleaning the tile floor within the portico beyond the Apse at the eastern end of the 2nd-century Basilica. (Whittington Avenue Site, 1988)

Col Pl I Pier base surviving at 90 Gracechurch Street, with 5x100mm scale standing on stone plinth.

Arcade piers in the redesigned Basilica: a major modification of the 2nd-century Basilica saw the solid Nave walls replaced by open arcades, comprising massive brick piers set on stone plinths.

Col Pl J The 5x100mm scale rests on a stone plinth from which the tile pier has been robbed: outline of tiles marked in mortar. (Area M)

Designs on the Basilica: fragments of painted wall-plaster.

Col Pl K (above) Traces of burning and graffiti. (West Antechamber)

Col Pl L (above) Part of a scrolling frieze. (East Antechamber)

Col Pl M (above) Parts of a robed figure (East Antechamber)

Col Pl N Part of wall decoration. (East Antechamber)

Col Pl O Life in the Basilica: the 5x100mm scale lies on a scorched and well-worn *opus signium* floor in the Basilica Northern Range. (Area W, looking east)

Col Pl P Rebuilding after the fire: the 5x100mm scale rests on a layer of burnt roof tile, representing a major fire in the Northern Range, over which the foundations of a partition wall have been laid. Fragments of the original walls of Room 1 can be seen in the bottom right and top left hand corners. (Area W, looking west)

the activity which took place immediately before a brickearth slab was laid over much of the site, upon which the first buildings were subsequently erected. The coin thus provides an important *terminus post quem* of AD 64 for those structures. Pottery from associated features (W15 S3 N8) is consistent with a date of AD 65–70/5 which is confirmed by the presence of Samian ware sherds (S3 W3) stamped by potters operating at La Graufesenque: Modestus, who was working from AD 60–75, and Crestus from AD 60–90. It would seem from the evidence of the coin and stamps that the activity represented here took place in *c*.AD 65–75, perhaps a decade or so later than the previous phase.

Unfortunately the assemblages from the buildings themselves were often too small to clarify the dating on their own. There was no evidence from Building 1 (S30). Building 2 produced a small group broadly datable to AD 55–70 (S28) with a noticeable lack of Highgate Wood 'C' ware, while the overlying dumps (S31) were dated to post–AD 65 by a Samian stamp of Patricius I (AD 65–90). By contrast, the equally small assemblage from Building 3 (W3) had pottery more typical of RCP1A (AD 50–60). The assemblage from Building 4 (S5 S6), which is later than Buildings 1 to 3, includes the first example of Highgate Wood 'B/C' ware, a fabric later than the 'B' wares but earlier than the 'C' wares, dating to *c*.AD 65–75. An external surface (N15) thought to be contemporary with this structure is dated after AD 70 by a stamp of Cotio (AD 70–85), who operated at La Graufesenque. Since the next major phase of development (see below) has been dated to *c*.AD 75, it seems that Buildings 1 to 4 were constructed after AD 65 but were rather short lived.

This activity at Leadenhall Court has helped shed light on our understanding of ceramic development during the early 70s and 80s. One of the main parameters for RCP2 is the technological change by the Highgate Wood potters from the use of grog (Highgate 'B') to fine sand (Highgate 'C') as a tempering for their vessels. But it was a gradual transition with both forms of tempering occurring together until the sandy wares superseded the grog-tempered pottery by the early 2nd-century (Table 6). A few sherds of Highgate 'C' were associated with the construction of Buildings 1 to 4, but this fabric was present in greater quantities after the demolition of those structures.

Buildings 5–14, 18 and 21: *c*.AD 75–80/85 *(Figs 9–11)*
The construction of Buildings 5–11 and 13–14 marks the expansion of the settlement over levels dated to *c*.AD 75. With the exception of Building 6, the structures were relatively insubstantial and consequently probably short lived. Although this and the succeeding levels produced well-stratified deposits containing large assemblages of pottery, the ceramics are undistinguished, and all broadly date to the period AD 70–100. Such homogeneity suggests that there is little redeposited early Roman material, an argument supported by the minimal development of the site prior to this phase of expansion. This lack of residual material is of particular relevance when examining the distribution of coins and stamped Samian vessels, which often continued in circulation long after the date of manufacture. Thus a coin of Titus (AD 77–8) provides a *terminus post quem* for the destruction of Building 7, and for its replacement with Building 18. Similarly, a Samian stamp of Severus I (AD 80–100) provides a *terminus post quem* for the midden-like deposits which accumulated in Buildings 16 and 21, and ultimately for Building 22.

It would seem from the dates of the destruction deposits that this development lasted for perhaps a decade. Further analysis of the coarse wares and the decorated Samian forms may well refine the dating of this pottery: indeed the complexities and large size of the assemblages from the Leadenhall Court sequence provide a unique opportunity for such a study. There is, for example, a subtle distinction in the incidence of forms in Highgate Wood 'C' ware. In the earliest phases of activity, the forms had been limited to bowls or lids, or occasionally beakers decorated with barbotine dots. However, deposits from Building 12 (N20) produced the first example of a jar form. This new vessel has a simple beaded rim (Table 8, IIA), more typical of the 'native' tradition, whereas 'Romanised' forms of decorated, necked jars are generally confined to 2nd-century assemblages.

Contraction and clearance: *c*.AD 80/85–100
(Figs 12, 13)
There is little evidence from the artefacts recovered from layers associated with the clearance of the site to suggest that the date of the activity represented is any later than *c*.AD 80/85. There are two coins of Vespasian, one dated to AD 69–79 from Building 22 (S39) and the other from the demolition of Building 6 (W17), dated to AD 71, but these layers also produced Samian stamps of AD 65–90 and 65–95. The ceramic assemblages contain little Highgate Wood 'C' ware and very few Dragendorff form 37 bowls, which post-date AD 70, whereas the earlier bowl form Dragendorff 29 is present in larger quantities (Table 7). As there are also a number of mid-1st-century

wares, it would seem that these levels largely comprise redeposited material.

A single sherd from a North African amphora found in a brickearth dump overlying the destruction levels of Building 6 (W17) is of particular interest. As a dating tool it is not very diagnostic as these vessels have a long date range, but its presence in London in such an early group warrants mention. Sherds in an identical fabric had previously been found in early to mid-2nd-century deposits at 25–6 Lime Street (LIM83) and an almost whole example of a 'Piccolo' form (Peacock & Williams 1986, class 33, fig 79, 153) came from a pit group dated to c.AD 140–60 at 28–32 Bishopsgate (Tyers 1984). The 'Piccolo' form has been found in early 2nd-century levels at Ostia in Italy (Carandini & Panella 1981; Panella 1973).

Basilica construction: c.AD 85/90–120+
(Figs 14–16)

Evidence to date the construction of the Basilica comes from levels associated with the last use of the brickearth and timber buildings on the site to the north of the new complex, as well as from the construction levels within the Basilica itself.

A coin of Domitian (AD 85) from the latest layers in Building 10 (N29) provides a *terminus post quem* for the later levels and for the latest use of Building 12 (N30). Although most of the associated pottery is broadly dated to RCP2 (AD 75–100), some of the coarse ware forms from overlying deposits suggest a later 1st-century date. A demolition deposit from Building 12 (N30) contained an example of a necked jar in Highgate Wood 'C' ware. This form is not like those generally associated with 2nd-century production (Table 8, IIE) as it is an unslipped, undecorated vessel. An occupation layer (N24) produced a similar jar, whilst unslipped and poorly-fired variants of the type IIE form were also noted in one of the latest layers in Building 10 (N28). In contrast, the overlying midden deposits (N31) contained the first example of the clearly 2nd-century jar form (IIE), together with other RCP3 pottery (AD 100–20), local mica-dusted wares, London wares and a Samian plate of Dragendorff form 18/31. In ceramic terms, this suggests a transition between the late 1st and early 2nd centuries, but the absence of RCP4 fabrics such as the products of the Black-burnished industries (BB1, BB2, BBS) suggests a date before AD 120 for the activity represented.

Nine Samian stamps recovered from deposits in this phase range in date from AD 65 to 95. However, it has already been shown that the associated coarse wares date to the later 1st and early 2nd centuries, which suggests either that the stamped vessels were in use for a long time or that the latest date in the range is the more appropriate. To sum up, the buildings in this phase are thought to be site huts associated with the construction of the Basilica. Since they were demolished in or by the early 2nd century, this implies that the Basilica programme was well underway by that date.

Evidence recovered from within the Basilica itself or from its primary surfaces supports an early 2nd-century date for the completion of the first phase of construction. Although most of the coins and pottery can be broadly dated to the period AD 70–100, it must be stressed that the majority of the assemblages considered here comprised material disturbed and redistributed by the Roman labourers during the excavation of the deep foundation trenches for the Basilica. This is illustrated by the identification of joining sherds from the same vessel, one found in the Basilica construction level (W32), the other from an earlier building (W30). There was a dearth of dating evidence from the levels within the Basilica, as has been noted on previous excavations (Marsden 1987, 74–5), but there were several small assemblages which merit consideration here. Construction dumps in the west (W26), the addition of a buttress (W60) and the laying of the floor in Room 12 (M64) all produced material datable to the early 2nd century, but no later 2nd-century wares.

A date of c.AD 120 is suggested by the presence of an abraded sherd of Black-burnished-style ware in the construction levels of the Nave (D32), in an assemblage which would otherwise have been dated AD 70–100. Unfortunately this group is contaminated by two sherds of medieval pottery, as part of the layer was cut by a post-hole truncated by modern activity.

Clearer evidence for a date of AD 120+/-5 for the completion of the Northern Range was recovered from deposits within the complex (N66). Although this horizon was truncated in Area N, analogous deposits were directly sealed by the primary surfaces elsewhere on the site. Overlying the final phase of midden material (N31) and demolition debris from the brickearth and timber site huts (N30) was a mortar spread containing sherds of Black-burnished ware (BB1, BB2), the earliest securely-stratified occurrence of this pottery on the site. It must be stressed that the exact date for the arrival of this ware in London is not certain, and to some extent our interpretation is influenced by the dates suggested for the introduction of Black-burnished ware elsewhere in Britain. Nevertheless, it appears in small quantities on several sites in layers sealed beneath fire levels dated to c.AD

120–5 (Marsh 1981, 222). Taken together, the ceramic evidence seems to show that construction work on the new Basilica began at the turn of the 1st century, and that the first phase was completed within a decade of AD 120.

First buildings north of the Basilica: c.AD 120+
(Fig 16)
A large assemblage was recovered from the make-up levels for the first road, which was laid after the Northern Range had been completed. The material was principally of early 2nd-century date, but included Samian stamps broadly datable to AD 70–100 and a coin of Domitian (AD 86). Pottery dating to AD 120 was absent. However, there was a Samian vessel more commonly associated with a mid- to late 2nd-century date. Joanna Bird suggests that the form '... is most like a Curle 11 (c.AD 70–140) though the lack of decoration would be more appropriate for an early Dragendorff 38. The fabric looks East Gaulish, probably from the earlier kilns, and a date of c.AD 100–35/40 would be a suitable date range.' Pottery from similar levels in Area W principally dates to the late 1st century, but this activity must post-date the construction of the Northern Range, and must therefore be at least early 2nd century.

A date of c.AD 120 for the first road in Area N is suggested by the presence of sherds of Colchester colour-coated ware with rough-cast decoration found in the gravel surface, although there was also a high proportion of RCP3 pottery. Study of the assemblage from the second road (N36) suggests a similar date, while the small assemblage from Road 3 (N38) also contained only RCP3 wares. Evidence from the broadly contemporary structures north of the new road, Buildings 24 and 25 (N34, N37), also points to AD 100–20, with a noticeable absence of Black-burnished and other later 2nd-century wares. However, they overlay an area of dumping (N65) from which a variety of Black-burnished ware (BB1) was recovered. Bearing in mind the uncertainty of the date of the arrival of this ware in London, a date of around c.AD 120 is suggested for these buildings. It would therefore seem that the Basilica, road and the associated buildings to the north were all functioning by approximately the same time.

The street and buildings were further developed in the 2nd century. An assemblage of RCP4 pottery from a layer of redeposited fire debris associated with Building 26 (N39) also included a Verulamium mortarium samped by Matugenus (AD 90–125), which fits well within a date range of c.AD 120–40. The absence of later fabrics and forms implies an early to mid-2nd-century date for the dumps of redeposited fire debris, which suggests that this fire represented to the north of the road is the same one identified within the Basilica itself, as discussed below.

Pre-fire occupation in the Basilica: early 2nd century
(Fig 17, Table 9)
The 2nd-century fire horizon within the Basilica provides a convenient datum common to the sequences recorded in the Nave, Northern Range and Antechambers where development of the complex as a whole can be assessed. Such pottery as there is from the pre-fire levels within the Basilica is mainly of early 2nd-century date (Table 9), the most diagnostic sherds deriving from a Verulamium region white ware ring-necked flagon with a slightly thickened upper ring (Table 8, 1B5). Similar vessels are thought to have been current c.AD 120–40. Comparable assemblages were also recovered from the fire debris horizon itself (Table 9). From the levels overlying the first fire horizon, Black-burnished wares were recovered in quantity, while other fabrics which became more common include Verulamium region coarse white slipped wares. By contrast, pottery from the Highgate Wood and Alice Holt kilns was less common after the fire. The forms are confined to early or mid-2nd-century types which, when combined with the factors just discussed, diagnose an assemblage comparable with those from several other sites in the City which have extensive fire horizons thought to represent the disaster of AD 120–25.

This raises the question of whether the Basilica fire identified at Leadenhall Court should be seen as part of that early 2nd-century conflagration which is thought to have destroyed at least 65 acres of the town (Marsh 1981; 221–6; Dunning 1945), and is often termed the 'Hadrianic Fire'. Whether all early 2nd-century fire deposits in London necessarily represent the same conflagration is a topic for future research. The assemblages from the relevant levels in the Basilica are not large, and the dates provided by externally datable artefacts are earlier than those suggested by the ceramic indicators: a precise date for the Basilica fire cannot therefore be established. However, the sudden influx of Black-burnished wares in c.AD 120 was a widespread phenomenon which is not peculiar to London, and the presence of such wares in the post-fire groups at Leadenhall Court is in effect the most precise indicator of date presently available.

While this could be taken to imply that the town fire and the Basilica fire were one and the same event, the excavators of the Leadenhall Court site conclude

Pottery Types	A number of records (0–50)	B number of records (0–50)
Alice Holt / Surrey	▬▬▬▬▬▬▬	▬▬▬▬▬▬
Misc amphora	▬	▬
Black-burnished ware 1		
Black-burnished ware 2		·
Black-burnished style		
Camulodunum-type 186 amphora	·	·
Camulodunum-type 189 amphora		
Misc colour coated wares		·
Central Gaulish other fabrics		·
Misc coarse wares		·
Dressel 20 amphora	▬▬	▬▬
Early Roman micaceous sandy ware	·	
Misc fine wares	▬	▬
Fine micaceous ware	▬	▬
Gillam-type 238 and developed mortaria	·	·
Misc grog-tempered wares		·
Haltern 70 amphora		
Hoo ware	▬	·
Highgate 'B' grog-tempered ware	▬▬▬	▬▬▬
Highgate 'B' and 'C' variant		·
Highgate Wood 'C' ware	▬▬▬▬▬▬	▬▬▬▬
Kōan amphora	·	·
London-type 555 amphora	·	·
Local micaceous ware		
London-type ware	▬	▬
Lyon colour-coated ware		·
Misc mica dusted ware	▬	·
Montans ware	·	
North Kent Shelly ware		·
Misc oxidised wares	▬▬▬	▬▬▬
Pelichet-type 47 amphora	▬	▬
Pompeian red ware 2		·
Pompeian red ware 3		·
Ring-and dot beaker	▬	
Rhône Valley mortarium		
Misc red & white slip ware	▬	▬
Samian	▬▬▬▬▬	▬▬▬▬▬
Misc sand-tempered ware	▬▬▬▬▬▬▬▬	▬▬▬▬▬▬▬▬
Amphora seal		·
Misc shell-tempered ware	▬	▬
Sugar Loaf Court ware		·
Verulamium region coarse white slipped ware	·	
Verulamium region grey ware	▬	▬
Verulamium region red & white slip ware	·	
Verulamium region white ware	▬▬▬▬▬	

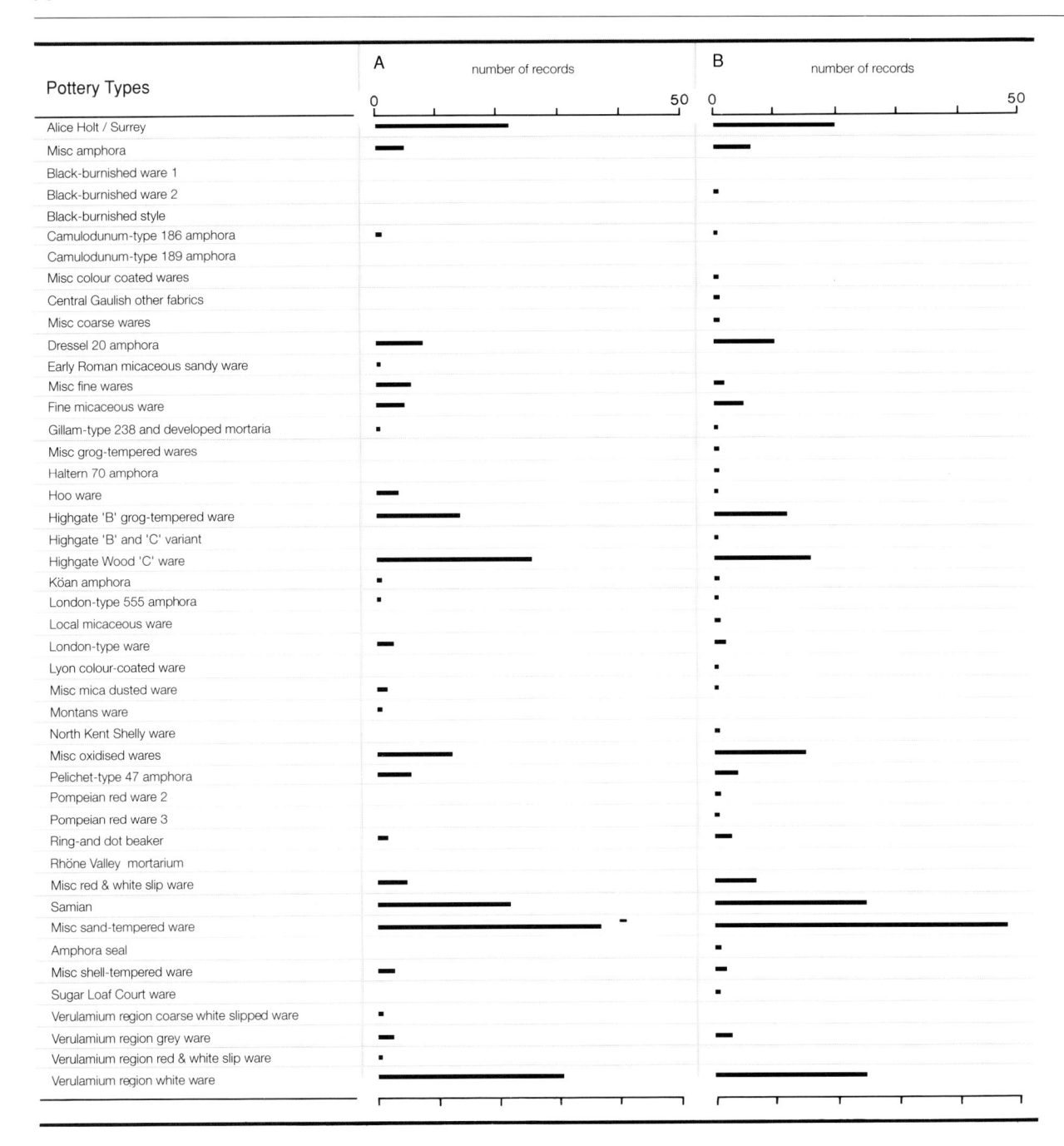

Table 9 Relative presence and absence of pottery types excavated within the Basilica on the Leadenhall Court site from assemblages representing: Column A = activity before the first 2nd-century fire; Column B = first 2nd-century fire horizon; Column C = activity after the fire. Note the changing quantities of Black-burnished, Highgate Wood and London wares before and after the fire (Column B): by comparing these patterns with Table 6, a date for the fire can be suggested

otherwise. Their argument is as follows. It has already been shown that the Northern Range of the Basilica was not completed or occupied until c.AD 120, after which a road was laid out with buildings to the north of it. Several phases of activity and occupation were recorded on the site after the initial construction of the complex, but before the Basilica fire. To the north, the street was resurfaced at least twice and Buildings 24, 25 and 26 had all been constructed and replaced before the conflagration. Within the Basilica, a major rebuilding programme had been undertaken and completed, one which saw the north wall of the Nave replaced by brick piers, the Antechambers completely altered, and the interior of the whole building replastered. It is possible that all those activities

assemblages from this building and the contemporary Road 4 (N40) are very similar. Both show a marked increase in the relative proportion of Black-burnished ware whilst that from Building 27 included the first example of a Black-burnished bowl with a rounded rim (cf. Table 8, IVH5), suggesting a date towards the middle of the 2nd century.

There is very little difference between the assemblages from Building 27 (N47) and the overlying debris from a later fire (N48). Material from the contemporary Road 6 (N42) is dated to c.AD 140–60 by the presence of a cup-rimmed flagon (Table 8, IB7, 8), a Samian bowl of form Walters 81, and an absence of later 2nd-century wares. Pottery from Building 28 (N49) contained a Samian stamp of the potter Imprito (AD 140–65), providing a positive *terminus post quem*. Subsequent developments, Building 29 (N50), the contemporary road (N43) and the next resurfacing of the street (N44) show no marked difference in the date of the associated ceramics, which have been broadly dated to AD 140–60/80.

The fire debris from Building 30 (N51) may be contemporary with a second fire horizon recorded within the Basilica. It contains several ceramic types not identified on the site in earlier levels, including Soller mortaria and hunt cups from the Rhineland. This group bears a marked resemblance to the large waterfront assemblage from the St Magnus House site (Richardson 1986) which is broadly dated AD 180–230. There is evidence of a major fire in London in this period, certainly later than AD 170–80 (Marsh 1981, 226), while a late 2nd-century fire has also been recorded on other sites, notably Watling Court (WAT78) in the western half of the town. While it is possible that the Basilica suffered in the same event, it must be stressed that Londinium, like all ancient towns with timber buildings and open hearths, was beset by many small and medium-sized fires: broadly contemporary fire levels recorded on several sites need not necessarily represent a conflagration which destroyed the entire town.

There is no apparent distinction between the date of the assemblage associated with Building 31 (N52) and that from the fire debris over Building 30. The material from the ninth and final resurfacing of the street (N45) was somewhat contaminated in antiquity, since the road was badly rutted, and included several partially infilled pot holes in its long lived and much worn surface. Most of the pottery broadly dates to the middle of the 2nd century, but sherds of Nene Valley colour-coated ware and Alice Holt/Farnham ware from deposits associated with the later use of the road

within and without the Basilica could have been completed within five years, but on balance it seems more likely that the Basilica fire occurred at least 10 to 15 years after the date of the initial completion of the complex.

Later buildings north of the Basilica: mid-2nd–4th century
(Figs 17–19)
Building 27 (N47) was constructed over the fire debris which marked the destruction of Building 26. The

can be dated from the mid- to late 3rd-century. By contrast, a disturbed area of the road produced Porchester D ware and late Oxfordshire colour-coated wares, which may be dated to the late 4th century.

Occupation of the buildings north of the street may have continued into the late 3rd to early 4th century. Pottery recovered from levels sealing Building 31 (N53) included a sherd of obtuse lattice decorated Black-burnished ware which is generally dated later than AD 230, as well as a mortarium (type M10) from the Oxfordshire kilns dated to AD 180–240. No later 3rd-century forms were identified in this assemblage or the one from Building 32 (N54). However, the sherd of a later type of Oxfordshire mortarium from the debris of a later fire (N55) can be dated AD 250 or later, while material from the silts which sealed the final road surface (N46) contained pottery dating from the mid-3rd to the early 4th century.

The series of shallow features cut into the silts over the street represent activity which demonstrates that the road was no longer operating as a thoroughfare. Pottery recovered from this phase (N58) produced an homogeneous 4th-century group with little residual material, and including several types dating to AD 350–400.

Later activity in the Basilica: late 2nd–4th century
(Fig 18)

In marked contrast to the well-stratified sequence of pottery recovered to the north of the road, little dating material was present in the contemporary levels within the Basilica itself, although a *terminus post quem* for the last use of Room 1 in the Northern Range (W55) is provided by a coin of Severus (193–211). A small group of pottery from the final use of Room 8 (S50) broadly dates to the late 2nd to mid-3rd century, and sherds of Alice Holt/Farnham ware from the final surfacing of the Nave (D36 D49) were of a type present in London from the mid-3rd century. It can therefore be suggested that the Basilica was in use in the late 3rd century, but there is little evidence to demonstrate activity here in the 4th. Taken together, it seems that the final occupation of the Basilica, the buildings north of the street and the last use of that road as a thoroughfare can be dated towards the end of the 3rd century or the very early 4th century at the latest. The evidence presented here suggests that demolition of both the Basilica and the buildings north of the street had taken place by or in the early 4th century.

Saxons and Normans *(Fig 20)*

A similar sequence of ceramic phases has been constructed for the post-Roman period (Vince forthcoming). The early Medieval Ceramic Phases (MCP1–MCP5) have been broadly dated from *c.*AD 850 to *c.*1150 by association with coins and dendrochronologically datable material from securely stratified contexts from a number of City sites including Pudding Lane, Peninsular House, Milk Street and Billingsgate Lorry Park (Horsman et al. 1988, 10–11), and may be summarised thus:

> MCP1: Late Saxon Shelly ware on its own: mid-9th to early 11th century.
> MCP2: Late Saxon Shelly ware with Early Medieval Sandy ware: early 11th century.
> MCP3: The same two wares with Early Medieval Sand and Shelly ware: early to mid-11th century
> MCP4: Early Surrey coarse ware with Early Medieval chalky wares but no Late Saxon Shelly: mid- to late 11th century.
> MCP5: Same two wares with London-type wares and coarse London-type wares and locally produced unglazed greywares: late 11th to mid-12th century

In contrast to the Roman levels, virtually no horizontally bedded medieval layers were recorded on the Leadenhall Court site. This was simply because the post-Roman ground surface had been comprehensively destroyed when deep basements were dug for the buildings which were demolished in 1986. However the truncated remains of medieval pits, wells and robber trenches were recorded, although few direct stratigraphic relationships could be established. Nevertheless, discrete groups of finds were recovered from them and although these assemblages cannot be dated as closely as some of the Roman phases, it did prove possible to assign a broad date to most of that medieval material. As a consequence, it was found that the earliest medieval features contained MCP2 and MCP3 pottery, showing that the Saxon reoccupation of this part of the City was later than the resettlement of the Billingsgate area, closer to the waterfront, where pits and buildings associated with MCP1 material were excavated (Horsman et al. 1988). Unfortunately, as is the case with many sites away from the waterfront, no medieval coins at all were recovered at Leadenhall, and so the dating of the post-Roman development relies heavily upon study of the ceramic material.

7 Inner city living

DOMESTIC BUILDINGS IN LONDINIUM

Gustav Milne, Chrissie Milne and Paul Wootton

The public buildings of Londinium have been the focus of much recent attention, with major excavations on the sites of the so-called 'Governor's Palace', the amphitheatre, the Huggin Hill bathhouse and the 2nd-century Basilica all within the last five years. However, the private buildings of Roman London also merit detailed study, not only in their own right, but also to determine how these humbler structures relate topographically, sociologically and chronologically to their more prestigious neighbours. Such an integrated approach to the pattern of building in the Roman town provides a fuller picture of the urban development than consideration of any one building or class of buildings on its own. Just such a study has been undertaken on the Leadenhall Court site following the 1984–6 programme of rescue excavations, which were initially designed to record the remains of the 2nd-century Basilica. The well-preserved sequence of Roman activity recorded beneath the Basilica is summarised in Chapter 2. Twelve phases of activity and the remains of 23 buildings were identified (Buildings 1–23), from which a clear picture was obtained of the growth of this central part of the town between AD 50 and 120. In addition, more fragmentary remains of a further nine structures were examined on the edge of the later Roman road to the north of the Basilica, and these were built between the 2nd and the 4th centuries (Buildings 24–32). In this chapter the form and function of these domestic buildings will be examined in more detail, focusing particular attention on the early Roman structures.

Form and function of the buildings
(Figs 25–9)

The 23 1st-century buildings exhibited a variety of forms, including single-roomed structures; multi-roomed strip buildings; and buildings of more complex structure. The form of Buildings 1–4 merits particular comment, since that group represents the earliest occupation of the site (Figs 7, 8 and 25). How 'urban' were those structures? Their form is clearly not that of the characteristically urban multi-roomed strip building, for example. Although no complete plan was recovered, these buildings bear at least a passing resemblance to the rural long-house type: small halls over twice as long as they were wide, perhaps 12 × 5m on average. Although it is not possible to say whether they represent barns, byres or farmhouses rather than urban dwellings, their general form and detached layout certainly seems to suggest a less intensive development of the area in this period when compared with the subsequent phases of settlement.

The three single-roomed buildings (14, 16 and 21) were the smallest type represented: Building 21 was only 3 × 3m for example (Figs 27 and 28). They were all positioned in yard areas at the rear of the properties fronting the main north–south thoroughfare (Figs 9–11). They were therefore probably used as storehouses or animal sheds rather than for domestic occupation.

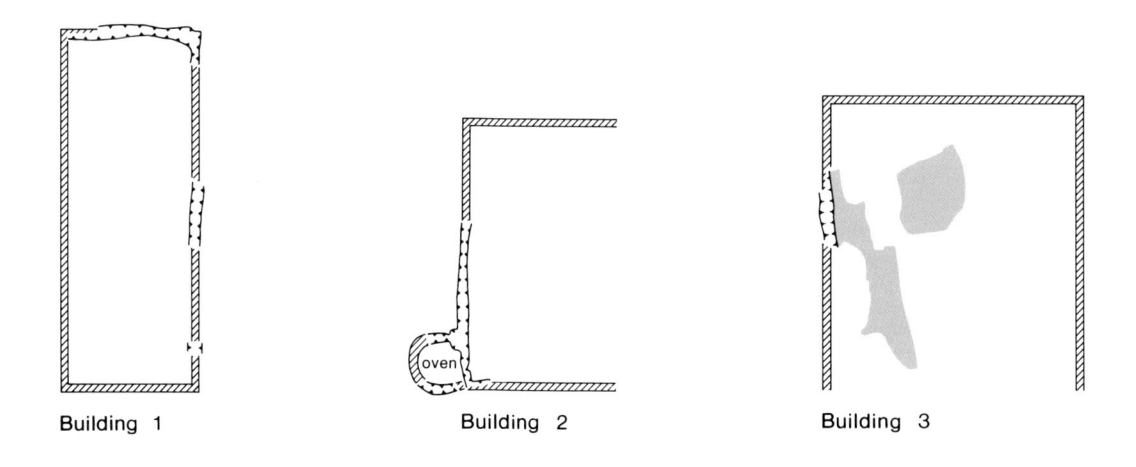

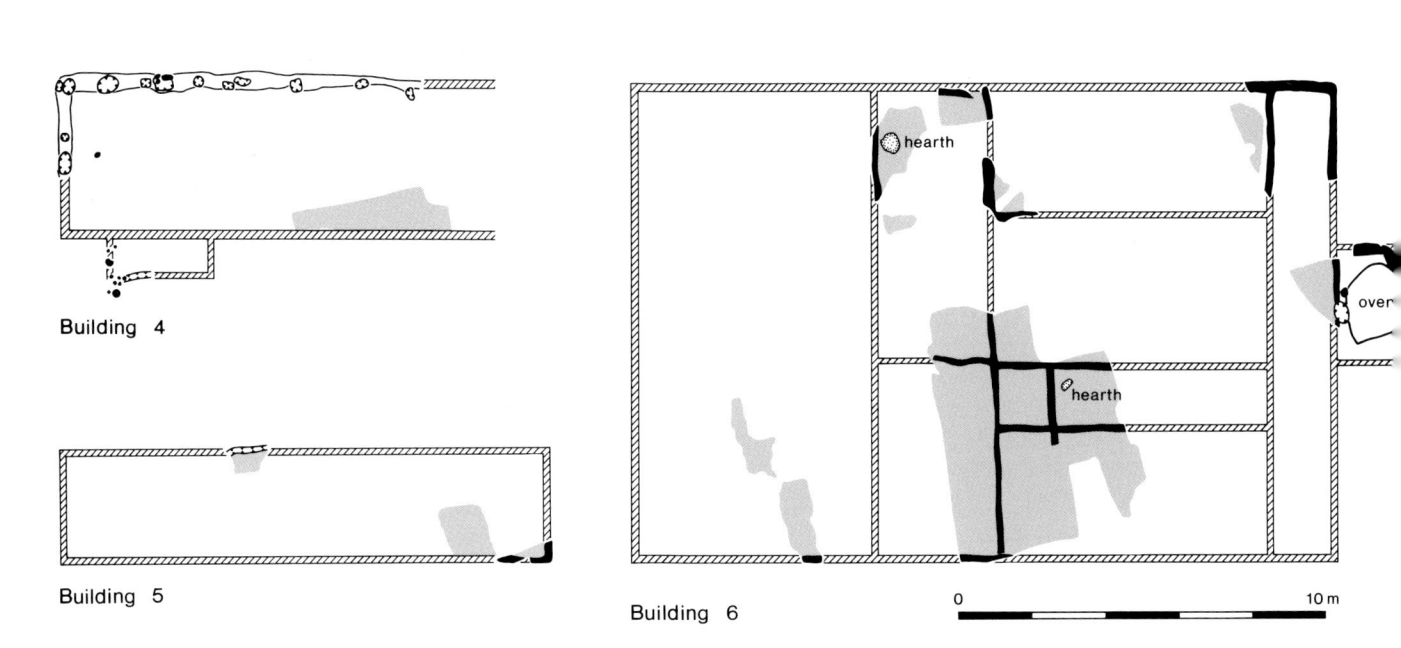

The multi-roomed strip building is now seen as one of the most common types of domestic vernacular building found in early Romano-British towns (Col Pl B). They comprise a single range of small rooms set one behind the other, and several such buildings were often laid out contiguously within long narrow urban property plots. On sites where the frontage has been recorded, the room immediately adjacent to the street is often interpreted as a shop with a workshop behind, and residential accommodation beyond that. Such structures are well known from recent work in London, as at the Newgate Street site (Perring & Roskams 1991), as well as in many other towns, such as Verulamium (Frere 1972). Six clear examples were recorded on the Leadenhall Court site (Figs 26–28; Buildings 9, 10, 11, 12, 15 and 23), while Buildings 7, 8, 17 and 18 may

Fig 25 Comparative plans of early Roman buildings 1–6. Extent of internal surfaces recorded shown with grey tone. Scale 1: 200

OPPOSITE ABOVE

Fig 26 Comparative plans of early Roman buildings 7–10. Scale 1: 200

OPPOSITE BELOW

Fig 27 Comparative plans of early Roman buildings 11–15 and 20. Scale 1: 200

also have been of this type. Unfortunately the western end of the buildings (i.e. the street frontage) lay beyond the limit of excavation and so the full length of these structures was not established. However, the seven-roomed Building 10 was at least 24m long, and a total length in excess of 30m may not be unreasonable. The average width of these buildings was 4m, and the rooms were usually square, often with a tile-based hearth to provide both heat and

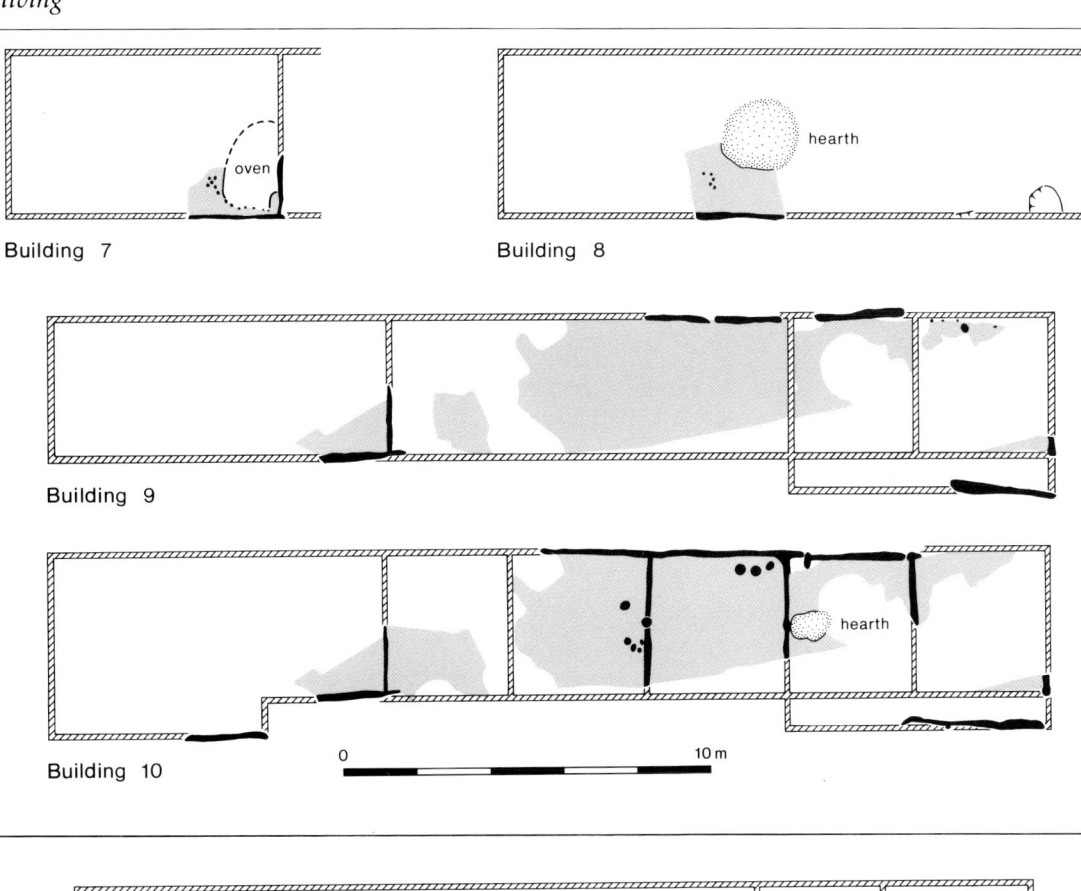

Inner city living

Building 7

Building 8 — hearth

Building 9

Building 10

0   10 m

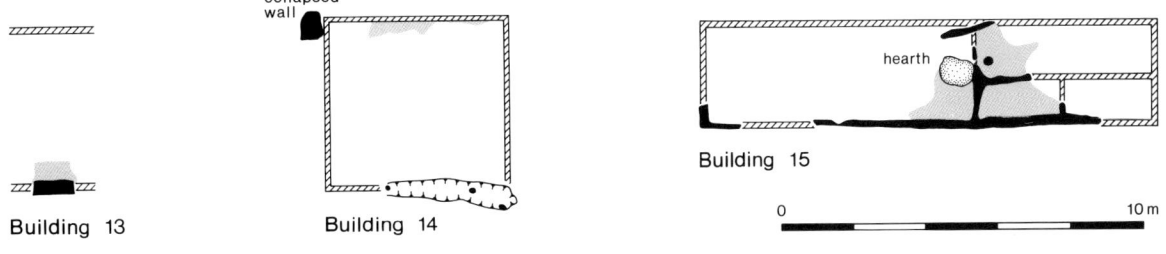

Building 11 — hearth

Building 20 — hearth

Building 12 — hearth, hearth, threshold

Building 13

Building 14 — collapsed wall

Building 15 — hearth

0   10 m

Building 16
Building 17 oven
Building 18 oven

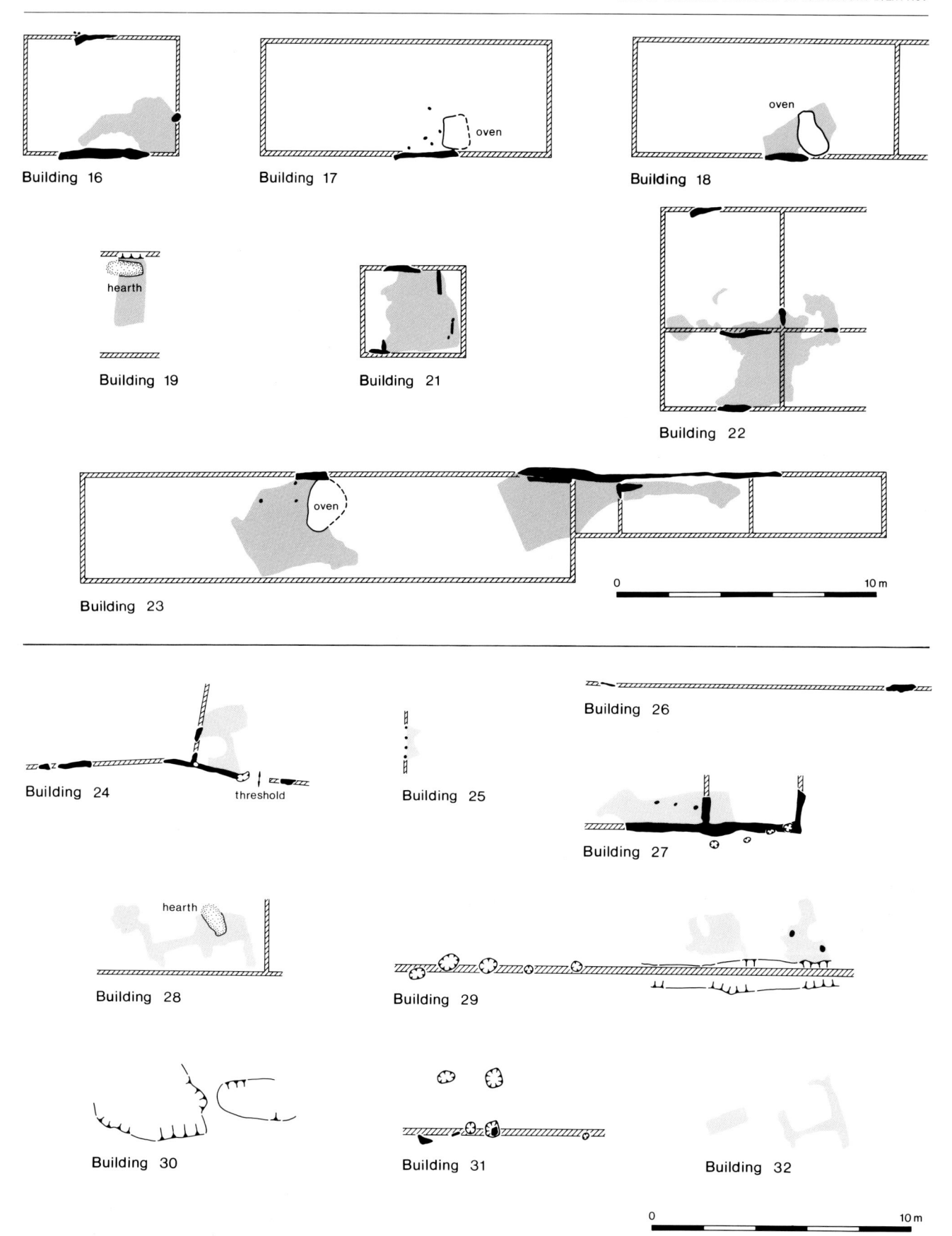

Building 19 hearth
Building 21
Building 22

Building 23 oven

0   10 m

Building 24 threshold
Building 25
Building 26
Building 27

Building 28 hearth
Building 29

Building 30
Building 31
Building 32

0   10 m

Inner city living

OPPOSITE ABOVE
Fig 28 Comparative plans of early Roman buildings 16–19 and 21–23. Scale 1: 200

OPPOSITE BELOW
Fig 29 Comparative plans of fragmentary remains of 2nd- to 4th-century buildings 24–32 fronting road to north of Basilica. Scale 1: 200

cooking facilities set against one wall (Col Pl D). The floors were simply surfaced and resurfaced with brickearth, and were rarely level. The doorways seemed to be in the side walls, opening out on to the narrow alleys which ran between the buildings, rather than in the partition walls themselves (Col Pl A). This is considered significant, since it suggests that the building was not occupied by a single family requiring access to all rooms, but that each room or block of two rooms may have formed an independent residential unit. Several different family groups may therefore have occupied each one of the strip buildings, perhaps renting the rooms from the landlord. Such tenants were presumably the new artisan class, the native British who flocked to the town having lost their farms and homes when ancient tribal estates were seized and the lands reallocated by the Romans. Such a landless class is of necessity itinerant, always moving to where work might be offered. This factor is also reflected in the modular construction of buildings, for they could be – and were – extended or contracted as required. Many of the buildings only lasted 5 to 10 years before being replaced, while none survived much more than 30 years.

The strip buildings may therefore be contrasted with the more spacious property excavated on the Watling Court site, in which a military diploma was found (Perring & Roskams 1991; Roxan 1983). That building was occupied by an auxiliary veteran, perhaps one of the more prosperous of the first Londoners, and one of the town's more willing inhabitants. There was only one structure on the Leadenhall Court site which could be favourably compared with that class of property: Building 6 (Fig 25). This was a timber-framed structure which had at least seven rooms, an internal corridor and a veranda at the rear. It was one of the few vernacular buildings which may have had a tiled roof since a number of tegulae and imbrices were recovered from an associated destruction horizon. It was also one of the few from which painted wall plaster was recorded (Col Pl C). The plaster was not applied over two to three layers of backing plaster as was standard practice elsewhere, but comprised a thin layer directly over the brickearth walling, which was then painted. The design seems to have included a white dado panel decorated with red, yellow and black splashes within a red border. Another unusual discovery was four fragments of a ceramic water pipe, a feature usually associated with the more substantial buildings in Roman London. Taken together, it seems that Building 6 represents the dwelling of a relatively wealthy citizen, and as such reflects the way rich and poor lived side by side in the early town.

The buildings: construction techniques
(Pls 23, 24)

Several construction techniques for domestic buildings have been recorded from Roman London, as has been noted in recent publications (e.g. Perring & Roskams 1991; Williams forthcoming). They range from the use of masonry footings with either a masonry, tile or even a brickearth superstructure, to a variety of timber and brickearth wall types. The 32 vernacular Roman buildings on the Leadenhall Court site were all built of the latter materials. At least three different construction techniques were represented, with some buildings incorporating walls of earth-fast posts, others stake and wattle, and others a timber framework. Occasionally different techniques were found in the same building.

Earth-fast post structures such as Building 2 had posts up to 0.35m in diameter, set into packed post holes at *c*.1.1m centres. The wall cladding may have incorporated wattle and daub infill, or brickearth mass walling poured between shutters and allowed to dry. The stake and wattle method of construction incorporated the driving of a series of stakes directly into the ground or a shallow construction trench. The stakes varied in diameter but averaged between 80 and 100mm, and were set some 0.5m apart. Wattles were then woven around the posts to provide a sturdy frame around which wet brickearth was packed and allowed to air dry. Some buildings (e.g. Buildings 10, 15 and 18) utilised mud bricks made from Brickearth (Pl 23), while evidence of external limewash rendering was recorded on Building 12. Nearly two-thirds of the strip buildings recorded were of a standard type and are thought to have been erected relatively quickly and at low cost. Contemporary comments on Roman wattle-walled buildings were made by the architect Vitruvius who declared: 'as for wattle and daub, I wish that it had never been invented. The more it saves in time and gains in space, the greater and the more general is the

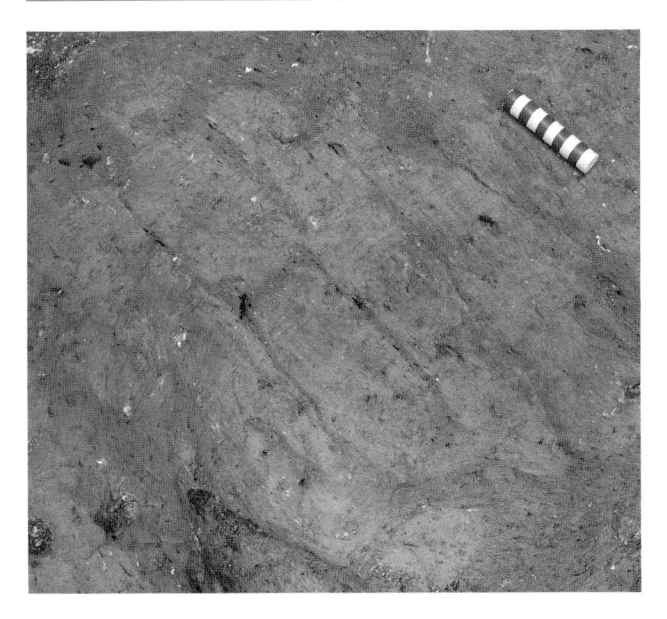

Pl 23 How Brickearth got its name: a collapsed wall built from air-dried mud bricks, made from locally quarried Brickearth. Sub-rectangular outlines of the bricks can be seen running parallel to 10x10mm scale. (Area N)

disaster that it may cause, for it is made to catch fire, like torches. It seems better, therefore to spend on burnt [fired] brick walls, than to save with wattle and daub and be in danger' (Morgan 1914, II, viii, 20). Clearly most of the inhabitants of buildings from the Leadenhall Court site did not have the money to erect fire-resistant brick houses.

Buildings with a timber framework were also common in early Roman London (Pl 24). A shallow construction trench was dug, into which was laid a timber base-plate with mortices cut into its upper face to support vertical timber posts, known as studs. On the Leadenhall Court site, fragments of decayed wood were all that survived of the base-plates, but few traces of upright studs were recorded. Much clearer evidence for timber-framed buildings in Roman London has recently been recorded. For example, the well-preserved wooden floor and foundations of a 2nd-century warehouse were discovered *in situ* in Southwark in 1988 (Dillon 1989), while on the Cannon Street Station site, timber base-plates, studs, wall-plates and tie-beams had been reused as foundation piles below a masonry wall (Goodburn 1990). At Leadenhall Court the infill material was usually either a form of wattle and daub, or mud bricks laid between the studs and bonded with wet brickearth. In some cases a further coating of brickearth or lime was painted on to the external surfaces of the finished wall for protection against the weather. In contrast to the stake and wattle buildings just discussed, walls which incorporated a timber framework – such as those of Building 6 – may have stood to a height of 2m or more, and may even have been two-storeyed.

Brick and tile fragments were recovered from the levels associated with the vernacular buildings at Leadenhall Court. This material came in a number of forms and fabrics, the majority of which were probably produced in tile kilns situated between London and St Albans. However, there is little evidence to suggest that many of the buildings were roofed in ceramic tile. Indeed, many of the walls recorded would not have been strong enough to support the weight. A considerable proportion of the brick and tile was used to construct the bases and walls of hearths and ovens, while much of the rest seems to have been reused as hardcore in the alleys and yards.

In the 1st century, then, it seems that the majority of domestic buildings in Londinium were of brickearth and timber construction, similar to the range of forms recorded on the Leadenhall Court site. However, there was a noticeable change in the 2nd and 3rd centuries (i.e. after the construction of the enlarged prestigious Basilica complex), for masonry buildings were built in several parts of the city. Recently recorded examples include those at Bishopsgate just to the north of our site (Milne et al. 1984), immediately to the east of the Whittington

Pl 24 Roman timber-framed building: the 5x100mm scale rests in a room defined by slots in which decayed traces of squared timber base-plates were recorded. (Building 6, Area W, looking south)

Avenue excavations (Appendix A) and at Lime Street (Williams 1984), to the west at Lothbury (Spence 1989, 22–3) and Austin Friars (Spence & Grew 1990, 14–15), and to the south at Pudding Lane (Milne 1985 138–41) and Billingsgate (Marsden 1980, 151–5). The floors of such buildings were frequently surfaced, not with brickearth, but with tessellated or mosaic pavements (Jones 1988) or *opus signinum*. It is this class of structure which has come to be identified in the public mind as the 'typical' Roman town house, although it is now known that, in London at least, domestic masonry buildings were virtually unknown in the 1st century. Indeed, brickearth and timber buildings continued to be built throughout the 2nd to 4th centuries, sometimes to a high standard, like the mosaic-floored building found at Milk Street in 1976. There are a number of examples of brickearth buildings replacing almost identical structures which had been burnt down in the 2nd century, such as those on the GPO Newgate Street and Watling Court sites (Perring & Roskams 1991) in the western half of the city. Clearly not all classes in Roman London had access to the same level of resources as the richer property owners in some of the eastern parts of the town.

With this thought in mind, it is significant that none of the buildings erected in the 2nd to 4th century on the far side of the road to the north of the Basilica seem to have used masonry walling, at least not within the area excavated at Leadenhall Court (Buildings 24–32). This could imply that it was a less prosperous zone of the town, although other explanations are possible. For example, given the limited area of excavation observed, it may be that some or all of the structures recorded merely represented porticoes or verandas aligned along the southern edge of prestigious buildings lying beyond the limit of excavation. Alternatively, our features might represent a series of shops or stalls, part of a market which may have grown up around the perimeter of the Basilica. Whichever interpretation is preferred, the occupation north of the road does not seem to have lasted much longer than that of the Basilica itself, for both seem to have ceased in the early 4th century.

The mechanics of urban development

This provisional study has also shed light on the mechanics of urban growth in Roman London. In particular, it highlights the overriding importance of centrally planned building programmes (rather than organic growth) to the overall development of the town, at least in the 1st and 2nd centuries. Before AD 65, the layout of the area indicates that it lay on the periphery of the settlement, the main focus of which lay to the south and along the river. The earliest ditches found on the site, together with the small cemetery beyond them, probably represent the northern limits of the original settlement. This suggestion is supported by the conspicuous absence of evidence for the Boudiccan revolt of AD 60, an event which is usually clearly marked by burnt debris on sites within areas of intensive contemporary settlement.

The earliest buildings (Buildings 1–4) may all have been of the long-house type, and seem to indicate a non-intensive, semi-rural phase of development spreading out over an area previously occupied by woods and fields. They do not appear to be built up to a major thoroughfare, but sit in the centre of an open field or yard. By contrast, the buildings introduced in the years between AD 75–100 mark a period of far more intensive occupation on the Leadenhall Court site. They include the ubiquitous multi-roomed strip building, so characteristic of fully urban settlement. This new development was aligned on and coincided with the construction of the earliest basilica and forum complex: that major building lay just south of the excavation area.

The layout of the insula examined in the recent excavations is therefore seen as an integral part of a comprehensive plan for this sector of the town, a scheme which clearly incorporated both public and private buildings. However, although constructed at one and the same time, the individual properties within the insula were developed quite separately thereafter: indeed the obviously unco-ordinated nature of the building developments within the insula reflects the varied incomes and interests of the owners and occupiers of the individual properties.

The clear signature of a central planning authority is obviously discernible both in the initial establishment of the insula in *c*.AD 75 and in the drastic replanning of the whole area in *c*.AD 100. In *c*.AD 75, a complete urban insula was laid out against a newly founded road in one dramatic act of expansion. However, some traces of the previous layout are detectable in the new plan, such as the alignment shared by the northern walls of both Building 4 and the later Building 6. Such evidence, slight as it is, could imply that Buildings 1–4 occupied a plot of land the bounds of which were laid out in AD 65 or earlier, but which was not fully developed for a decade.

If that argument is accepted, then it can be seen that the AD 100 redevelopment was exceptionally sweeping, for it paid no heed to any buildings, roads, property boundaries or even established alignments and orientations. Although the construction of the strip buildings in AD 75 was precisely contemporary with that of the first phase of the civic centre, the form and modest status of most of those brickearth buildings might seem somewhat inappropriate for such a prime urban location in the insula adjacent to the basilica itself. It is perhaps not surprising that these strip buildings were so unceremoniously cleared when preparations were made for an even more prestigious civic centre in AD 100. However, that redevelopment should not be seen just as a slum clearance programme for the simple reason that it cut so absolutely across all previous boundaries. This scheme was surely of far greater consequence, since it saw the heart of Londinium completely replanned. Possible reasons for this are discussed in Chapter 11, and need not detain us here. What this chapter has demonstrated is that evidence from our excavations shows how Londinium's growth was controlled by major development plans, designed by an authority with extensive powers and considerable resources. Its expansion was not therefore gradual and organic: it would seem that Roman London grew by decrees, not degrees.

8 Civic centre redevelopment

FORUM AND BASILICA REASSESSED

Trevor Brigham

In Chapter 2, the development of the 2nd-century Basilica was assessed, in so far as the recent work on the Leadenhall Court site allowed. Now the focus will be widened to consider the implications of that important sequence for the rest of the Basilica and for its Forum to the south. To do this, the records of many other sites in the vicinity were examined, including those compiled by Henry Hodge and William Miller in the 1880s, and the most recent excavations at Whittington Avenue in 1988–9 (Figs 2, 30). As a consequence, it has proved possible to make a reassessment of the forum development recently discussed by Peter Marsden (Marsden 1987). In the light of this latest information, new reconstructions of the complex at various stages are proposed in this and the following chapter.

Construction of the 2nd-century Forum-Basilica *(Fig 30)*

The development of the civic centre of Roman London began in AD 70–80 with the building of the first forum, a comparatively modest structure occupying an area of some 100 × 50m (Marsden 1987, 22–36). Within a generation, it was deemed that that structure should be replaced by a larger, more prestigious complex. The construction of the 2nd-century Forum-Basilica required the clearance of a large area of the contemporary town centre. Part of this was occupied by the earlier forum, and was therefore already owned and administered by the town. To the south and east, the new site was bounded by the main east–west and north–south through roads; the latter may have operated from the early years of the settlement, although a narrower, but more direct route flanked the east side of the 1st-century complex. The width of the Forum-Basilica was apparently determined by symmetry, the central entrance to the forum being located at the head of the early road from the bridge. The 2nd-century Basilica itself was placed squarely on Cornhill, the highest point in the town. In addition, new roads were to be constructed along the western and northern sides of the complex. By the mid-2nd century, the new Forum comprised the Basilica to the north, with eastern, western and southern wings enclosing a courtyard on its southern side. The length of the initial construction process – up to 30 years – reflected the complexity of the project and the major investment of resources which it represented, while the subsequent modifications to the plan show that it continued to incur considerable expense.

The new scheme to be presented here suggests that the sites for the Forum and for the Basilica were cleared at the same time. However, the 1st-century civic centre probably remained standing for some time, since internal colonnades were added to its south wing and inward facing aisles, presumably as an interim measure. Since the two fora coincided in the south, the corresponding wing of the second Forum could not have been constructed immediately, a hypothesis supported by its different construction. It is suggested that the East and West Wings were constructed at the same time as, or shortly after the second phase of the Basilica, and that the outer walls

From Roman Basilica to Medieval Market

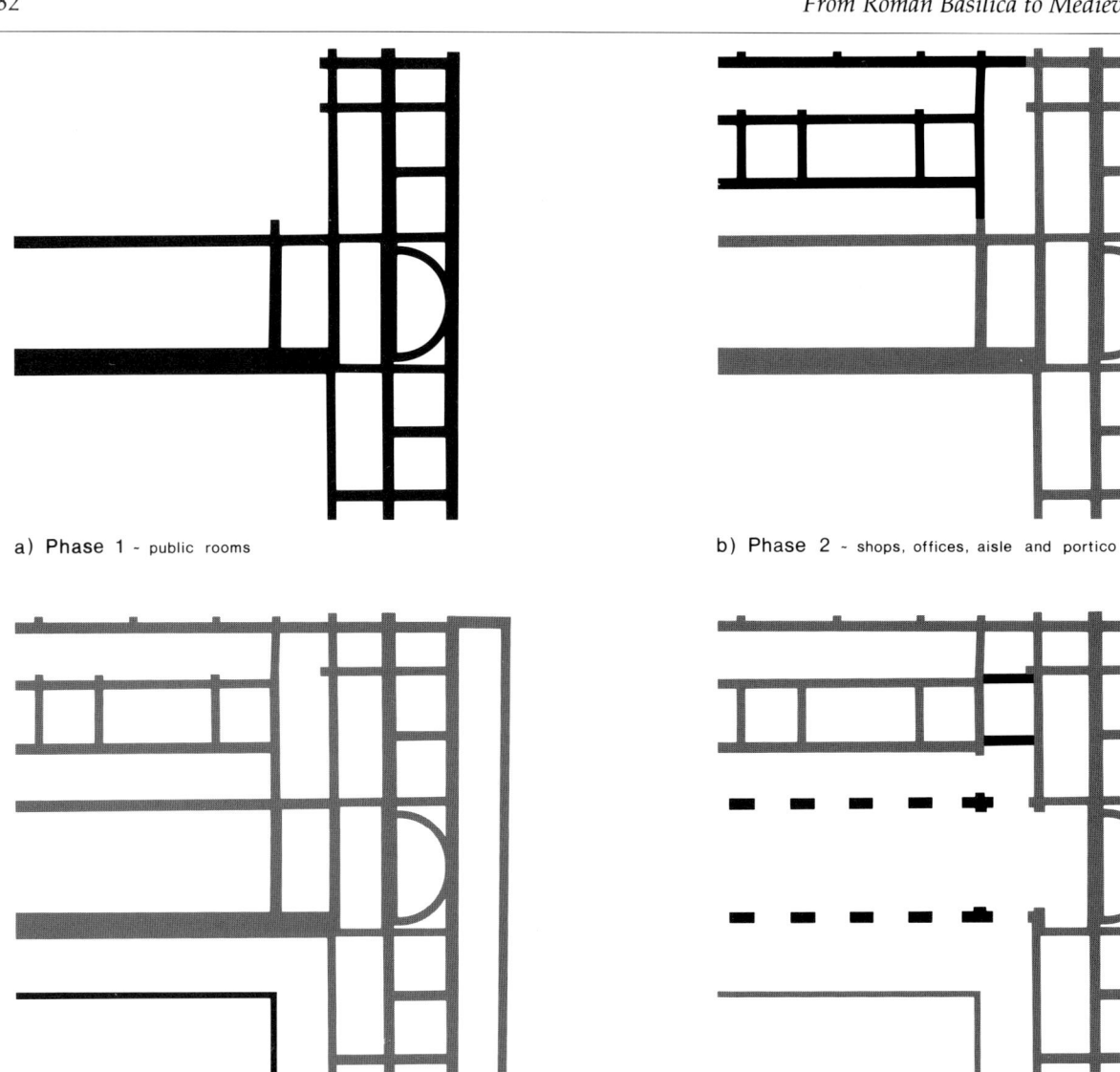

a) **Phase 1** - public rooms

b) **Phase 2** - shops, offices, aisle and portico

c) **Phase 3** - forum completed

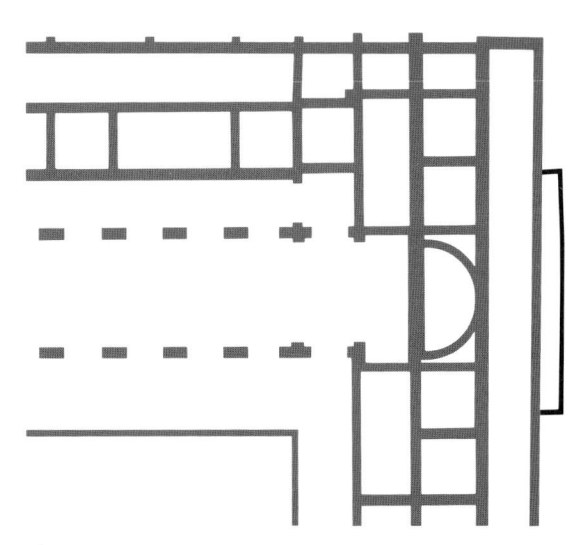

d) **Phase 4** - reconstruction with piers

e) **Phase 5** - new portico (post fire?)

Fig 30 Construction and development of part of 2nd- and 3rd-century Basilica, combining the evidence from the Leadenhall Court project with that collected by Hodge and Miller (1880–2) and from the Whittington Avenue site (1988–9): see Figs 2 and 3, Sites 1, 2 and 3. For each phase, new walls are shown in black, walls retained from previous phase in grey tone: cf. Fig 35. Scale 1:1,000

Pl 25 Building the Basilica: the first phase. The 5x100mm scale stands on the offset foundation of this internal buttress, which has no tile course at that level: cf. Pl 26. (Area S, looking south-east)

Pl 26 Building the Basilica: the second phase. The 2x100mm scale stands on the offset foundation of this Northern Range wall, clearly separated from the superstructure by four tile courses: cf. Pl 25. (Area S, looking east)

of the wings continued north to form the outer porticoes of the Basilica. The South Wing was added only after the first forum was demolished, and a hitherto unrecognised inner portico was then added, connected to the South Aisle of the Basilica. Significant variation was apparent in the details of construction and dimensions, even between several sections of the same Forum wall. For the most part, this seems to represent primary construction rather than later reconstruction work, suggesting that the project was built in stages over an extended period.

Foundations

Study of the Basilica foundations has revealed the use of slightly different building techniques suggesting that there were two phases of construction, with work on the public rooms such as the Nave and Apse commencing first (Fig 14). To the east of Gracechurch Street, a double foundation formed the south wall of the Nave. It has been suggested that the southernmost was an attempt to buttress the original northern wall, which was extensively patched (Marsden 1987 43–4). However, the southern foundation was offset at the standard level of 13m OD, whereas the northern foundation was offset at 12.5 to 12m OD where it was recorded by Hodge at 3 Gracechurch Street. This implies that it was the northern wall which was the addition. In this regard, it is notable that the line of the southern foundation coincided with that of the south wall of the eastern antechamber, whereas at the west end of the Basilica it was the northern foundation which coincided with similar walls. The slight curvature noticeable in the western section before it passed under the street was later corrected by a line of brick piers. The pier which survives at 90 Gracechurch Street rests mainly on the northern foundation, but laps the southern. This implies that the double foundation was an attempt to rectify a mistake at the laying-out stage, presumably because the construction site was initially divided by the north–south street which was still in use. The difference in levels of both the top and the base of the extra wall also suggests some kind of error. Other unusual features associated with the southern wall, include semicircular and straight foundations bonded into it. These presumably divided the infill within the Nave into more stable pockets and prevented the weight of the material in that foundation raft from thrusting directly against the wall, a variation of a technique suggested by Vitruvius (Morgan 1914, 189–92, VI, viii.7).

Superstructure

The superstructure was not as uniform as might have been expected, nor did the variations correspond completely with the two phases of foundation. A common construction consisted of four courses of broken, reused brick, narrower than the foundations, below seven courses of squared ragstone facing (*petit appareil*) which supported a layered ragstone and mortar core. A single course of broken brick capped the top of the first 'lift' at 14.2m OD. Above this level, Hodge's illustrations show that the second lift was narrower still, consisting of four brick courses followed by four ragstone courses, capped by two of brick at 15.2m OD. There was no offset at this level, and it seems probable that thereafter the superstructure was a repeated pattern of two brick courses followed by four of ragstone, each lift being 0.7m. Variations in the number of tile and ragstone courses occurred, however, in the north Nave wall, the wall between Rooms 14 and 15, the office partitions west of Gracechurch Street, and the south wing beyond a brick culvert inserted to drain water from the south aisle roof. Though the reasons for all the variations are not always immediately apparent, they do provide further support for the suggestion that different workmen were used on the eastern and western parts of the Basilica, for example. No brick courses or offsets were observed in the outer wall of the eastern range, although it survived to 13.3m OD. This foundation was 1.4m wide, narrower than the main external wall of the Basilica, which implies that the range was an addition to the north wing. The eastern range was structurally a continuation of the Forum portico, and may therefore have been contemporary with the second phase of Basilica foundations. The wall between Rooms 7 and 8 exhibited trowel marks striking the vertical joints of its east face, possibly to key a vanished stucco coat: similar examples have been observed by the author in the basilica at Caerwent.

The Basilica in the 2nd and 3rd centuries
(Fig 30)

The development of each part of the Basilica will now be summarised, relating the sequences recorded from 1880 to 1989 to that emerging from the Leadenhall Court site. This new scheme differs substantially from the published plan (Marsden 1987, figs 26, 28) in ways which fundamentally affect not only how that building might be reconstructed, but our view of how it was actually used. The four main differences are:

(1) The Basilica was not built in one phase, but had a complex development: neither of the aisles were part of the primary scheme for example.

(2) The Basilica plan was not symmetrical, for there was only one apse, at the eastern end of the Nave, rather than two, since the Western Range of offices probably continued northwards to join the Northern Range.

(3) There were not two ranges of offices on the northern side of the Basilica, but one. Access to the most northerly rooms (e.g. Rooms 1/4) could not be gained from the Nave or offices, but only from the street to the north. They are now interpreted as shops, separated from each other by temporary partition walls, of a type which could be found on all other sides of the Forum.

(4) There was a portico beyond the Apse.

The public rooms: Nave, Antechambers and Apse

The Nave was by far the largest room in the Basilica, and the development of its floor sequence was mirrored in the other public rooms. The initial surface was a thin mortar layer at 13.2m OD, probably a subfloor beneath a suspended timber platform resting on the second wall offset at 14.3m OD. Continuing subsidence caused by the compaction of earlier features required compensation over much of the Nave area subsequently, and damage was also caused to the walls, for a buttress was added to the north end of the east wall. However, another buttress attached to the south end of the wall on Miller's plan suggests that both may have had a decorative function, perhaps supporting engaged columns, for example. The next phase saw the walls around the Nave replaced by brick arcades allowing direct access to the north and south aisles, demonstrating that the aisles were unequivocally additions to the original plan. An exception was the central part of the south wall, which appears to have been retained. The uneven brickearth slab laid over the demolition debris lapping the piers and sealing the truncated walls presumably acted as a subfloor beneath a second timber platform, constructed at the same level as the old one.

The brickearth surface was scorched by the extensive 2nd-century fire which badly damaged the Basilica. Evidence for the fire or the ensuing destruction was found over a wide area, including the Antechambers, Apse and North Aisle. The Nave was eventually cleared, an *opus signinum* floor laid over the destruction debris, and the walls repaired and replastered. This floor was worn by heavy use, patched or replaced several times by thin surfaces. Then followed a period of neglect, characterised by the build-up of up to 0.4m of grey silts containing thin trampled brickearth, mortar and *opus signinum* surfaces. Subsequently, a second *opus signinum* slab was laid, with some evidence of timber structures where a series of posts was driven into the new floor. Notably, Hodge recorded in a section labelled 'North Excavation W(est)' (Marsden 1987, fig 41) a thin tile floor on an equally thin concrete bed immediately over the silts. This was not seen elsewhere, although he also noted a fragment of white tessellated pavement over the south wall near the surviving pier, possibly contemporary with a tessellated floor seen in the Eastern Antechamber. Once again, silts built up, particularly in the subsiding areas. A third *opus signinum* floor was then laid which, as Hodge also recorded, used broken tiles pressed into the surface to prevent the *opus signinum* from wearing down too quickly. The final activity recorded in the Nave saw the construction of several closely spaced clay post pads directly over the new, clean floor in the same area as the earlier post holes: they may have supported a timber platform.

In the Eastern Antechamber, a rounded foundation was inserted into the rubble over the sleeper wall between the two Antechambers. It is suggested that this supported one or more columns for a decorative triumphal arch, replacing an earlier, larger opening which may have been damaged by the fire. An *opus signinum* floor was laid over the rubble, but instead of being sealed by up to 0.4m of silts as in the other public rooms, Hodge noted 0.9m of 'soft soil' divided centrally by a line of broken brick. Over this was the mortar make-up for a tessellated pavement, followed by a thin tile and earth make-up for a final *opus signinum* floor at 15m OD. None of these features were recorded during the 1986 excavations in the same room, suggesting that they were truncated in the 19th century. The very high floor level suggested by the Hodge sequence implies that there were steps up from the Western Antechamber, leading to a similar floor level in the Apse. The number of floors was the same as in the other public rooms, which suggests that the sequences were contemporary.

In the Apse itself, the thin brickearth and mortar surfaces were affected by subsidence to such an extent that, with the exception of a clear fire level, it was difficult to correlate them with any other public room sequence, including Hodge's observations immediately to the east. Most of the deposits probably represented subfloors beneath a timber platform. A central masonry foundation carrying an offset pier was recorded by both Hodge and Miller, and may have carried a raised timber floor, or supported an internal feature such as a statue or column. If Hodge's evidence for a high floor level in the Eastern Antechamber is accurate, the Apse must therefore have been entered at the same or a higher level. The presence of plaster above the second offset (14.3m OD) suggests that the initial (pre-fire) timber floor was at this level, the same as elsewhere. After the mid-2nd-century fire, a new timber floor must have been constructed, despite the fact that solid slabs were laid down elsewhere. This would explain why the 1m thick post-fire dumps seen elsewhere were absent. The new floor level in the Eastern Antechamber suggests that the post-fire Apse floor would have been positioned at or above the third brick course (15m OD), which was also the level to which the walls survived, a relationship which was common elsewhere

The Eastern Range

In addition to the two sections drawn by Hodge in 1880, three areas were excavated in the Eastern Range at Whittington Avenue in 1988–9, together with parts of the eastern and northern wall foundations (Appendix A). All the sequences of thin brickearth and mortar floors showed a marked general resemblance to those in the street-front room along the north side of the Basilica and the east portico of the Forum. However, variation in the detail of those sequences suggests that the range was subdivided into separate areas, probably by timber partitions, since there were no signs of masonry crosswalls. In contrast with the Northern Range, the first floors were at 13m OD, the same height as those in the public rooms and the contemporary street surface. However, the final floors were at 13.7m OD, which was level with the primary floors along the northern side of the Basilica. This discrepancy in heights simply reflects the need to maintain a level floor surface along the Forum wing which extended downhill for 150m to the south.

There was clear evidence for internal structures within the range including a series of gullies in the north–eastern corner, culminating in two post trenches set at right angles. These may represent a corridor 1 to 2m inside the east wall (assuming that that wall still stood), and other posts were recorded at various phases in different parts of the range at this distance from the wall. Localised burning reflected the extensive use of braziers or other forms of heating. Near the Apse, the many small circular intrusions recorded in two successive phases of occupation may have been marks left by tripods or stands: in one area, four of these features defined a small square around a patch of scorched brickearth against the east wall, and could have been associated with a raised iron grate.

The Eastern Portico

Opposite the centre of the Apse, Hodge recorded a tessellated floor at 13.2m OD which was later replaced by a tiled floor at 13.7m OD. Since such substantial floors have not been observed anywhere else in the eastern range, they may represent an entrance way which was formalised by the addition of a portico, possibly after the mid-2nd-century fire. The new portico extended the eastern range by over 2m and spanned the width of the public rooms from opposite the north aisle to a corresponding distance southward, some 30m in all, with the Apse directly in the centre. The narrow outer wall was 0.5m wide, constructed with a shallow mortared rubble foundation 0.4m deep and 0.7m wide. Immediately over the foundation at 13.2m OD was a double bonding course of brick, followed by three courses of ragstone and two of brick. Significantly, the top course was level at 13.6m OD and thus may have supported a colonnade, since there was no evidence that the wall had been carried any higher. Both faces were plastered, although the bricks may have been left exposed. Hodge noted that the south end was constructed entirely of brick, and this may therefore have marked the junction with a return wall.

A deep timber-lined covered drain ran beneath the portico alongside the original outer wall of the Basilica. This may have carried rainwater from the roof of the Apse and other eastward-facing roofs. Pieces of a marble wall panel were found packed behind the lining (Pl 33). A mortar floor was laid over the top of the drain at 13.4m OD, patched and later replaced by a fine *opus spicatum* (herringbone tile) pavement at the same level as the top of the outer wall (Col Pl H). This may have remained in use for a considerable time, but the western half was badly damaged when the underlying drain collapsed. The resulting subsided area was filled by a series of compensatory dumps chiefly of building materials. Although this material may have been brought on to the site from further afield, it may well represent major alterations incorporating the demolition of the eastern wall and roof. A level floor was restored making use of these dumps, which also covered the surviving eastern section of herringbone floor. All later activity was at a higher level than the eastern wall top, which implies that the wall was no longer operative. Hodge's section labelled 'At Arch A' appears to have been drawn through the drain and dumped material and clearly shows later mortar floors.

The west end of the Basilica *(Fig 2)*

Much less is known about the west end of the Basilica, although a number of excavations have taken place there. At Site 24 part of the Nave, North Aisle and offices were investigated. The offices were similar to those recorded at Leadenhall Court but with no counterpart to the double-length Room 3/7; parts of two square rooms were seen, and the corners of two others. The floor sequence in the Nave and North Aisle was also similar to that to the east, indicating that these were the same rooms. The Nave was traversed by a north–south wall, the counterpart of Wall 13/14, flanked by piers. However, the aisles continued westwards, there being no counterpart to Room 11, the Western Antechamber, the Apse or even Room 6. The western end of the Nave was not therefore a mirror image of the east end. By contrast, it seems that the west wing of the Forum continued northwards across the end of the Nave, since the small room recorded immediately north of St Michael's Cornhill was the same size as the offices in that wing, precisely half the width of the Nave. Such a room layout shows that there cannot have been a monumental western entrance to the Basilica, such as Cirencester is thought to have had (McWhirr 1981, 28–31). Indeed, the range of rooms at this end of the London Basilica seem to have been carried right through to the Northern Range, or so the evidence from Site 25 suggests (Marsden 1987, 85–9). Here one complete square room and parts of three others were recorded, of which the easternmost was almost certainly the west end of the long portico-like Room 1/4.

The South Aisle *(Fig 2)*

The South Aisle sequence (Marsden 1987, 100–1) has also been reinterpreted, and it is now thought to be the product of several phases. The south wall of the 'aisle' was first identified in the Gracechurch Street tunnel excavations in 1977 (Site 13), where its foundation was 1.9m wide and lay 8.8m south of the Nave. There was no indication that it continued in either direction despite some confusion with a foundation recorded to the west by Hodge (Marsden 1987, fig 46). It is suggested therefore that only the central section was 1.9m wide, and that it continued substantially reduced in width to east and west, being represented by a short section of 0.9m-wide wall at Site 22 (Marsden 1987, fig 77). Since the brickearth slab scorched in the 2nd-century fire and the associated debris sealed the northern part of this wider central foundation, this central part of the aisle must have been built before the fire. It is now suggested that this thicker-walled section formed part of an imposing entrance, a primary feature, to which the thinner walls were subsequently attached and extended to form the South Aisle proper. Immediately to the north at 3–6 Gracechurch Street, Hodge recorded a 2m-thick buttress or column base, possibly associated with this entrance, which terminated at the west end but continued eastwards beneath the street.

The use of piers shows that the South Aisle was at least partly open fronted, although the pier may actually have supported the east side of a central arched entrance. It is now apparent that none of the South Aisle wall fragments connect with Hodge and Miller's Wall No 5 (Marsden 1987, fig 43: the extension of wall 14/15 at Leadenhall Court), but these may well be contemporary with the two previously unrecognised inner porticoes to the east and west Forum wings. These were erected during the final stage of the Basilica construction programme utilising walls which, significantly, were the same width as the narrow sections of the South Aisle wall.

Within the South Aisle, the earliest recorded deposits were several superimposed layers of gravel, the uppermost layers of which sealed the rubble covering the already truncated Nave wall. Since it has already been shown that the Aisle was laid out after the Nave was constructed, the lower gravel layers must have been laid at the same time or before the construction of the 2nd-century Basilica. The latter is quite possible, since the Aisle was positioned directly over the street which bordered the north side of the 1st-century Basilica, and its metallings may have been incorporated into the 2nd-century make-ups. If this interpretation is accepted, it assumes that the presence of those cambered gravels obviated the need for the construction slabs, initial mortar floor and the make-ups which sealed the truncated walls elsewhere in the complex. The later history of the South Aisle broadly reflected that of the Nave and North Aisle, although the presence of gravel sealing the *opus signinum* floor over the mid-2nd-century fire level implies that the Aisle was more of a covered terrace than a room. Grey silts covered the gravel, over which was a second mortar surface, but unfortunately the floor sequence did not survive above this point.

The Northern Range *(Fig 2)*
It is now thought that a single long room extended along virtually the whole length of the northern side of the Basilica. One possible cross-wall recorded by Hodge, apparently at the western boundary of the Leadenhall Court site, was almost certainly a buttress which had been plotted too far to the north. The long northern room may originally have been designed as a portico, but it was soon subdivided by lath-and-plaster partitions into a series of shops fronting the street to the north.

To the south of the shops, but not connected to them, was a single range of offices (Rooms 2, 3/7 and 8) which shared a pattern of development closely reflecting events in the Nave and other public rooms. However, one difference was that, although furnished with a primary mortar floor at the same level as that in the Nave, this was probably not hidden beneath a raised timber floor, since fragments of *in situ* painted plaster occurred at this level in Room 2. Subsequently, a thick brickearth slab was laid for a mortar floor or make-up layer, sealing such plasterwork as had not already been removed. The mortar was covered by a thin brickearth floor which was scorched in the mid-2nd-century fire. As elsewhere, further mortar floors were laid over the ragstone and mortar demolition deposits. After a second fire, the roof also collapsed, and was left where it fell, to be used as levelling material. In the debris, an east-west foundation was constructed of reused bricks 2m north of the southern wall of the room, although its superstructure and any related floors were later removed. It is not clear whether the roof was replaced, or if the brickwork was part of a separate structure occupying the shell of the room. This was not the end of occupation, however, and a mortar slab was laid for a brickearth floor whose extent respected the Basilica. Immediately to the east, observations in the Gracechurch Street Tunnel in 1977 showed that silts built up on the collapsed tiles, and were sealed by two mortar floors. The final mortar surface was also sealed by silts, this time followed by collapsed mortar and wall plaster representing the 'soft-stripping' of the walls after a period of neglect. This was followed by the demolition of the south wall to the level of the final surface opposite the second offset. Both the wall and silts were sealed by a layer of darker earth containing tiles and ragstone rubble (Marsden 1987, 59).

In the room to the west of Room 2, a north–south ragstone and tile partition was inserted into demolition deposits similar to those associated with the mid-2nd-century fire (Marsden 1987, fig 62). Floors reached 14.2m OD to the east of the wall, the sequence here being similar to that in the other offices. To the west, by contrast, a white mortar floor was laid and superseded by a tessellated pavement over 1.2m of rubble, presumably at 15m OD. The south wall was rebuilt in brick, possibly around this time, and survived to 15.4m OD, while the north wall west of the partition survived up to the third brick bonding course at 15.2m OD. However, the west wall only survived to 14.4m OD, although there was no evidence to suggest that the tessellated floor passed over it. Taken together, the high level to which the floors and walls survived, the unusual nature of the surfaces themselves and the central position of this particular room suggest that it was used as a shrine or similar feature. A room on the central axis of a basilica was often set aside for the tutelary deity. Significantly, the only other known tessellated floor at such a high level lay in the Eastern Antechamber.

Construction of the 2nd-century Forum
(Figs 2, 31)

The construction and development of the 2nd-century Basilica was only part of an even more extensive civic centre redevelopment which saw the 1st-century forum demolished and replaced by a much larger structure attached to the south side of the Basilica. How this was achieved and what that new complex looked like will now be considered. The 2nd-century Forum consisted of three wings enclosing a rectangular courtyard, some 100m east–west and 85m north–south, the evidence coming from 13 sites investigated from 1881 to 1977 (Fig 2). The East Wing was recorded on Sites 3, 4, 6, 8, 9 and 10, and the West Wing at Sites 16, 18, 19 and 20. The layout of the South Wing is much more difficult to disentangle than the others, despite extensive observations at Sites 10, 16 and 17, as well as Site 11, 168–70 Fenchurch Street (this site is incorrectly labelled as no 160–62 Fenchurch Street in Marsden 1987, 14, fig 8). Site 16 also belonged partly to the West Wing, although it is not clear where the precise distinction lay, while evidence for the courtyard comes principally from Site 13. Re-examination of the records from those 13 sites has suggested some differences from the scheme published previously (Marsden 1987, 41, fig 26). The most notable changes proposed are: the later addition of inner porticoes to the East and West Wings, probably as the final stage of construction when the South Aisle of the Basilica was built; suggestions as to the form of the monumental entrance in the South Wing; the feature once thought to represent an ornamental pool is now seen as part of a colonnaded walkway which effectively divided the courtyard in two. These modifications were more than minor changes in the architectural form of the complex, since they clearly affected the way the Forum was actually used.

Taken together, the evidence shows that the Forum walls were characterised by notable variations in their build and coursing, showing more than one phase of development and the use of different construction teams. In the first phase, the East and West Wings presumably incorporated three ranges of rooms comprising two sets of shops or offices with an external portico, but there is evidence to suggest that an inner portico facing the courtyard was subsequently added. These two wings may have been joined in the middle by a walkway which spanned the central courtyard. The South Wing seems to have comprised a single range of rooms with internal and external porticoes and a major monumental entrance.

In general, the walls diminished in width south of the Basilica's south wing as far as Site 8. Instead of brick courses laid directly on the foundation, two to four ragstone layers were followed by brick. The difference in construction from the Basilica may have been caused by the need to compensate for the slope of Cornhill, whereas in the Basilica the foundation itself provided a level platform; it is clear that there was a considerable slope southwards towards the Thames. Alternatively, recent work at Whittington Avenue seems to suggest that the Forum wings were added to the Basilica as a later phase of construction, although, like the Northern Range, they were clearly part of the original plan.

The East and West Wings *(Fig 2)*

It was once thought that the East Wing comprised three sets of rooms: the external portico facing east, the central rooms, and the inner portico which opened on to the courtyard. However, a re-evaluation of the records from Site 4 revealed two sections of rubble-filled robber trench (Trenches 15, 17/18), 8m to the west of the former 'inner portico'. These were paralleled by similar foundations relating to the West Wing, and it is suggested that two extra porticoes existed in the courtyard. It seems probable that both were part of the final additions to the original scheme, adjoining the South Aisle wall of the Basilica. That wall may have been built at the same time since it did not extend east as far as the internal range on Sites 3 and 4. It is now suggested, therefore, that the East Wing consisted of two internal ranges of rooms, the eastern- and western-central ranges, between two porticoes.

At Site 4, the west wall of the western-central range comprised two sections which overlapped by 7m immediately to the south of the brick culvert and walls recorded at Site 3. Changes in construction either side of this point suggest that the east wing was added to the Basilica as part of a separate phase. The wall of the outer portico which continued the line of the Eastern Range at Whittington Avenue (Appendix A) may represent an integral part of that same development.

Similar sequences of *opus signinum* floors, the first or second of which had been affected by fire, were recorded in the eastern portico and east-central range on Sites 3 and 8. This suggests that these ranges were interconnected. By contrast, the surfaces in the west-central range were of mortar and chalk (Site 8) and it seems that those rooms opened inwards, towards the courtyard.

Civic centre redevelopment

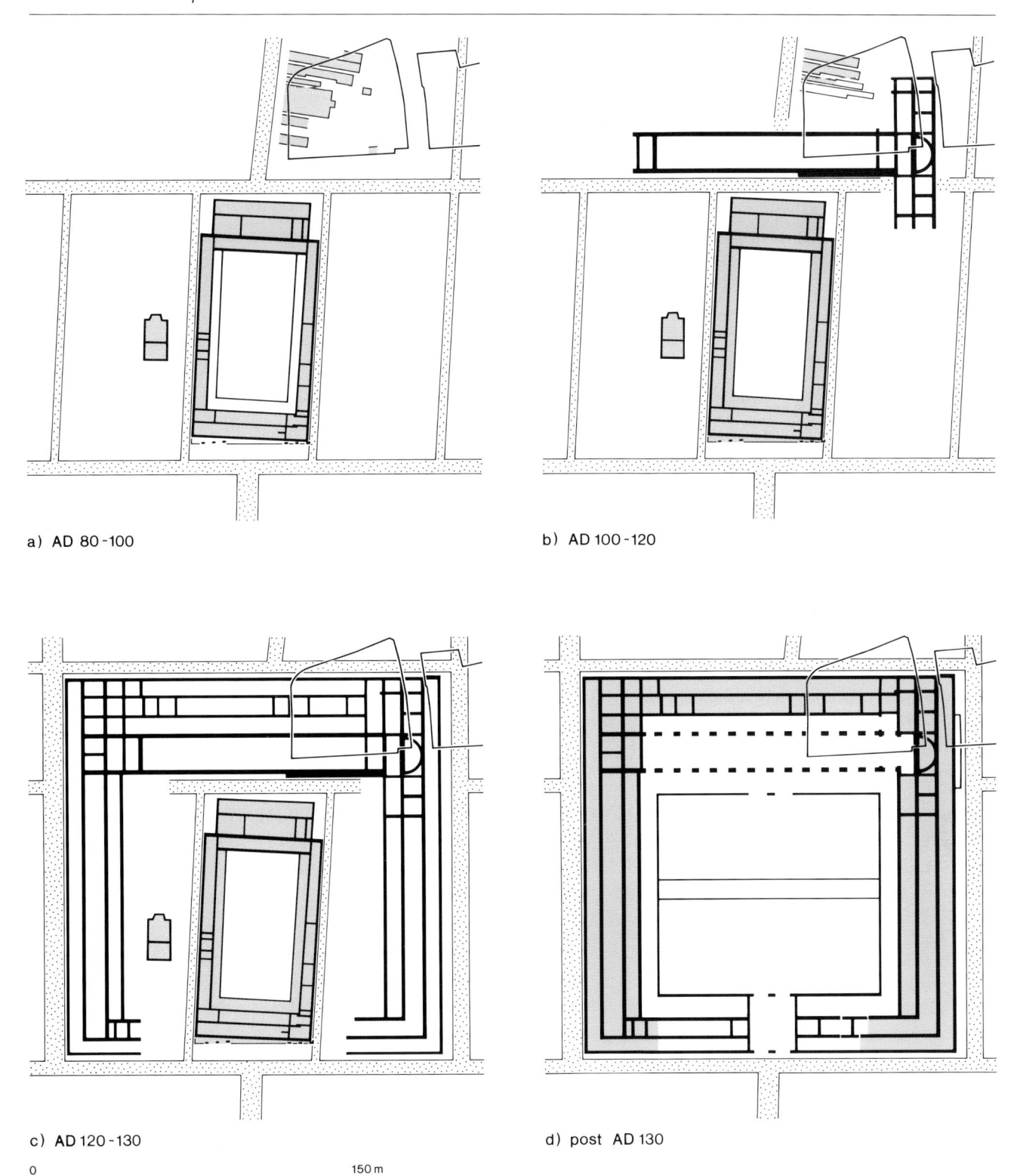

a) AD 80-100

b) AD 100-120

c) AD 120-130

d) post AD 130

0 150 m

Fig 31 Civic centre redevelopments in the 1st and 2nd centuries: plan series to show how developments illustrated in Fig 30 recorded on the Leadenhall Court and Whittington Avenue sites (shown in outline, top right) have been related to: a) 1st-century forum; b) construction of larger Basilica in early 2nd century; c) construction of larger forum around earlier complex, still standing well into the 2nd century; d) modifications to new forum and basilica after demolition of 1st-century complex: aisles are added to Basilica, a colonnaded walkway to Forum. Scale 1: 2,500

Less evidence is available for the West Wing. However, mortared ragstone rubble and a ragstone foundation 0.9m thick were recorded on Sites 18 and 20 some 8m east of the wing, representing a wall running to the west of the 1st-century temple associated with the first forum. It marks the presence of a wide inner portico, showing that both wings comprised two sets of inner rooms set back to back, but both opening outwards into porticoes.

The South Wing and monumental entrance
(Figs 2, 32)

The structural history of the South Wing is complicated by the remains of the first forum, including a series of yellow-mortared brick piers on ragstone bases on Sites 11 and 17. Marsden considered that they marked the addition of a colonnaded inner portico to the forum and the realignment of its south wing parallel with the street frontage: similar changes were observed in the other wings. However, ragstone was not widely used for foundations until the early 2nd century in London, which suggests that these piers substantially post-date the construction of the first forum, which otherwise rested entirely on flint footings. Another ragstone foundation (Site 11, Wall E) ran parallel to the first forum (Marsden 1987, 139, fig 103) and may have been a precinct wall for the small temple to the west, which also had a ragstone footing attached to its south-west corner. It is therefore suggested that the first forum must have continued in use well into the 2nd century, to allow for the incorporation of those ragstone foundations.

Straddling the remains of those demolished structures was the South Wing of the new Forum. It comprised three ranges: a central row of rooms with porticoes to north and south. Two rows of pink-mortared brick piers were constructed in the outer (southern) portico and two rows of similar but smaller piers replaced some of the yellow-mortared examples in the inner (northern) portico. It is possible that both groups helped support a monumental entrance in the middle of the South Wing (see below); however, the presence of a disturbed column base in the northern portico implies an internal colonnade, while the larger foundations of the southern portico carried piers. One of these piers to the west of the entrance was probably T-shaped, and it is suggested that the north side of this portico was separated into booths or shops facing the street, as is recorded in fora elsewhere. However, the piers and column bases were apparently confined to the central area, which implies that the booths may have been guardrooms or market officials' offices flanking the entrance.

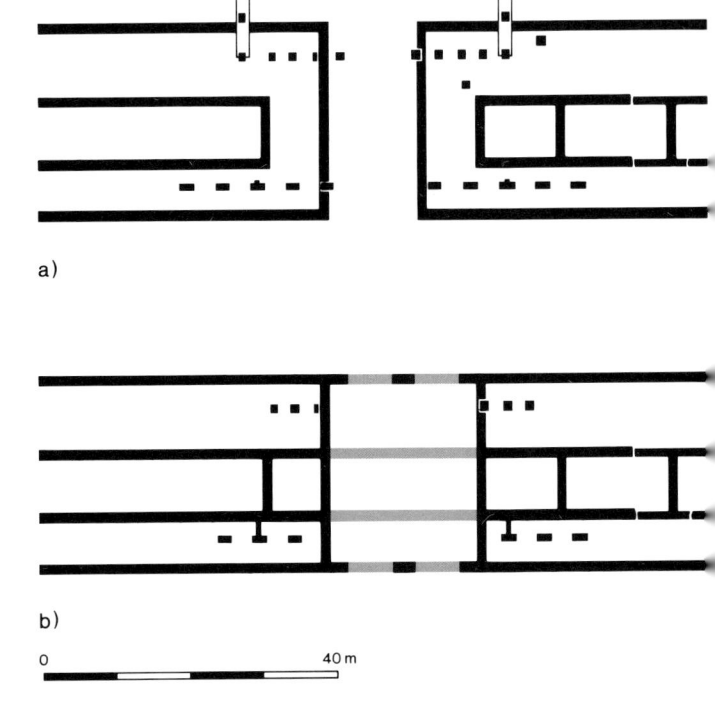

Fig 32 Two interpretations of evidence for a monumental gateway in the southern range of the Forum as suggested by: a) Brian Philp (Philp 1977) and b) Trevor Brigham. Walls and piers found and conjectured are shown in black, with sleeper walls which were not carried above ground level shown with grey tone

The possibility of a central entrance was raised by Marsden (Marsden 1987, 62), but although an artist's impression appears in his report, evidence for it was not discussed. A section of north–south wall uncovered on Site 17 defined the east end of a room in the central range. It had been plastered and painted on both sides, and seems to have continued north and south to meet the outer walls of the South Wing, but did not return east. At Site 11, the west wall of the central range also seems to have continued north, with no sign of an eastern return. These two walls therefore seem to define the sides of a 20m-wide central entrance. Although the superstructure of the central range did not extend across the entrance, observations in the tunnel (Site 13) demonstrated that the foundations did continue, probably to support the door arches. It is likely that the entrance took the form of a large cross-hall, with two or three separate openings which could be closed off to seal the Forum at night.

The South Wing was characterised by the extensive use of brickwork in the outer walls. At Site

17 for example, the south wall consisted of four courses of ragstone, six courses of brick, two of ragstone, six of brick, two of ragstone, then four further brick courses set in buff mortar. It was truncated at 14.6m OD, higher than the general level of survival elsewhere in the Forum and Basilica. The continuous nature of the superstructure must have restricted access to this section of the portico, which contrasts with the standard picture of an open colonnaded walkway: however, it is possible that continuous walls were confined to the area of the main entrance.

Although the extensive use of pink mortar and brick facings could suggest that the South Wing was remodelled at a time when brick was more commonly used than ragstone, it seems more likely that the whole wing was the final addition to the Forum complex, its construction delayed by the demolition of the corresponding wing of the first forum. A similar conclusion was reached by Peter Marsden, but arguing from the presence of straight joints within the foundations of the south wing (Marsden 1987, 42). The reversal in the proportions of brick to ragstone in this part of the structure contrasts with the early phases of the Basilica construction: since brick was invariably used in later additions to that structure, the use of brick in the primary work on the South Wing therefore suggests that this notable change in building style actually took place during the protracted period in which the civic centre was being constructed.

The Forum courtyard *(Fig 2)*
The levels beneath the yard contain most of the evidence for the 1st-century forum-basilica, with the exception of the south wing which lay beneath the corresponding wing of the second Forum. The first forum seems to have had a split-level courtyard, with the main part almost 1m below the northern section (Marsden 1987, 31–2). This response to the slope of the hillside was also reflected in the differing floor levels within the basilica itself and within the forum wings, a situation which enhanced the profile of the basilica. The courtyard for the 2nd-century Forum was initially formed by dumping gravel up to 1m thick at a level of 13.2m OD, as was recorded at Site 5. In the north, this level was consistent with that of the streets flanking the first basilica and the higher, northern part of the earlier yard. It seems, then, that the introduction of these gravel dumps levelled off the area enclosed by the new Forum, presumably after the earlier complex had been demolished.

Although the first forum walls were sealed at this level, the floors of the basilica nave and south aisle on Site 4 lay above this, at 13.8m OD and 13.6m OD respectively. If demolished immediately, therefore, the remains of the first basilica and the contemporary temple to the south-west (which survived to a height of at least 13.4m OD) would have formed obstructive mounds. It seems likely, therefore, that the first basilica remained in use for at least a short period after its forum had been demolished, presumably until its successor was fitted out.

Study of the field records from Site 13 (cf. Marsden 1987, 65, fig 54) highlights the difference between the sequences in the northern and southern halves of the new yard. In both areas, the gravel itself may have formed the first surface, although it was sealed in places by mortar floors. In the north, the primary surfaces were sealed beneath 0.7m of grey silts comparable to thinner layers of similar material within the Basilica. This horizon may have been dumped in one or two increments, perhaps to raise the northern courtyard level above the remains of the first basilica.

Directly south of the second Basilica, the grey silts were sealed by white limestone slabs bedded on mortar, which may have formed a substantial pavement broadly level with the floors in the public rooms, but some 0.6m higher than the surfaces in the northern part of the Forum and Eastern Range. To the south, the slabs were replaced by a mortar floor over which was a surface of broken tiles or bricks at the same level as the limestone, extending south for at least 16m. A limestone gutter at the same level as the limestone pavement ran alongside the Basilica, and probably carried rainwater from the South Aisle roof into the brick culvert set into the East Wing of the Forum. The courtyard floors and this gutter were sealed by the ubiquitous dark grey silts, suggesting that they fell into disuse when the Basilica was abandoned.

The silts in the gutter were overlain by part of a collapsed brick pier from the South Aisle wall. This pier may have been a springer for an entrance arch leading into the Basilica as it had a dressed west face, and was in line with the east side of the monumental entrance to the Forum in the South Wing (Fig 34).

In the southern half of the courtyard, the sequence was more complex. The series of thin gravel and mortar floors punctuated by grey clay or pebbly soil was similar to that of the public rooms in the Basilica, except that gravel was used instead of brickearth for the initial make-up deposits. This may reflect a gradual accumulation or a deliberate raising of the ground level, but the general nature of these deposits both internally and externally seem to suggest neglect during the later phase in the life of the public building.

The evidence therefore suggests that the ground level in the northern half of the courtyard next to the Basilica was higher, and was provided with hard-wearing limestone and tile surfaces. In the south, the level was raised more gradually and was more frequently repaired. This implies that this courtyard, just like the 1st-century forum, operated on two levels. The need to identify the division led to the reinterpretation of the feature observed in 1977 some 37m south of the Basilica. This comprised the remains of what has been interpreted as a 7.4m-wide 'ornamental pool' (Marsden 1987, 64–5 fig 55), consisting of two parallel walls lined externally with clay and internally with mortar. The feature contained a series of floors, mostly of mortar or *opus signinum*, one of which had a quarter-round skirting of the same material. A later floor was of chalk blocks bedded in grey clay. The interpretation of this feature as a pool depends principally upon the extensive use of clay which, it was argued, was used to render the structure water tight. However, clay was often used as a bedding material for floor surfaces, and need not have functioned solely as a water-proofing agent. That said, the clay cladding against the walls could have been used to prevent water entering the floored area, rather than vice versa. It is therefore suggested that the 'pool' was part of an east–west walkway which bisected the Forum courtyard. The low, flat-topped walls may have carried a colonnaded roof (Figs 31d and 33).

Several factors provide further support for this hypothesis. A foundation recorded some metres to the west of the south wall of the feature was of similar dimensions, being 0.8m wide, and comprised ragstone and yellow cement with a south face of large undressed blocks (Site 18). A depth of 0.7m was uncovered, with only a slight foundation, but the top was level for a tile course or as a sleeper wall at 13.2m OD, the same height as the 'pool' walls, and in accord with the Basilica offset and the primary surface of the Forum. A buttress for the wall was found 3.5m to the west, which was of similar construction with a 0.8m south face extending north for at least 0.5m to the line of the east–west wall. This buttress was truncated at 12.6m OD by a later robber trench, but was traced to a depth of 12.1m OD. The relative shallowness of these foundations suggests that the feature was cut through the courtyard gravels, and this in turn suggests that the walkway was constructed as a secondary feature some time after the completion of the main complex.

The walkway would have linked the Forum wings, and the nature of the floors (mainly *opus signinum*) reflects this, as does the later use of chalk blocks in clay, since similar chalk surfaces were recorded in the East Wing of the Forum and the eastern range of the Basilica. There must have been entrances through the Forum wings constructed as part of the original plan before the corridor which linked them was built. Significantly, there was a 50% increase in the depth of the outer wall foundation in the East Wing at the precise point where the north side of the entrance would be (Site 6). That the courtyard sequence was noticeably different to north and south of the walls (Marsden 1987, section 13) provides further support for the interpretation of the feature as an extensive walkway dividing the yard in two.

Streets and public utilities

At Site 22, the later surfaces of the north–south street immediately to the west of the 1st-century basilica were at the same level as the lower ones of its successor, between 12.7m and 13.1m OD. To the north, the corresponding east–west street beneath the south aisle of the later Basilica also reached 13.1m OD. These were sealed by material presumably related to the construction of the 2nd-century Basilica. A section recorded in the tunnel (Site 13) seems to show a similar pattern: layers of metalling up to 13.3m OD overlain by the mortar make-up which elsewhere followed the mid-2nd-century fire. Another section further north may show part of the north–south street leading to Bishopsgate (Marsden 1987, section 9), immediately beneath the construction make-ups of the street-front range of Basilican rooms. If the two ends of the Basilica were constructed on two discrete sites as suggested above, the street may have remained in use initially, even if only as a service road for the delivery of building materials. It would have passed through a central gap in the foundations as has already been suggested in the South Wing of the Forum. It is likely that such arrangements would have been terminated before the construction of the Basilica superstructure. The western and northern streets were not replaced until *c*.AD 130, but the eastern route already existed in a narrower form, and would have been able to take diverted traffic: this road was widened after the rest of the street system was completed.

The new streets incorporated drains and a system of water mains, which were replaced at frequent intervals. The water mains were formed of square wooden pipe sections, bored down the centre and held together with iron rings hammered into the ends of adjoining sections. The wood had decayed, leaving a series of voids and a 'flange' of rust around the linking rings. At Leadenhall Court, the pipes were restricted to the north of the street with the open drains to the south, collecting run-off from the Basilica roof. At Whittington Avenue, however, pipes existed on both sides and also crossed the T-junction to run beneath the north—south street.

It is not clear where the water originated or what it fed, but the pipes presumably continued northwards along the street, possibly leading out of the town at Bishopsgate, and along a gravel ridge ultimately to the springs which fed the River Walbrook in the Clerkenwell area. Alternatively, the water may have been raised by mechanical methods, and stored in a tank or water tower (*castellum aquae*), perhaps at Bishopsgate. South and east, the pipes may have fed public drinking fountains, possibly in the Basilica or Forum, and some of the buildings which flanked the complex, although no distributor lines were found. However, the water main found at the Bank of England (Wacher 1978, 104) pointed towards Cornhill, and may have been connected to the Leadenhall supply. The pipes there were of the same dimension, with collars 76mm in diameter and a bore of 51mm. Two diameters of water main are known from London, a large one, and a second of half the diameter, to which the Leadenhall and Whittington Avenue pipes belong. As such they were probably not primary mains, and certainly could not have provided enough water for bath-houses, most of which were situated on the spring-lines on the banks of the Thames or the Walbrook.

Demolition of the Forum-Basilica

Peter Marsden's study of the fate of the London forum concluded that there was 'absolutely no archaeological evidence to date the period when the complex ceased to be used, and became a ruin' (Marsden 1987, 67). Fortunately, the more recent work has enabled this particular problem to be addressed. Although it was a major public building, it now seems that the Basilica suffered from neglect in the later 2nd and 3rd centuries. This suggests that the necessary political will or finance required to maintain the seat of local government was lacking, and Chapter 12 considers some of the causes of this reversal of fortune. Nevertheless some occupation and repair work did continue in most areas of the Basilica, even after Room 1/4 was badly damaged by fire in the mid-3rd century. Thereafter, however, it seems that the Basilica had entered a cycle of terminal decline, which ended in c.AD 300.

The final phase of occupation in the Nave was represented by clay post-pads which may have supported a timber platform laid over the last *opus signinum* floor. In the northern and eastern ranges, a sequence of thin surfaces and hearths continued up to c.AD 300, but evidence from the eastern portico suggests that it was demolished in the mid-3rd century. This followed the clumsy restoration of extensive damage to the *opus spicatum* pavement caused by the collapse of a large underfloor drain. The site of the portico was then occupied by iron smelters, represented by hearths and deposits of slag, who were probably melting down fittings such as hinges, clamps, spikes and window grilles from the Basilica itself. Similar levels found at Silchester have been interpreted as representing a later use of that basilica for commercial or industrial purposes (Fulford 1985). In London, activity continued in the former portico, probably until the end of the 3rd century, utilising some type of lean-to structures. It is possible that similar structures were also constructed in the adjacent Eastern Range, where two substantial timber-framed walls joined 1–2m inside the masonry outer wall. It is not clear, however, whether they represented an addition to the Basilica before demolition or a replacement. The final floors in most areas lay at the second wall offset level, c.14.3m OD, with some exceptions: 13.7m OD in the eastern range, and approximately 15m OD in the Eastern Antechamber, Apse and central offices. Where later deposits were preserved, the floor surfaces were sealed by fine light and mid-grey silts. These deposits were largely composed of wind-blown dust, graphic evidence demonstrating that the maintenance mechanism, which had served sporadically for many years, no longer operated.

Similar silts sealed the final road surface to the north, as well as the Forum courtyard to the south, showing that neglect of the Basilica had spread to its immediate environs, although wheel ruts in the street indicated that some traffic continued, presumably associated with the occupied buildings to the north. No occupation debris was apparent in the small surviving areas of the Basilica silts, which suggests that the building was no longer used, although its civic ownership may have prevented the inroads of squatters. Once abandoned in this way, the fate of the Basilica was sealed, for the Roman authorities were strict about the removal of redundant structures which might be regarded as a fire risk or a danger to passers-by. Furthermore, the site and the building materials might have a more profitable use.

In the extension of Room 1/4 recorded on Site 13, large fragments of wall plaster and mortar embedded in the silts imply that the walls were soft-stripped in advance of demolition. Such a procedure would account for the lack of *in situ* plaster elsewhere in the Basilica. Although later activity has obscured much of the evidence, the superstructure then appears to have been demolished consistently to within 0.2m of the second offset at 14.3m OD, the same level as the final Basilica floors. This is confirmed at sites as far west as 68 Cornhill (James 1987) and also beneath Gracechurch Street (Site 13), where a section of the central Northern Range wall was sealed immediately above the second brick course by dark grey silt containing roof tiles, ragstone and mortar. These layers also sealed the lighter grey silts referred to in the previous section.

Unfortunately, the relationship between the demolished walls and dark grey silts did not survive at Leadenhall Court, but horizons of light and dark silts were recorded elsewhere on the site, and had clearly once covered the entire Basilica area. Within the Nave, the build up of silts, mortar and tiles was sealed by collapsed roof tiles, rubble and, ultimately, by deposits of dark grey silt. The few sections of collapsed wall remaining in the Nave and recorded in the 1880s and the 1980s seem to have fallen from the clerestory above the brick arcading, their varied construction testimony to the frequency of repairs in this major building. In the Eastern Antechamber, Hodge records that the final floor was directly sealed by rubble, and the room may therefore have been maintained until the final demolition, after which the remains were sealed by the ubiquitous dark grey silts.

Three areas in which the walls survived to up to 15.4m OD, significantly higher than the general level of truncation, were recorded outside the area of the Leadenhall Court excavation. Two of these coincided with the areas of high floors in the Eastern Antechamber/Apse and central office range. The first and most important of these comprised part of the Apse (Marsden 1987, 45, fig 31, Walls 4E, 8). The survival of further sections of superstructure in the area suggests that the Apse may have remained more or less intact to at least the second offset level until the construction of the 15th-century Leadenhall and the Tudor cellars associated with later phases of that building. At that time, sections of the superstructure were cut through, but even so Hodge was subsequently able to record substantial survival of walls in the area which now lies beneath Whittington Avenue. This fact, coupled with the special treatment of the adjoining Antechamber (notably in the provision and survival of tiled and tessellated floors and high-quality wall plaster), suggests that the Apse was of sufficient importance to be retained after most of the Basilica had been levelled.

The second area incorporated several walls now beneath Gracechurch Street, including the brick-built westward extension of the south wall of Room 2, clearly an addition to the original Basilica walls (Marsden 1987, 53–60). The upper brickwork could represent repairs to the Basilica or a later building erected on the site after the demolition of the Forum. As in the Apse/Antechamber area, there was a raised tessellated pavement in the western half of the adjoining room, and it has already been suggested that there may have been a shrine or a feature of similar importance here. These walls may therefore have survived after the remainder of the range was demolished. This may be the origin of the legend that the church of St Peter Cornhill was a Roman foundation, since the chancel lies over the 'shrine' room. The present church is shorter than its medieval forerunner, which extended further east.

Part of a brick pier on the south wall of the Nave also survived above the general truncation level, and is preserved in the basement of 90 Gracechurch Street (Col Pl I). Little significance should be attached to its survival however, in view of its apparent isolation. Stumps of the piers would not have formed much of an obstacle once their arcades had been removed, although most were robbed for their bricks and limestone plinths at a later date.

It is assumed that the Forum was demolished as part of the same process, although the little evidence there is comes only from the Eastern Wing. At Site 8 the western wall of the outer portico was demolished to 14.1m OD and sealed by a thick burnt deposit. At least two interpretations are possible: either part of the structure was destroyed by fire and not replaced, presumably because the Forum's decline was already recognised and accepted; or the Forum had already been demolished, and the burnt deposit was related to a later timber structure on the same site. In the portico, the latest brickearth and mortar floors were at 14.3m OD and may have belonged to such a later building, since they were separated by dark occupation material from what elsewhere appeared to be the final *opus signinum* surface in the Forum, which lay at 13.9m OD. However, in the south-eastern corner of the wing (Site 10) a 1.15m sequence of gravel, sand and mortar surfaces reached 14.3m OD, also unusually high; but although there was no evidence of a break in continuity, a slot with post holes similar to the Whittington Avenue example and a nearby wheel rut suggest some change of function. In the west-central range at Site 8, the final chalk floor at 13.9m OD was overlaid by ragstone and tile rubble reaching 14.5m OD, which must represent local demolition work. At the north end of the outer portico in the section labelled 'South Excavation W(est)', (Marsden 1987, 50, fig 40), Hodge noted six layers of roof tiles and mortar, presumably abandoned by demolition workers, above a thick layer of 'black earth and tile debris'.

It seems, therefore, that the Basilica and Forum were razed following a period of abandonment around the end of the 3rd century. At this stage, possibly only the Apse and the shrine were retained, but for how long is uncertain. Most of the enormous quantity of building material released by the demolition of the civic centre was systematically removed for reuse elsewhere, probably in other public works programmes, such as the construction of part of the riverside wall or the masonry structures erected on the terrace to the rear. There is some slight evidence for structures built over the levelled site, but none seem to have lasted for a substantial period. For example, walls surviving to a high level and apparently postdating the Basilica were recorded at Site 24 (Marsden 1987, 83; fig 63). These abutted the south wall of the Northern Range, and crossed the demolished walls of the offices and the North Aisle. Although the date of the walls is not clear, they were on the Basilican alignment, not that of the medieval street.

The majority of the area, including the road to the north and ultimately the site of Building 32 (Fig 19), was then sealed by dark grey silt which contained 4th-century pottery and early 4th-century coins. Thereafter there is little archaeological evidence for intensive occupation of the site until pits were cut into these late Roman levels c.AD 1000, by which time the position and alignment of the Basilica had been long forgotten.

9 Reconstructing the Basilica

Trevor Brigham with Naomi Crowley

What did the Forum actually look like when it was completed? It is surprising that no detailed, methodical attempt has ever been made to reconstruct the superstructure of the London Forum: the complex has been argued to be the largest of its type in Britain, while the Basilica itself was one of the biggest buildings north of the Alps. Several scholars, most notably Peter Marsden, have attempted to establish the extent and plan of the complex: indeed, he brought together much of the material upon which the reconstruction offered here is based (Marsden 1987). Although a number of artists' impressions have been commissioned over the years, these have done little more than provide an impression of the structure: the actual height and proportions of the building were all too often obscured by perspective or early morning mist. The data available, even before the most recent excavations took place, were considerable when compared with the evidence for the basilica at Verulamium for example, for which Professor Frere has suggested several reconstructions (Frere 1983). However, work at Leadenhall Court and Whittington Avenue has added considerably to the evidence for both the external and internal appearance of the 2nd-century Basilica in London and has shown that it underwent a more complex structural development than was previously thought. Working from the revised ground plan, a reconstruction of this remarkable building from floor to roof line has now been attempted for the first time.

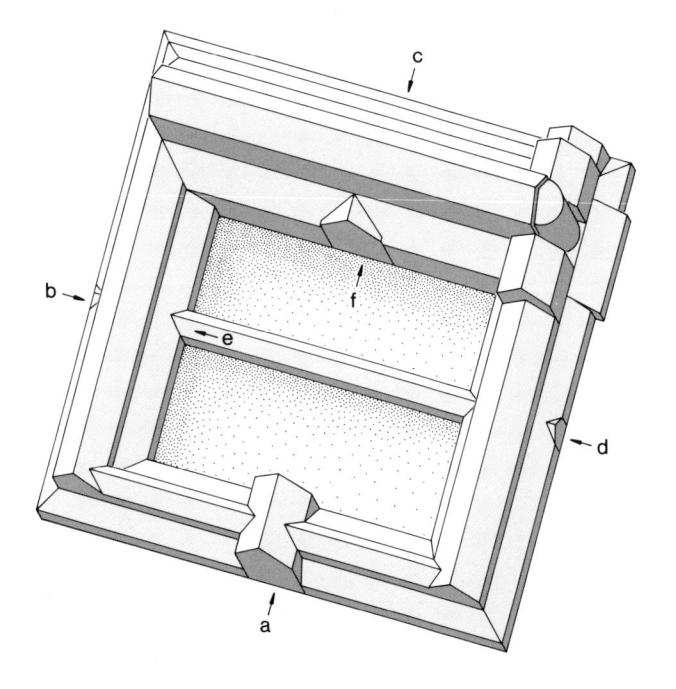

Plan and proportions
(Figs 33, 34)

First, the field records were analysed to determine the order of construction and to establish the sequence of development already described and illustrated in previous chapters. The next step was to compile an accurate, scaled ground plan of the Basilica, and one of the first problems to be solved was the basic form

LEFT
Fig 33 Outline reconstruction of 2nd- to 3rd-century Forum and Basilica. Letters indicate position of elevations shown on Fig 34. Scale 1: 1,250

OPPOSITE
Fig 34 Reconstructed elevations of 2nd- to 3rd-century Forum and Basilica. For positions of the elevations, see Fig 33. Scale 1: 1,000

Reconstructing the Basilica

a) External facade of Forum

main entrance to Forum from bridge road

b) External facade of West Range

c) External facade of Basilica

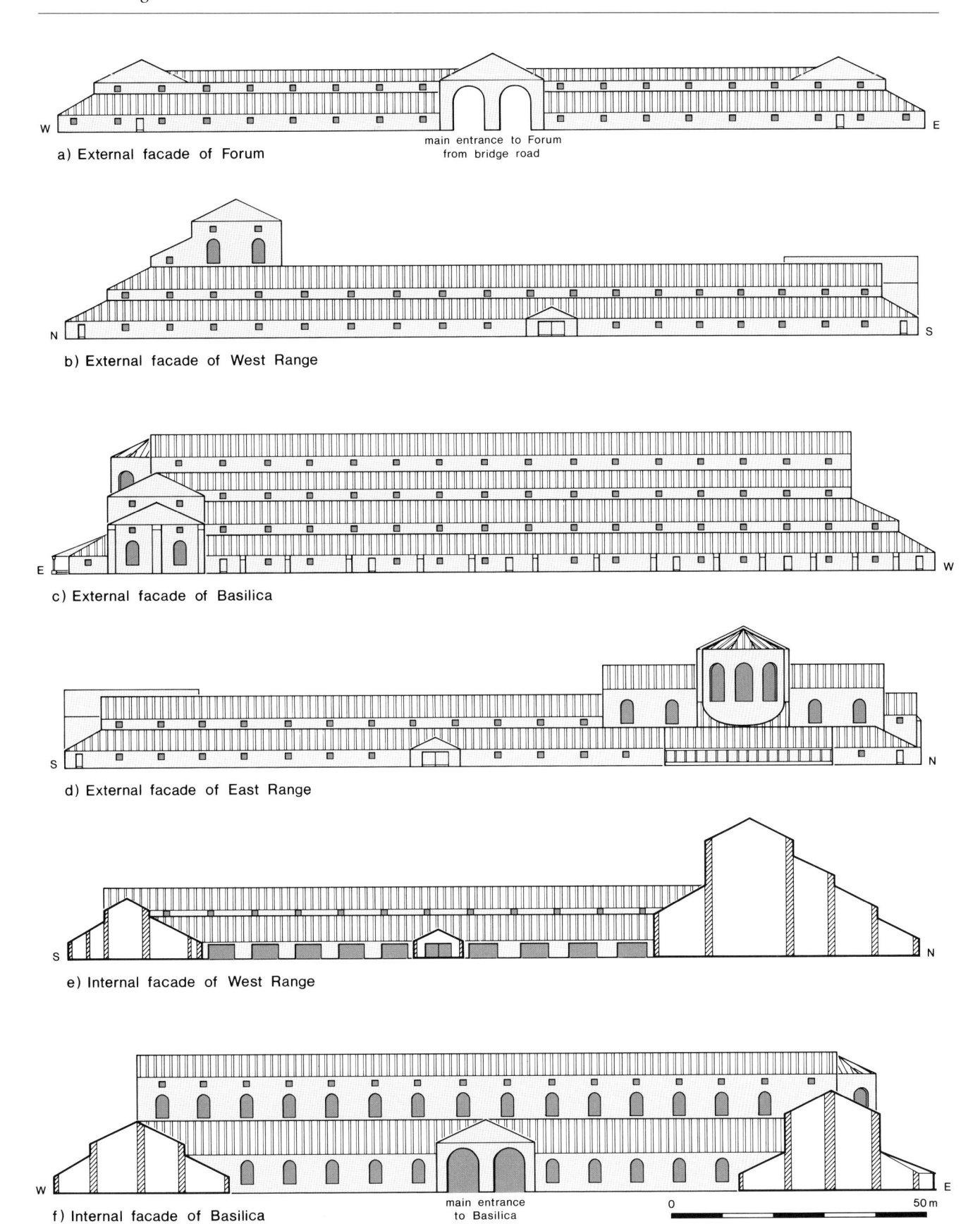

d) External facade of East Range

e) Internal facade of West Range

f) Internal facade of Basilica

main entrance to Basilica

0   50 m

of its west end. Previously this had always been illustrated as a mirror image of the east end, but the information now available suggests that the west end was different internally, lacking an apse and associated wings. In this respect, the London Basilica would have resembled Cirencester, which had a single large apse, although it had an open colonnade at the opposite end, where the London Basilica apparently had further offices. Having established the plan, consideration could be given to the superstructure.

There are obvious problems in determining the number and height of storeys in any building when working only from a ground plan, the more so if that plan is incomplete. Nevertheless, a recent study of villas demonstrates the probability that buildings with two or more storeys were commonplace in Britain, the evidence for which 'may come in the form of upstanding masonry, unusually broad foundations, the addition of buttresses and small rooms which served as stairwells or, perhaps more important, by questioning the intent of the architect' (Neal 1982, 157). Following these criteria, it is clear that the dimensions of the Basilica foundations and superstructure and the presence of buttresses were significant to the form of the building. Thus although a particular wall taken in isolation cannot be used to demonstrate a particular height of superstructure, the existence of a range of widths implies that there was internal consistency to the design. Having established this, it is possible to suggest a corresponding range of wall heights. The presence of buttresses suggests the direction of thrust of various walls, and therefore the direction of the roof in that particular area.

The different gauges of the foundations were modified further by the use of offsets at the two lowest brick bonding courses, which reduced the width of the superstructure substantially. This left the main section of the walls between 50 and 70% narrower than the foundations. Since the Roman architect Vitruvius suggested a comparable reduction of 50% where columns were to be used (Morgan 1914, III, iv.i), this implies that the Romans treated walls and columns in much the same way when calculating loads. The foundation can therefore be equated with the stylobate of a colonnade, the first lift with the plinth, and the main wall with the column shaft. Although there were no further offsets apparent, the walls may have tapered inwards in the same way that columns were treated for aesthetic reasons, but in this case to reduce their weight. The Basilica may have been given a running cornice, approximating to the architrave of a colonnade.

The east–west walls of the Basilica were more substantially constructed nearer the Nave, presumably in proportion to the increasing height of the building. The walls which crossed the 14m width of the Nave and Antechambers had to carry the additional burden of gables and the central roof ridge without the aid of buttresses, and it was here, consequently, that the thickest walls were constructed, with the most massive separating the Apse from the main body of the building. The latter must have supported both the main Basilica roof, that of the Apse itself, and the end gable.

The available planned data suggests that the approximate height of the Basilica can thus be calculated working from a constant set of values. A reconstructed cross-section through the Basilica with a roof-pitch of 1:2 (around 25 degrees), clerestories of a minimum 1.5 to 2.5m, and a minimum height for the northern street-frontage of 3.5 to 4m, gives a height of 25 to 26m for the apex of the nave roof. This figure would obviously be subject to alteration if the roof pitch was less steep, or the height of the clerestories was different. Nevertheless, it is worth noting that it lies between the 29m suggested for the Verulamium basilica (Frere 1983) and the 22m for Silchester (Boon 1974, 114), the former based on much less substantial evidence than for London. Significantly, the height of the London Nave would therefore have been one quarter of its length and twice its width.

The roof
(Fig 35)

Judging from the increasing widths of foundation and superstructure through the Northern Range, North Aisle and Nave, it is probable that the roofs of these areas rose in a series of tiers, allowing each interior to be lit by clerestories. The extra width and buttressing of the northern external wall suggests that some of the load was also dispersed outwards through the series of cross-walls dividing the offices and possibly through vaulting in the street-front rooms. The orientation of the east wall of Room 5/9/11 and its buttress suggest that the long axis of the roof of Rooms 6 and 10 lay north–south; given the width of the foundation, it is likely that there was a high wing projecting north from the Antechambers. Possibly this was balanced by a second wing to the south which would have terminated immediately south of the brick culvert, emphasising the Apse which lay

Reconstructing the Basilica

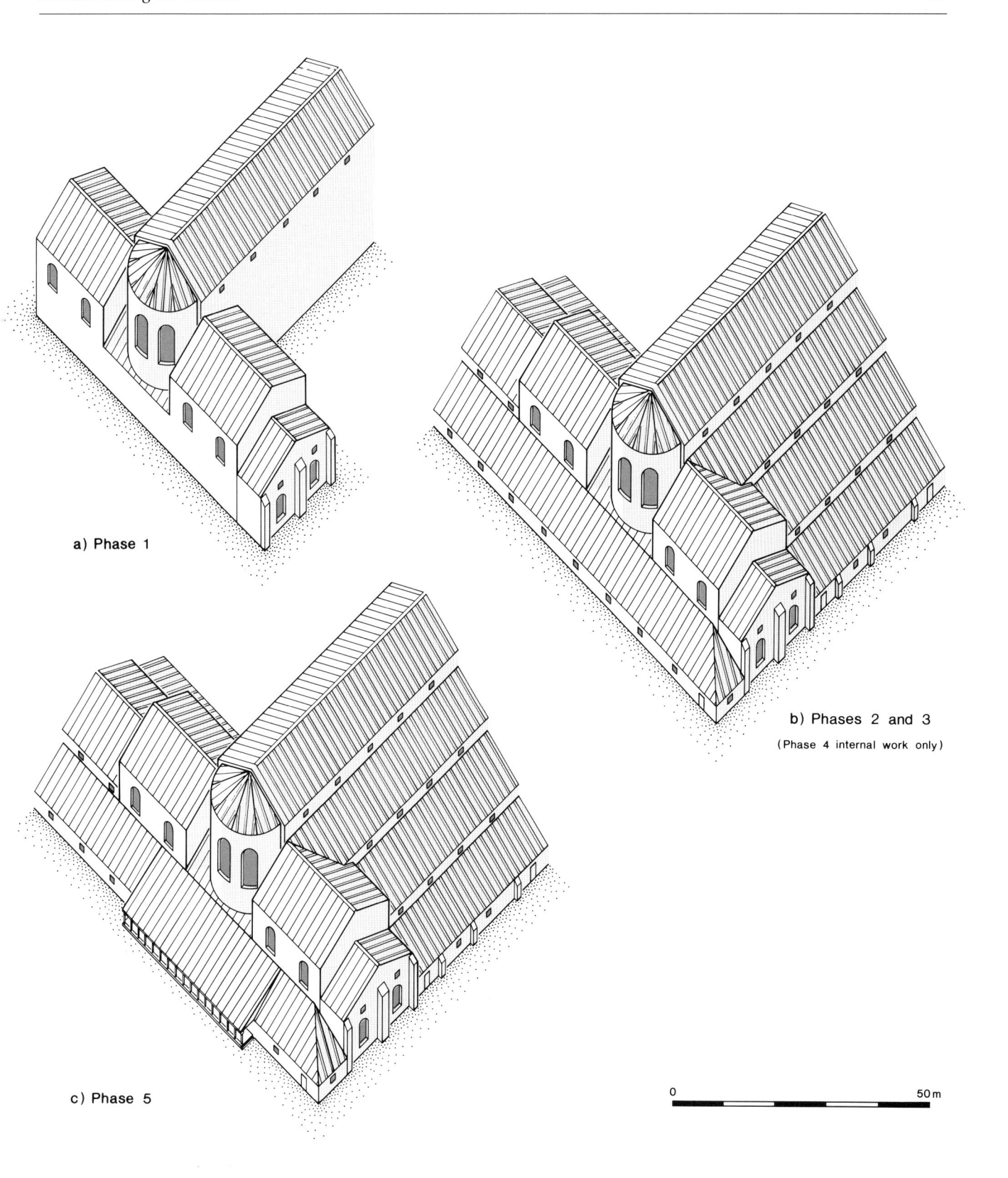

a) Phase 1

b) Phases 2 and 3
(Phase 4 internal work only)

c) Phase 5

0   50 m

Fig 35 Reconstructed projections showing development of the north-east corner of the Basilica in 2nd and 3rd centuries; cf. Fig 30. Phases 1, 2, 3 and 5. Scale 1: 1,000

between, although this may have been part of the Forum proper, rather than a section of the Basilica. The Apse almost certainly had its own half-domed roof, and its presence was further stressed by the later addition of an eastern portico projecting 3m beyond the adjoining eastern range. The east wall of the portico probably carried a low colonnade to support the roof.

Most of the tile used in the Basilica was supplied by tileries in the London/St Albans, Radlett (Hertfordshire) and Eccles (north Kent) areas. The roof was of plain red tile, although the Nave and Western Antechamber were partly covered by white tile, slipped red in order to resemble standard tegulae; examples of these tiles were recovered from collapsed sections of the roof after the first major fire in these areas. Since no slipped tile was recovered from deposits representing the original roof, it seems that they were only used after the first major reconstruction as a substitute for broken stock which could not be replaced, particularly if local stocks of suitable red tile were exhausted by extensive new building work elsewhere. It was not a cheap substitute, and was probably more expensive to produce. Several roof tiles recovered from the Basilica and later road make-ups were stamped PPBRLON (*Procurator Provinciae Britanniae Londinii*), suggesting that they were specially produced by a municipal brickworks. By contrast, the bricks used in the walls were mainly fragments salvaged from demolished buildings, and included bossed bricks (*tegulae mammatae*). It is possible that the bricks used in the later piers may have been specially brought in, since Hodge recorded the presence of 'inscribed' bricks in the example at 90 Gracechurch Street, although that adjective could refer to keying, tally marks or signature marks, all of which are frequently found on bricks from many City sites. Of especial importance is a unique type of brick first identified at Leadenhall Court (Fig 36). These quadrilateral red bricks were not cut to shape, but were made in moulds, presumably especially for the Basilica. Although none were recorded actually in the surviving superstructure, it seems clear that these bricks were employed in the initial construction phase of the 2nd-century Basilica.

External appearance
(Fig 34)

London's Basilica was an imposing structure, probably with accommodation on several levels; the available space in both the wings and the office range could easily have been increased by inserting extra floors. Apart from the east wall of the portico, which was plastered, and a fragment of pink plaster on the outside of the north wall of the eastern range, there is no evidence to suggest that the Basilica was decorated externally. The grey of the ragstone would have contrasted with the regular red brick courses and roof. Lintels, and the dressing of windows, doorways and walls was probably also executed in brick, for structural rather than aesthetic reasons.

The external buttresses must have been carried above ground level, since successive road side ditches were diverted around them. However, it is not clear whether they were raked back, rose vertically, or carried engaged columns, as Merrifield suggests (1983, 68). Sections of collapsed masonry from the upper Nave walls imply the use of a mixture of materials and mortars, possibly in repair work of several periods, which may have affected the outer appearance.

Internal organisation of space

Internally, the original form of the public building suggests a series of chambers linked by doorways. However, the demolition of the north and south Nave walls enabled the central space to be opened out with the insertion of arcading around the Nave. This represents a major change in the plan of the Basilica, which had only just been completed. Brick was selected for the new piers, even though this meant removing large areas of the original walls, since it is a stronger material than cement rubble and well suited for use in continuous arcading in the absence of

Fig 36 Quadrilateral moulded red brick manufactured for the Roman Basilica. Scale 1:4

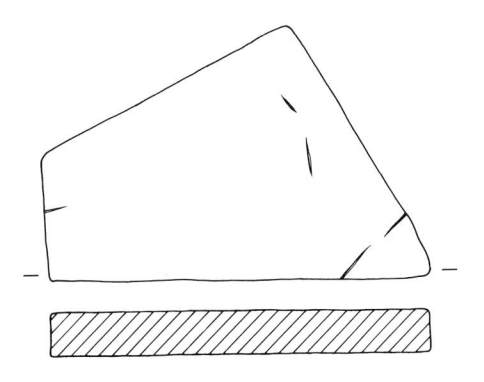

ashlar. The weight of the new piers was distributed on slightly larger limestone plinths. It would have been feasible to perform the alterations without demolishing the upper fabric, by inserting the piers into openings cut into the lower walls, and by supporting the wall by 'needles' (horizontal beams set in slots cut through the wall) resting on props. The intervening arcades could then be completed in two sections. The original doors were almost certainly situated above the second offset, and were thus destroyed. Many of the other walls at the east end of the Basilica were probably cut back to form similar piers, edged in brick and replastered, opening out the Antechambers and Room 11. Of all the walls in the public rooms, only the chord of the Apse and the walls in the wings were apparently untouched.

In the Northern Range, continuous stretches of superstructure divided the offices and the street-front rooms. No doorways were found, suggesting that the offices were not interconnected, and that there was no access to the street-front rooms. The offices were reached only through the North Aisle; the street-front rooms solely from the street.

Floors

Initially, the public rooms were probably provided with raised timber floors resting on the second offset at 14.3m OD. Substantial post pits in the earliest mortar floor and subsequent brickearth slabs suggest that the joists in the Nave were in 5m lengths. During the post-fire reconstruction, however, these were replaced by *opus signinum* laid on solid rubble in the Nave, Aisles and Antechambers, and also in the offices, which do not seem to have had a timber floor. The level of the late floors recorded by Hodge in the Eastern Antechamber suggests, however, that the Apse retained a suspended floor, probably now at the level of the third brick course. The northern and eastern street front rooms were characterised by thin brickearth and mortar surfaces throughout. The level of the final floors in all rooms appears to have determined the point at which the walls were truncated as the Basilica was demolished.

Hodge noted tiles in the east end of the Nave and the eastern range, tessellated floors in the Nave (white), eastern range, and Eastern Antechamber. A herringbone-pattern (*opus spicatum*) tiled pavement recorded by both Hodge and Miller in the eastern portico has recently been excavated at 1–4 Whittington Avenue, and a tessellated pavement was excavated in the office to the west of Room 2 in 1922.

The Basilica appears to have been heated by braziers; scorch marks were visible on many of the floors laid in the offices and street-front rooms. Although underfloor heating systems were provided in some basilicas for the apse and curia, there is no evidence of it in London, despite the fact that the Apse floor was probably raised and could therefore have accommodated heating ducts. Fragments of box tile recovered from some rooms were probably imported as part of general make-up deposits.

Interior decoration
(Figs 37, 38; Col Pls K, L, M, N)

It has been suggested that the Basilica was largely undecorated (Marsden 1987, 52). However, study of the wall plaster recovered from various destruction deposits dramatically contradicts that view. It is now clear that great efforts were made to lighten the public rooms, while the Eastern Antechamber was intended to be a contrasting and striking focal point, leading the eye towards the Apse; there is unfortunately no evidence for the nature of the decoration in the Apse, although the walls were plastered, possibly as a base for marble veneers (Pl 33). The offices were given different colour schemes, with the larger Room 8 perhaps having a slightly higher quality design. The street-front range was normally red and white or pink and white.

In situ evidence for interior decoration is sparse, but includes dark blue painted plaster from the dado level of Room 2, mixed painted panels from a room beneath Gracechurch Street and a 50mm-thick plaster coat in the Apse above the second offset (Marsden 1987, 53–60). However, loose plaster has recently been recovered from several rooms, dating from both before and after the first major alterations and the mid-2nd-century fire. Study of the painted wall plaster from these various destruction levels has provided evidence of four successive schemes used to decorate the Basilica, and also gives some idea of how the allocation of internal space operated.

Scheme 1
From the debris associated with the first major alterations, it is suggested that the street-front Room 1/4 was originally decorated with a plain pinkish-red colour. The neighbouring office, Room 3, was

plastered twice in the initial stages, the second scheme being yellow panels with a red and white border, surrounded by black interspaces. Yellow panels had also been employed in the office next to Room 2, where they had a black border (Marsden 1987, 140–1). The Western Antechamber contained both red and yellow panels with a thin white border, separated by grey interspaces with a green (possibly floral) design. By contrast, the North Aisle contained black panels decorated with green and yellow swirls and bands, surrounded by a pink border, and red panels with yellow and white borders.

Scheme 2
After the structural alterations had been completed, the building was redecorated. Room 1/4 now had a plain red and white design. The office, Room 8, was painted with white panels, bordered with grey, and with some pale green, pink and red patterning. The west end of the Nave and West Antechamber may have been painted predominantly white, with yellow outlined panels. The North Aisle contained red panels with yellow and red bands meeting at 120 degrees and some plain fragments painted with 'Egyptian' blue.

Scheme 3
The Basilica was redecorated once again before being severely damaged in an extensive fire in the 2nd century. Most of the plaster recovered came from thick make-up deposits which were used in reconstruction work. These suggest that, before the fire, Room 1/4 was painted plain white and pink. Room 8 appears to have contained two distinct designs: green panels, and red panels with a green floral design and a yellow border. In the Nave and Western Antechamber, the main panels were plain white with red and black borders. In the Nave, the dado was probably also white, divided by thin black bands. Red reeds, red wavy lines, black splashes, pink and green flowers appear to have decorated some panels. One fragment, perhaps part of the dado, bore red wavy lines, black bands and red, white and black splashes. A white plaster quarter-round moulding, possibly part of a cornice, was also found.

The scheme used in the Western Antechamber consisted of red bands meeting at angles on a white background. These may have been part of a trellis design. Some of the fragments were burnt and scratched as well as marked by grafitti, which suggests that they came from the base of the wall, possibly the dado, of the Antechamber (Col Pl K). The Nave plaster was not affected by the fire, although the burnt sections may well have been reduced to powder, forming the bulk of the matrix of the make-up.

The main area of interest at this stage was the richly-decorated Eastern Antechamber, although the paintwork may have been executed in the preceding phase. Most of the plaster belonged to a scheme of red panels bordered by lines of both green and yellow pennants. These were surrounded by a second border of a thin white band with yellow surroundings. The red panels were decorated with curving green leaf stalks, and yellow, pink and black flowers, highlighted with white to give a three-dimensional effect (Col Pls L and N). It may be part of this design that is represented by plaster fragments in the British Museum (RCHM 1928, 127). It is not clear whether these elements formed a conventional panel design or a scrolling upper frieze design with the pennants hanging downwards (Fig 37). Red plaster with a bevelled border in expensive 'Egyptian' blue indicates the decoration employed around openings – either doors, niches or arcading. The dado may have been red with thin yellow lines. The room also contained fragments of a robed figure design, with flesh pink tones associated with green, red, pale blue, 'Egyptian' blue, yellow, brown and white pigments. Three fragments may have been part of an arm, shoulder and leg, indicating a large figure (Fig 38; Col Pl M). A second design contained red, yellow and orange with white highlights adjoining an area of red stripes on a yellow ground. This may depict some kind of drapery or background composition for the figure. Since all of these designs had a highly polished surface, were unweathered and included many joining fragments, they must have derived from the Antechamber. A small, rougher group of yellow ochre and green floral designs on a cream ground may have intruded from a neighbouring room or represent the remains of an earlier scheme.

Scheme 4
Following the 2nd-century fire, the Basilica was redecorated, although only small quantities of plaster were recovered. Room 8 was painted red with yellow borders. The Nave contained some red and white plaster, while the Eastern Antechamber was at least partly white with red bands. There is no evidence for the final decor of the Basilica.

Reconstructing the Basilica

Fig 37 Interior decoration of Basilica, Scheme 3: a) possible reconstruction of scrollwork. Scale 1: 8; b) detail of painted plaster showing part of frieze and scrollwork. Scale 1: 2; c) painted wallplaster from another section of the Eastern Antechamber. Scale 1: 2

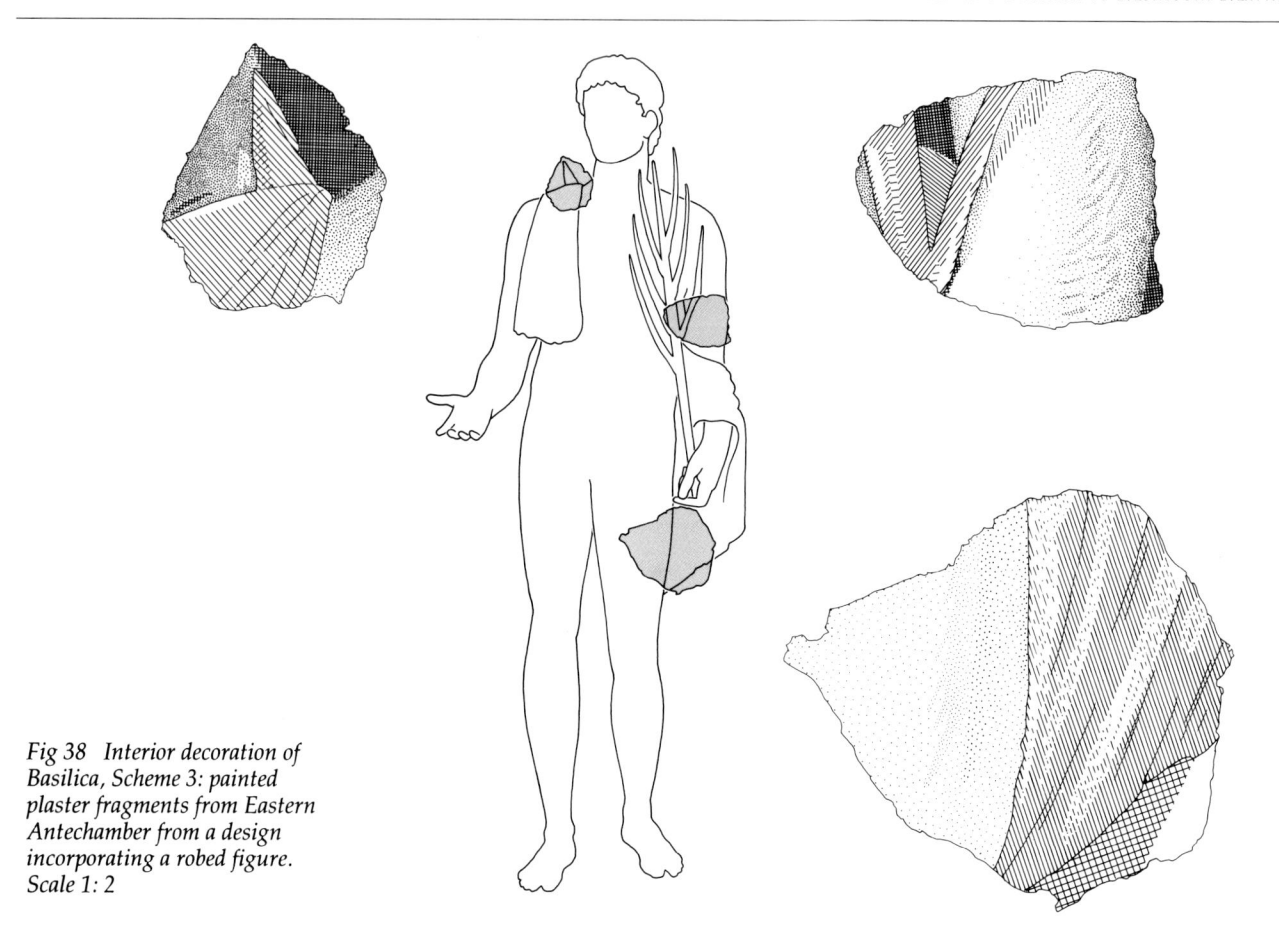

Fig 38 Interior decoration of Basilica, Scheme 3: painted plaster fragments from Eastern Antechamber from a design incorporating a robed figure. Scale 1: 2

The Forum: plan and design

There is less evidence for the plan of the Forum and a correspondingly high degree of uncertainty about its appearance, as outlined in the previous chapter. The east and west wings initially comprised three ranges, and an extra inner range was added some time after the main structure was completed. This implies that the three main ranges were self-contained structurally. They appear to have comprised two ranges of shops or offices with an outer portico, which suggests a high central range spanning the rooms, and a lower roof to the portico. This would be mirrored by a lean-to roof over the extra inner porticoes. This interpretation is favoured by the similarity in width of the extra porticoes, the South Aisle of the Basilica and the inner portico of the south wing, which, it is suggested, were also constructed slightly later than the east and west wings and Basilica. An 8m-wide inner portico was therefore created around the four sides of the Forum courtyard. The roof of the slightly wider portico in the south range was apparently supported by a row of columns or piers inset by around 2m from the external wall. A row of larger piers was set around 3m in from the south portico wall, although in this case they may also have marked separate areas, subdivided by masonry walls running north from some of the piers.

It seems likely that the two central ranges of rooms in the east and west wings were not accessible one from the other, and that they each opened outwards onto their individual porticoes. This is suggested partly by the presence of a continuous superstructure in the wall which divided the east wing at Leadenhall Market. In the south wing, where there was a single range of rooms, the situation is less clear. On balance, the rooms are likely to have opened inwards on to the wide inner portico, since the outer portico may have been partly subdivided by walls attached to some of the piers, perhaps using timber partitions. In this respect, the south portico of the Forum resembled the north portico of the Basilica, the street-front range.

The position of the Forum opposite the road to the bridge, and the known elements of the layout, combine to suggest a central entrance in the south range, although the foundations of the main walls continued beneath. The side walls of the entrance were 20m apart in all, although the opening itself was presumably narrower, perhaps a single arch of a similar width to those spanning the Basilica Nave. There is no evidence to suggest general access to the external portico, which instead seems to have had a fairly continuous superstructure. It is more likely that only a few entrances were available, lockable at night or at other times in order to control access. The possibility of a central walkway which divided the courtyard north from south implies the existence of side entrances: significantly, the outer wall foundation deepened in the eastern range as if to accommodate the springing of just such an arch.

The height of the porticoes and the central range were probably comparable with that of the street-front rooms and offices of the Basilica's northern range, but lower than the projected wings to north and south of the Apse, which are more likely to have been comparable with the North Aisle.

Loose wall plaster survived in some interior areas, and one north–south wall which formed the east side of the central entrance had surviving plaster on both faces. Unfortunately no further details are available, but the colour scheme was probably similar to that of the corresponding sections of the Basilica: largely red or red and white in the porticoes, and brighter in the central ranges, with more yellow and green present.

10 Basilica studies
Trevor Brigham

Previous chapters have discussed the plan, history and form of the Basilica in London; in this chapter consideration will be given to the origins of the forum-basilica plan in Britain, to the function of these important buildings and to the relationship of the civic centre to the town it served.

Development of the forum-basilica plan
(Fig 39)

For the origins of the forum-basilica, we must, of course, look to the Continent. In Italy, the earliest examples probably developed from Greek prototypes, which consisted of an agora and stoa, although the stoa was replaced by the aisled hall or basilica, which was normally attached to part of the forum. In the Spanish, Asian and north African provinces, a similarly informal plan was usually adopted, possibly influenced by the Greek origins of many of the settlements. However, Professor Todd has assembled material which demonstrates that in some provinces the main elements of the forum, basilica and often a temple (*capitolium*) began to be grouped in a more standard way from the 1st century BC (Todd 1985, 56–66). At Bolsena in central Italy, the basilica faced the forum plaza, which was unenclosed. At Veleia in Cisalpine Gaul a temple lay opposite the basilica, with the open forum between, an arrangement also seen at Glanum in Narbonensis in the late 1st century BC. The next development was the enclosure of the forum courtyard and envelopment of the temple, by means of porticoes or wings attached to the basilica, as at Julium Carnicum in Cisalpine Gaul. The basilica at that site was long and narrow, with a single row of columns down the centre. This type has also been excavated at Clunia in Tarraconensis and at Iader in Dalmatia (possibly late 1st century BC to early 1st-century AD). Virunum in Noricum was similar and may be late 1st-century AD, but this consisted of two separate structures – a basilica with two forum wings, separated from a slightly narrower enclosed temple precinct by a gravelled area. This double-precinct plan became the dominant form throughout Gaul, Germany and the Danube provinces. Three of the best-known continental examples are the tribal capitals of Lugdunum Convenarum (St Bertrand de Comminges), Augusta Raurica (Augst) and Lutetia Parisiorum (Paris), all of the early to mid-2nd century, contemporary with London's second Forum-Basilica (Todd 1985).

The forum-basilica in Britain
(Fig 40)

The origins of the Romano-British forum were summarised by R G Goodchild who argued that its plan derived from the principia of army forts (Goodchild 1946, 70–7). Atkinson had previously considered that the use of a standard design reflected the backwardness of British civil development (Atkinson 1942, 360), although Goodchild suggested that the provincial nature of Britain's urban settlement alone would not account for this. In Britain, as elsewhere in the Empire, each forum-

Fig 39 Interpretive plans of Roman forum and basilica at Augusta Raurica and Virunum: B = Basilica, F = Forum, T = Temple. Scale 1: 2,000

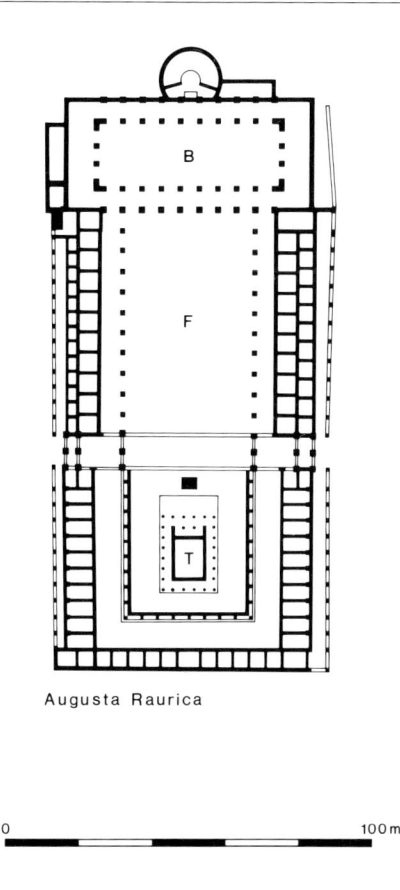

basilica complex was unique, although often there was a general family resemblance to others in the area.

In Britain, the situation was somewhat different from that on the Continent. The double-enclosure plan was not common in Gallo-Germany at the time of the Claudian invasion, and Todd suggests that for this reason it was not adopted in Britain. Although the earliest British fora have left little trace, excavations at Silchester have revealed a late 1st-century timber structure of similar size and layout to the well-known mid-2nd-century masonry basilica which succeeded it (Fulford 1985). Reconstructions of the Colchester temple-precinct, however, suggests that the double-enclosure was probably known in Britain, although not apparently adopted for general use. Here, a large courtyard surrounded the temple of Claudius, and it is now suggested that a smaller adjoining one contained a basilica, the two being separated by colonnades. If true, this is a unique discovery, possibly dating to the early post-conquest period, and Crummy suggested that the basilica was for the administration of the imperial cult (Crummy 1984). The actual town hall and forum lay elsewhere – probably on the site of the former principia in Insula 18, although the large public building in Insula 20 is another contender.

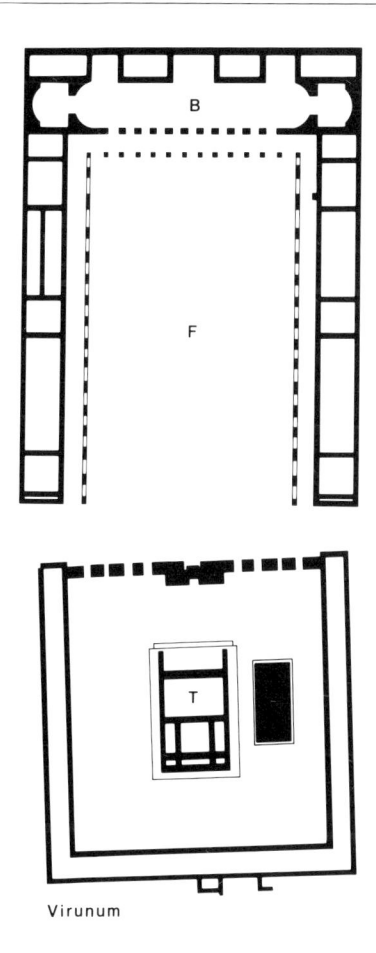

The first forum-basilica in London, and the much larger structure from Verulamium, were among the earliest examples constructed in masonry, the latter being dedicated in AD 79 (Frere 1983). This rather idiosyncratic structure does bear some resemblance to continental complexes, with a relatively long forum and a transverse basilica opposite a temple placed centrally in the forum wing, but it apparently lacks the division into two enclosures. Temples were not normally attached to British fora as primary features, but here the existing example was later flanked by two others. In London, the small temple next to the first forum-basilica may have been associated with it, despite being separated from it by a street. The Colchester double-enclosure and the hybrid Verulamium building are both unique in Britain and, in view of the more normal layout adopted in the following decades, may reflect the development of a local

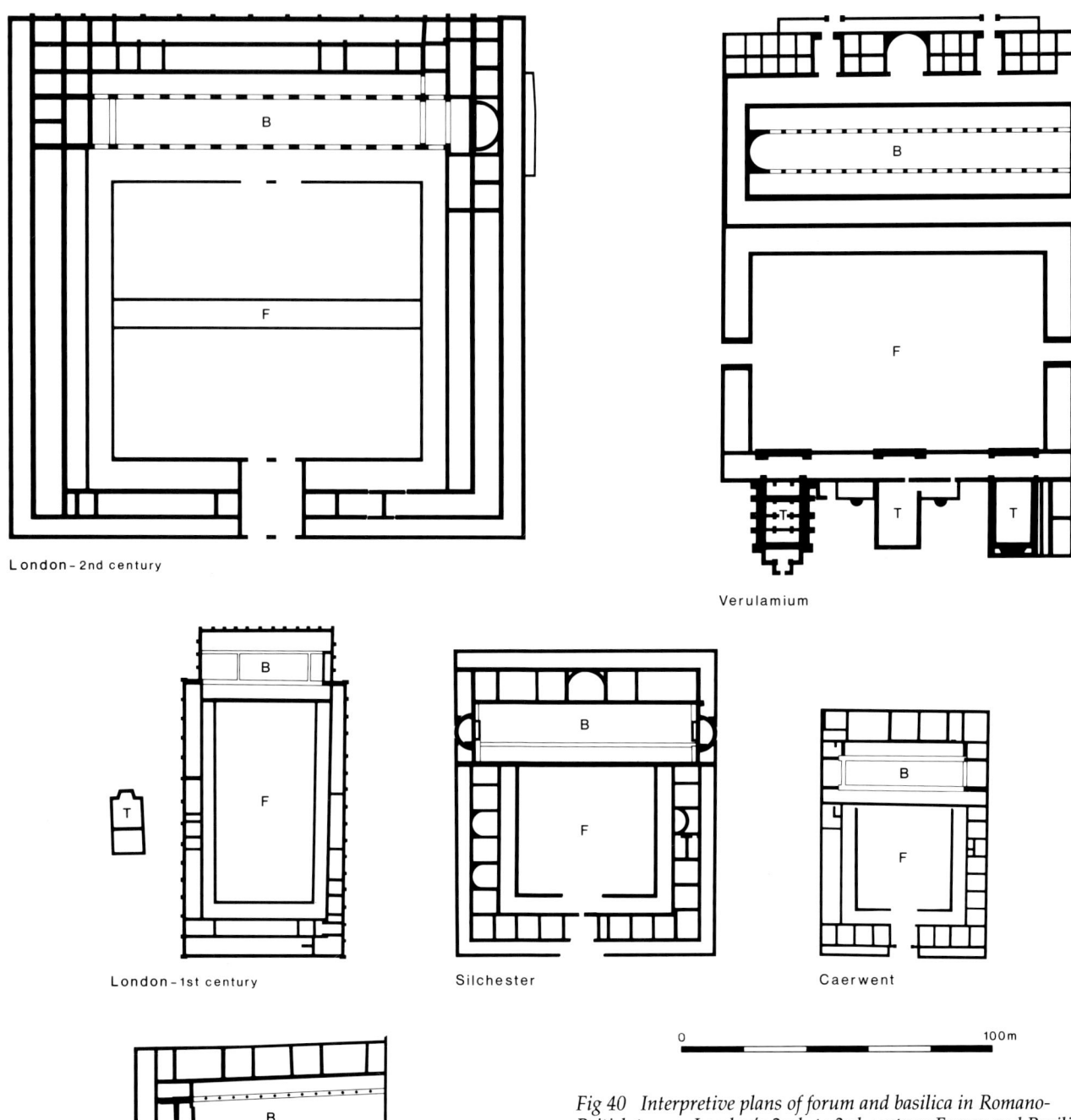

Fig 40 Interpretive plans of forum and basilica in Romano-British towns: London's 2nd- to 3rd-century Forum and Basilica compared with Verulamium; London's 1st-century Forum and Basilica compared with Silchester, Caerwent and Wroxeter. B = Basilica, F = Forum, T = Temple. Scale 1: 2,000

response to the particular conditions prevailing in the province. Fora built from the later 1st century onwards were closer in form to the timber structure at Silchester, the chief difference being that the forum became a squarer enclosure, with the position of the temple taken by a third forum range. The lack of a temple may, as Goodchild suggested, reflect a divorce between civil administration and the imperial cult in

Britain, which led to temples being positioned on separate sites. The presence of a small temple next to the 1st-century London basilica and the existence of a separate basilica-temple complex for the imperial cult at Colchester both suggest this to be the case, although the temples at Verulamium imply that this did not occur immediately.

Civic forum-basilica complexes are attested in varying degrees of detail in 15 Romano-British towns: the provincial capital London, the coloniae of Lincoln (Jones & Gilmour 1980) and Gloucester (McWhirr 1981), the *civitas* capitals including Canterbury, Chichester and Winchester (Wacher 1974; Todd 1989b) and even the *vicus* (small town) of Godmanchester (Green 1975). The fora were recorded in sufficient detail to allow a reconstruction of the main aspects of their plans in eight *civitas* capitals: Verulamium (Frere 1983), Caistor-by-Norwich (Frere 1971) Silchester (Fulford 1985), Cirencester (McWhirr 1981), Exeter (Bidwell 1979), Leicester (Hebditch & Mellor 1973), Wroxeter ((Mackreth 1987) and Caerwent (Brewer 1988).

All these examples consist of a single square or rectangular courtyard surrounded on three sides by colonnades and on the fourth by an aisled hall. One row of offices usually lay along the opposite side of the aisled hall, with further offices or workshops/shops fringing the forum colonnades. Ambulatories were often provided around all four outer walls, although these were absent at Caistor, and elsewhere were replaced by a second set of rooms. Most of the halls had partitioned areas at one or both ends, which probably acted as tribunals for the town magistrates, and often had floors raised above the general level. In most cases, these areas were rectangular, but in the case of London, Cirencester, Silchester and possibly Leicester, apsidal chambers were provided. However, apses appear to have been the exception, being replaced at Silchester, for example, by rectangular rooms. A large room, which may have acted as the curia or council chamber, has been identified at Exeter and Caistor where it lay at the end of the main hall. At Silchester, a central apsidal room leading from the basilica has been interpreted as the town shrine, presumably copying its 1st-century timber predecessor (M Fulford, *pers comm*). A similar rectangular room was excavated at Caistor.

The date of much of the construction of British fora is rarely easily determined, particularly since evidence from Silchester suggests that in some cases they copied timber precursors. Despite the unreliability of some of the dating evidence, however, it is clear that British forum-basilicas were mainly constructed in the later 1st and 2nd centuries. An inscription from Verulamium suggests that the forum there was completed in AD 79, around the same time as the first London basilica and the example at Caerwent. For Gloucester and the second London basilica, a date of AD 95–100 is suggested for the start of construction, which in the case of London was probably completed around AD 120–30. At Winchester, Cirencester and Exeter, a late 1st- to early 2nd-century date seems likely for the construction of those civic centres. The forum-basilicas at Leicester and Wroxeter were built in the early 2nd century, with a dedication inscription in the latter suggesting a date of *c*.AD 130. At Silchester, a late 1st-century timber basilica was replaced in stone in the mid-2nd century. Beneath the timber basilica was what may have been an early market building, although equally, this could have been a forum-basilica, developing from a post-conquest principia, according to Professor Fulford. At Caistor, the forum-basilica may have been late 2nd-century, perhaps replacing an earlier building which was recorded beneath. The forum here was destroyed by fire and completely rebuilt after a long interval to a different plan a century after the main period of building ended, although the new basilica may have been raised on the original foundations. This scatter of construction dates seems less marked than in many other provinces but, together with the geographical distribution, perhaps explains the morphological variation.

The often-remarked resemblance between the British type of forum-basilica and military principia is striking, particularly when compared with complex structures from legionary fortresses such as Caerleon, Neuss, Lambaesis and Xanten. The principia had its origins in Republican military camps as a combination of the commander's tent and an open space in front for addressing troops (Johnson 1983). Their translation into drystone in the 2nd century BC can be seen in primitive form at Pena Redonda and Castillejo in Spain, where they bear little resemblance to later examples (Johnson 1983, 126, fig 96). The earliest principia of 'standard' plan are those of the Augustan timber fortresses of Haltern and Neuss, and by the time of the Claudian invasion of Britain, they had achieved recognisable form. The double enclosure plan forum-basilica had already been developing for some time on the Continent, however, and it was from there that the British type appears to have gained its inspiration. Similarities between principia and fora are probably a result of parallel evolution, a case of two similar forms being determined by related but distinct functions.

The Basilica Ulpia in Rome had a superficial resemblance both to British fora and to military principia. This has been convincingly explained as due to Trajan's career as a soldier, and his consequent adoption of military forms for civilian purposes (Sear 1982, 158–60), but the Basilica Ulpia was too late to have influenced design in Britain, although its construction was contemporary with that of the second basilica in London.

The nature of northern urbanisation

Although there is general agreement on the actual functions of fora and basilicas, there is less of a consensus about their status and relationship to the settlements which they served. Large centres such as Rome and Corinth were endowed with a number of examples of each. In the case of Corinth, several identical basilicas were built in the agora, suggesting that each housed separate, well-defined functions. Similarly, some of the functions of a forum may have been shared with a number of specialist markets or *macella*.

Wightman has suggested that the late 1st-century rush to construct civic centres in Gallia Belgica was due to an anxiety to comply with the pressure from individual emperors or legates to carry through the Romanisation (or urbanisation) programme (Wightman 1985, 80), in contrast to the more positive pro-Romanisation move by the natives in Britain suggested by Reece (Reece 1981). The forum-basilica should be seen as the embodiment of Romanitas, although there was no standard plan in the province of Gallia Belgica, despite some common elements (Wightman 1985). This strongly suggests that urban settlements made individual commitments to construct their civic complex, with little central interference, a situation which also seems likely in Britain.

Reece, by contrast, suggested that the provision of public buildings and the initial planned nature of towns was one of the outward manifestations of a more positive wave of pro-Romanising feeling which swept parts of Britain early in the occupation. Once established, he argued, the towns became self-perpetuating to some extent, deriving much of their wealth from trade and taxes, rather than from exploitation of their hinterlands. Outside the *territoria*, which were too small to circumscribe much more than a cemetery zone and some agricultural land, the countryside remained separate, and perhaps aloof from the urban areas except as a market for their produce. The towns remained more a part of the Empire than part of the province.

This hypothesis certainly explains some towns' apparently shallow attachment to the soil of Britain. Their dependence on trade was their downfall, particularly after the late 2nd- and early 3rd-century economic downturn. Reece saw such towns as marginal institutions in this period, unable to weather the storms of financial and political upheaval which marked the 3rd century. Continuing public expenditure must have fallen heavily on the few remaining men of curial class who were still obliged to form the administration. There seems to have been an inevitable movement towards the consolidation of holdings within towns, possibly as the initial impact of Romanisation diminished and trade began to fall away. Evidence from Gallia Belgica demonstrates that in Avenches and Trier, Beauvais and Reims, large masonry town houses were displacing the artisans' narrow strip buildings from as early as the reign of Claudius, and certainly by the late 1st century; in Britain this did not occur until the mid-2nd century.

The later development of British towns may be accounted for by the ripple effect of economic change suggested by Reece as proceeding from the centre of the Empire. In London, trade dwindled, leading eventually to the abandonment of the wharves (Brigham 1990b; Milne 1985). The remaining population may have engaged in agriculture as a source of subsistence or livelihood, which may explain the universal presence of dark earth in areas which had been cleared of buildings. Certainly the demolition of little used and expensively maintained facilities such as the forum-basilica becomes more easily understandable. Perhaps the only surprising aspect is that the London Basilica should have survived to the end of the 3rd century.

Proportional representation
(Fig 41)

It has long been thought likely that the dimensions of a forum-basilica must have been at least partly dictated by the town's size, status or wealth (e.g. Frere 1967; Mackreth 1987, 134–5). As an example of this school of thought, Professor Wacher argues that: 'As befitted a tribe [the Silures] which must have been impoverished by long years of fighting against Rome, the forum and basilica [of Caerwent] were built on a modest scale... In this respect the tribe resembled the Iceni... and there is a remarkable similarity in the development of their capitals... [Caerwent and Caistor-by-Norwich]' (Wacher 1974, 378). The suggestion that a *colonia* or *civitas* would have constructed as large a civic centre as was reasonably affordable at the time was then tested, first by studying those two towns.

If the areas of Caistor and Caerwent are compared with the area of their fora, an apparent discrepancy is found. At Caerwent, the town enclosed by the wall seems to reflect accurately the extent of the earlier occupied area. Here, the forum-basilica is approximately 1/50th the size of that later walled area. At Caistor, the 3rd-century walled town had a 1:25 relationship with its forum-basilica, which seems disproportionately generous. However, the defended area was much smaller than the settlement as originally planned, the extent of which can be partly determined through the visible outline of the former street grid. The original extent of the earlier town is not precisely known, but the street system suggests that the area was intended to be considerably larger, approximately twice the size of the extant walled town. This would place the forum-basilica somewhat closer to the 1:50 ratio. It is unclear whether or not the planned area was ever fully occupied, but it could be suggested that the forum-basilica was constructed to serve a population which did not expand as much as initially projected.

On the surface, therefore, Wacher's hypothesis is correct, and significant variations in the scale of fora may therefore be anticipated, reflecting variations in financial and political fortunes. However, a study of Romano-British towns shows that the size of the forum-basilica was probably determined by factors other than affordability. For example, if the Caistor forum was constructed for a larger projected population, then it might be suggested that it was future expectations which were fundamental to the design of fora, rather than current financial restraints. It is suggested here that the main determinant was, in fact, an estimate of the expected maximum population, and that there is a relationship between the planned extent of a settled area and the dimensions of the forum-basilica itself. Affluence, or its absence, could still be manifested, but in the form or the quality of decoration and the efficiency of maintenance.

This hypothesis implies that the size of a settlement does not necessarily reflect the size of population, but that in some cases, a larger population was clearly planned for than was achieved. This could reasonably be included in any equation, where the planning was demonstrably contemporary with the construction of the forum-basilica. This is also relevant where extra areas, such as the *vicus* at Gloucester and the walled *colonia* of Lincoln were included as part of the settlement area before the construction of the forum-basilica. Ribbon development was not counted as part of the settlement area, since it was presumably uncontrolled, and therefore unplanned.

It is unfortunate that in many towns, the size or even location of the forum-basilica is partly guesswork, while the extent of the occupied area is difficult to determine exactly, since the area enclosed by later defensive works sometimes bears little relationship to the initial settlement. In certain cases, as at Wroxeter, the defences were much larger than the occupied nucleus, and their position was determined by topographical factors (Barker 1985). The forum-basilica is therefore extremely small for the area, but not when looked at in relation to the occupied nucleus.

At Silchester and Verulamium, several defensive circuits of different periods existed. In the former case, the ramparts enclosing the early settlement were levelled and extended greatly in the later 1st century (Fulford 1984). The 1st-century timber basilica was therefore constructed to service the smaller occupied area of the first town. The enlarged later 1st- to late 2nd-century town did not receive a basilica to match, however, which suggests that although the defences were extended, the occupied area did not expand greatly, according to Professor Fulford, although there may have been plans to attract a larger population. Instead, the timber basilica was replaced by a mid-2nd-century masonry structure, which was only marginally larger than its predecessor, and was presumably designed to serve a similar population. This accounts for the position of the basilica in an insula which was disproportionately large, a fact noted by Wacher (Wacher 1974, 262). The insula was the correct size to build a structure more in proportion to the enlarged town, and that may have been the original intention. In the late 2nd century, masonry walls restored the town to a size similar to that of the 1st century. At Verulamium, the early defended area was roughly doubled in size, and a similar expansion in population may have been planned, although once again, the area is unlikely to have been fully occupied (Frere 1972).

In the case of Gloucester, the basilica simply replaced the principia of the underlying fortress, just as houses slowly replaced barracks (Hurst 1972, 66–7).

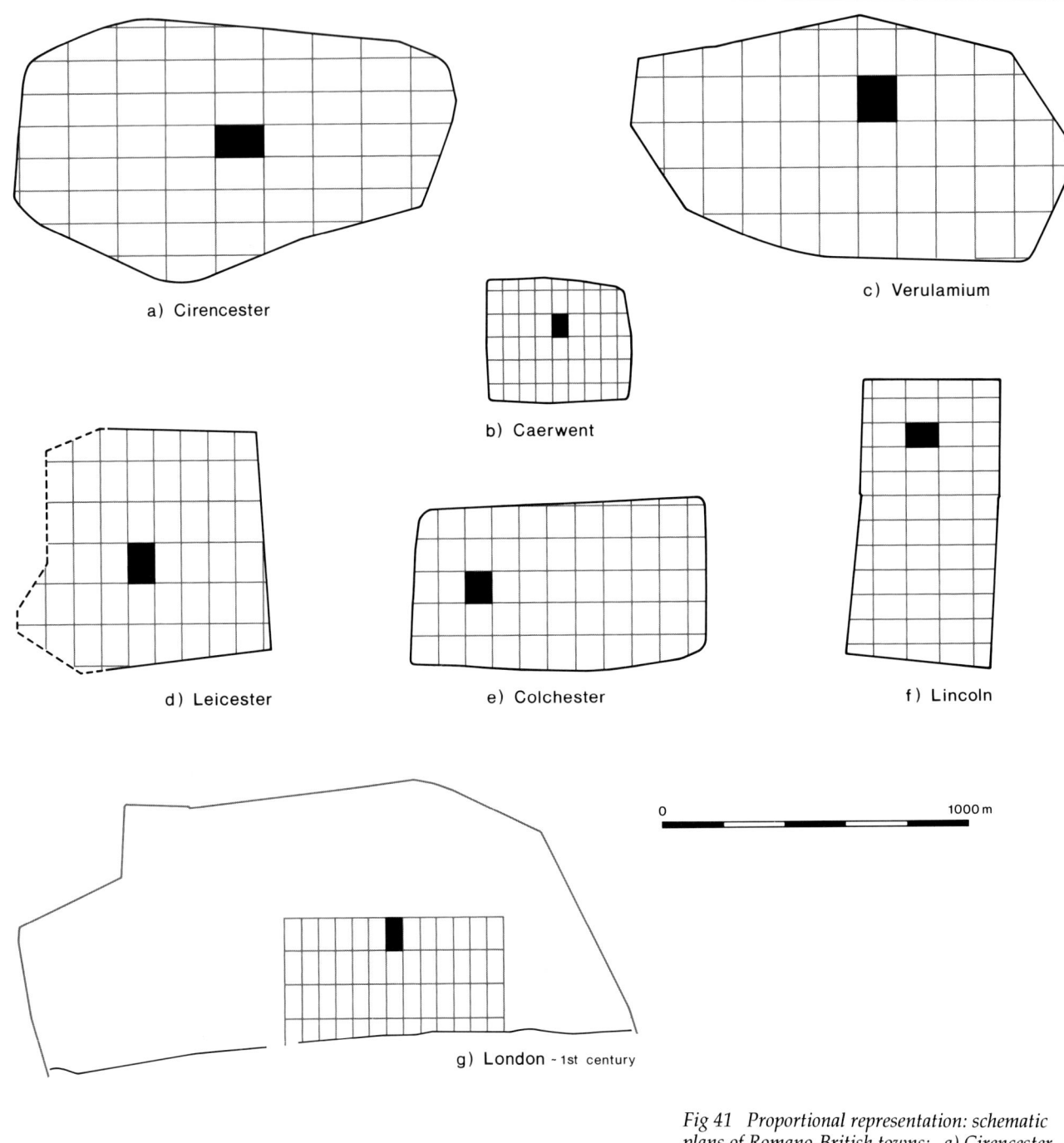

Fig 41 Proportional representation: schematic plans of Romano-British towns: a) Cirencester, b) Caerwent, c) Verulamium, d) Leicester (with conjectured wall line shown dashed), e) Colchester and f) Lincoln, showing that the forum insula occupies an area of c.1: 45 to 1: 50 of the size of the town it serves: the largest town has the largest forum. If this ratio was consistent, then it would imply that the settlement served by g) the 1st-century forum in London (possible extent shown within grey line of later town wall), was substantially smaller than h) the town served by the 2nd- to 3rd-century forum. Scale 1: 20,000

The disproportionate 1:25 relationship of the principia and fortress was thus maintained. However, there was a prosperous and extensive extramural settlement here, which would have justified the retention of a structure this large. If the current theories about the position of Colchester's basilica in Insula 18 are correct, the complex there was also probably large enough to serve the expanded *colonia*, provided it occupied the full area of the insula. At Lincoln, the forum-basilica was also presumably constructed to serve the extended settlement after the addition of a walled *vicus*, although the exact dimensions of the building are still unknown.

In those few cases where reasonable certainty exists, such as Verulamium, Caerwent and Silchester, there seems to have been a relationship of around 1:45/1:50 between the area of the forum-basilica and the occupied area of the settlement at the time the complex was planned or constructed (Fig 41). This seems to hold for towns with less clear evidence, such as Leicester, Colchester, Lincoln, and possibly the planned area of Caistor-by-Norwich. It seems likely that a more or less fixed ratio was the result of deliberate policy, for reasons implied by Vitruvius in an earlier century, and in a different part of the Roman world: 'The size of a forum [courtyard] should be proportionate to the number of inhabitants, so that it may not look too small a space to be useful, nor look like a desert waste for lack of population' (Morgan 1914, V, 1 .ii). Since the area of the courtyard also determined the minimum length of the encompassing basilica and forum wings, it is not too surprising that the area of the entire complex also bore a relationship to that of the town.

In the case of London, there are two successive fora of very different scales. The 1st-century forum-basilica was constructed to serve a much smaller settlement. It was around 109 × 55m, which makes it small by comparison with other British structures, and closest to that of the *civitas* capital of Caerwent. If 1st-century Londinium was of comparable size to Caerwent, around 18 hectares, the early planned settlement could fit neatly into the area from Cornhill southwards to the Thames and from the Walbrook eastwards to the point where the angled Colchester road hit the regular street grid. This area contained the known nucleus of the oldest settlement, and included the forum-basilica, as well as the bridge and harbour, based around the only section of regular street grid. It was also fronted by the 1st-century quay, which did not extend far either east or west. However, it excludes the early Roman settlement on the opposite bank of the Thames at Southwark.

The enlarged 2nd-century Forum-Basilica was constructed for an extended settlement whose exact limits are unknown, although a 1:50 relationship allows two possibilities. The first is that the planned area of occupation may have corresponded with most of the later defended town, but not including the western enclave, where cemeteries may have remained in use into the 2nd century. That western area was, however, incorporated by the time the walls were built c.AD 200. Instead, the comparable area of 2nd-century Roman settlement in Southwark might be added to the calculations. A second option is that the planners did not include Southwark, since the *pomerium* was already established at its maximum extent by that date, and must have been marked by earthworks. There were unoccupied zones within these limits, including parts of the south-eastern, south-western and north-western quarters, and it may well have been intended to expand into these areas at some date, since there were no insuperable problems attached.

If the hypothesis proposed here is confirmed by further work, it should become possible from the remains of a forum-basilica to calculate the area of a town, where that area is imperfectly known, as at Leicester. It should conversely be possible to calculate the area of a basilica using the size of a settlement as a guide, as at Colchester. Some examples are illustrated in Fig 41, but in most towns more detailed information obtained by careful archaeological investigation is required to relate the forum-basilica to its settlement, and in a wider context, to the hinterland which it also served.

11 Reconstructing the medieval market at Leadenhall

Mark Samuel

The discovery of a medieval masonry wall surviving to its full height of 11m is a rare event in London, where fires and redevelopment have destroyed virtually all the fabric of the ancient secular City. It was therefore with some excitement and not a little disbelief that archaeologists began stripping off wall plaster in a derelict building in Gracechurch Street in January 1985. Medieval stonework was revealed not just in the basement but all the way up to the fourth floor. That wall was part of the 15th-century Garner which was assumed to have been entirely demolished over a century ago. How the wall managed to survive has been discussed in Chapter 3, a remarkable story in its own right. This chapter summarises the evidence from which the Garner was reconstructed and the process of reconstruction.

Trading places

Superficially, the size and the plan of the 15th-century courtyard market parallels that of the 1st-century forum. Religious ritual played much the same role in civic life, although over 1,000 years separate the two; there was a temple on the western side of the Roman market and a chapel on the eastern range of the medieval Garner. Both civic buildings occupied the same hill-top site, only to be swept away in subsequent developments. But it must be stressed that there were also major differences between the form, function and fate of the Roman forum and the medieval building, as well as in the data available for their study. Nevertheless, as much can be learned by contrast as by comparison. For example, the reconstruction techniques used for the medieval building may be contrasted with those used for the Roman basilica (see Chapter 9). For the medieval study, the archaeologist was able to relate site records to documentary, pictorial and cartographic evidence, a luxury not available for the Roman period. Just how successful this different methodology was will now be considered, as the evidence for the 15th-century Market and Garner is described.

Archaeological evidence

By December 1986, the archaeologists had collected a superficially unprepossessing body of data, from which a reconstruction of the 15th-century building would be attempted. There were 177 moulded stones, the fragment of the west wall of the west range of the quadrangle, and a series of truncated chalk foundations. Each of these three elements will be summarised, after which the process of integration is outlined. A more comprehensive account is deposited in the Museum of London archive (see also Samuel 1989).

The recording of the upstanding wall fragment was a piecemeal process, involving the photogrammetric recording of part of the west face in July 1985 (Pl 27) and the manual drawing of the remainder in September of the following year. The east face was recorded floor by floor during the demolition of the Metal Exchange Buildings from October to November 1986 (Pl 28). Although the external wall of the Garner

Pl 27 Courses, lifts and put-log holes: the external (west) face of the 15th-century Garner wall, revealed inside a 19th-century office building in Gracechurch Street when the plaster was stripped off. This is the ground floor section; the head of the 5x100mm scale rests against the dressed plinth.

included no doors or windows, the record made of it greatly increased the accuracy of the reconstruction, for it showed, in exquisite detail, how the Garner was built. For example, it revealed the nature of the stone and mortar used, the depths of the lifts, and the nature of the scaffolding. The wall fragment preserved a set of dimensions which were common to the entire complex. It was possible to show that it stood 9.35m above the plinth (which was itself 1.5m above the contemporary ground level), that the ground floor was *c*.5m high, and that the upper two storeys were each just under 3m (Fig 42). In addition, on the east face the positions of joists and corbels were discovered. These marked divisions between bays of the building, as well as the levels of the roof and floors.

The Garner was probably built as a single entity. It was uniformly constructed in a series of 36 lifts (which survived in the west wall fragment). The lifts frequently corresponded to features such as the bases or tops of windows, the level of the moulded plinth, corbels or cornices. In the same way, the external ashlar courses of the 15th-century Guildhall in London correspond to the courses of moulded stones forming the blank tracery. In both civic buildings, the lifts regulated the course of construction and were accurately determined in advance.

The chalk and mortar foundations from the north and west ranges were recorded during the controlled excavations (Pl 18) while part of the east range foundations were observed during the subsequent watching brief. Generally, the trenches into which the mortar foundations were poured were neatly dug with sharp corners and vertical sides, their flat bottoms cut down to the surface of the undisturbed natural Brickearth. By contrast, the Basilica foundations were not dug down to such stable deposits, a lack of foresight that was to have grave consequences. The plotting of these medieval foundations showed for the first time how the Garner was positioned in relation to the modern City.

116 *From Roman Basilica to Medieval Market*

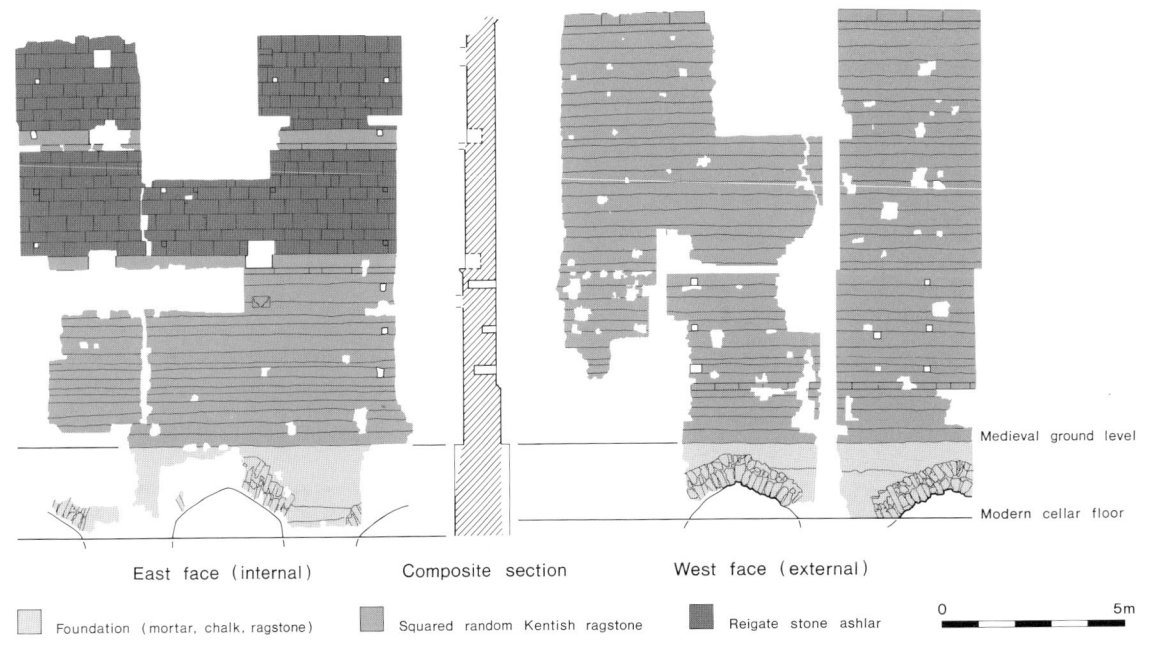

East face (internal) Composite section West face (external)

Medieval ground level
Modern cellar floor

Foundation (mortar, chalk, ragstone) Squared random Kentish ragstone Reigate stone ashlar

0 5m

Reconstructing the medieval market at Leadenhall

OPPOSITE ABOVE
Pl 28 Facing the 15th century: internal ashlar face of second-floor granary revealed after modern plasterwork and a fireplace were removed in the Metal Exchange Buildings in 1986

OPPOSITE BELOW
Fig 42 Elevations of part of the west wall of the 15th-century West Range: internal face, profile, and external face, to show lifts and different types of stone used: see Fig 23. Scale 1: 200

BELOW
Pl 29 Building with the past: this cellar wall is built of stone from the northern range of the 15th-century Garner, demolished in 1794. It incorporates moulded stones from the arcading, window surrounds and even from the spiral stairs. West (internal) face with 5x100mm scale. (Area N)

BOTTOM
Pl 30 Building with the past: cross-section looking north through cellar wall, showing reused moulded stones. The 5x100mm scale rests on a chalk foundation of the demolished 15th-century Garner

Pl 31 Collecting the evidence: archaeologists carefully dismantle a cellar wall (cf. Pls 29 and 30) to recover the moulded stones reused in it. Part of an arcade pier and a corbel can be seen next to the pick-axe. (Area N, looking south-east)

The moulded stones recovered from the Leadenhall Court site were fragments of the northern range of the 15th-century Garner. They had been reused in cellar walls of terraced houses built on the site immediately after the range's demolition in the 1790s (Pls 29 and 30). Some of this material was extracted from walls within the controlled excavation (Pl 31), but much was collected during the machine clearance of the site. This was a far more hazardous operation, and many stones must have been lost in the process, which frequently badly scarred those which were retrieved. Nevertheless, 177 moulded stones were saved and recorded in detail, most representing parts of arches, columns, doors, two- and three-light windows and two spiral staircases.

Medieval masons carved all architectural features with uniform profiles by using a template called a 'moulding'. This uniformity allows great scope for archaeological reconstruction, as the fragmented pieces can be reconstituted on the basis of shared mouldings.

First, each aspect or face of the moulded stones was drawn at 1:2. They were then recorded and catalogued using special recording sheets permitting a basic classification of the stones according to a series of keywords. Visual comparison of the drawings remains the final test of relationships. Next, the stones were sorted into types of moulding. Those which formed part of a window, door, stair tread or similar element were grouped together. The 47 groupings

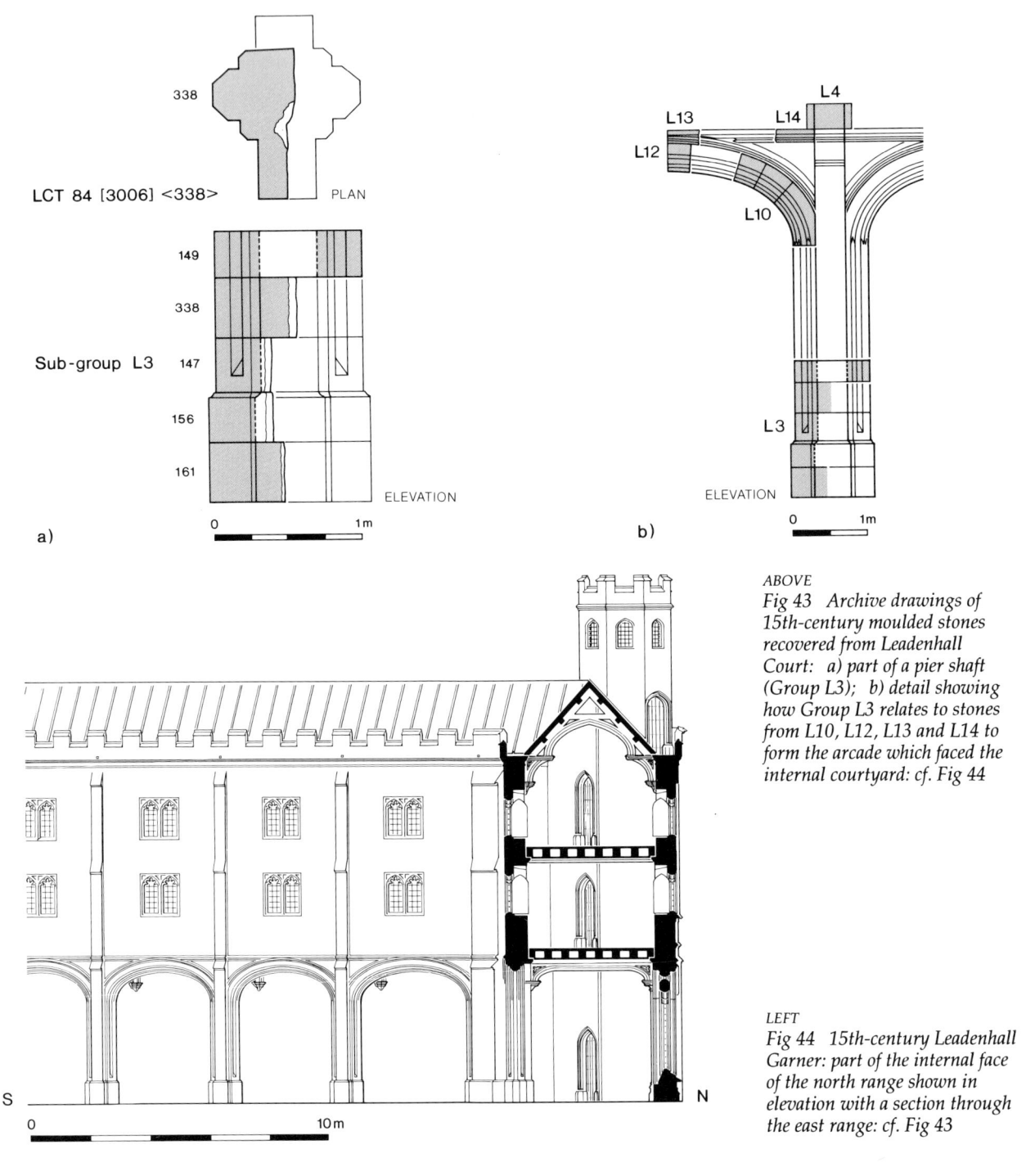

ABOVE
Fig 43 Archive drawings of 15th-century moulded stones recovered from Leadenhall Court: a) part of a pier shaft (Group L3); b) detail showing how Group L3 relates to stones from L10, L12, L13 and L14 to form the arcade which faced the internal courtyard: cf. Fig 44

LEFT
Fig 44 15th-century Leadenhall Garner: part of the internal face of the north range shown in elevation with a section through the east range: cf. Fig 43

thus formed were then examined to see if larger, more complex architectural features (such as the corner of the north range) might be reconstructed by combining them (Figs 43–46).

It was clear at this stage that the moulded stones derived from a monumental building in the Perpendicular style, but before more detailed reconstruction could proceed two more items were needed. One was an accurate three-dimensional skeleton outline of the building on to which the elements represented by the moulded stones could be attached. The second was far more detailed information concerning the appearance of the greater architectural embellishments, where the archaeological evidence was inadequate. Another class of evidence now came into its own.

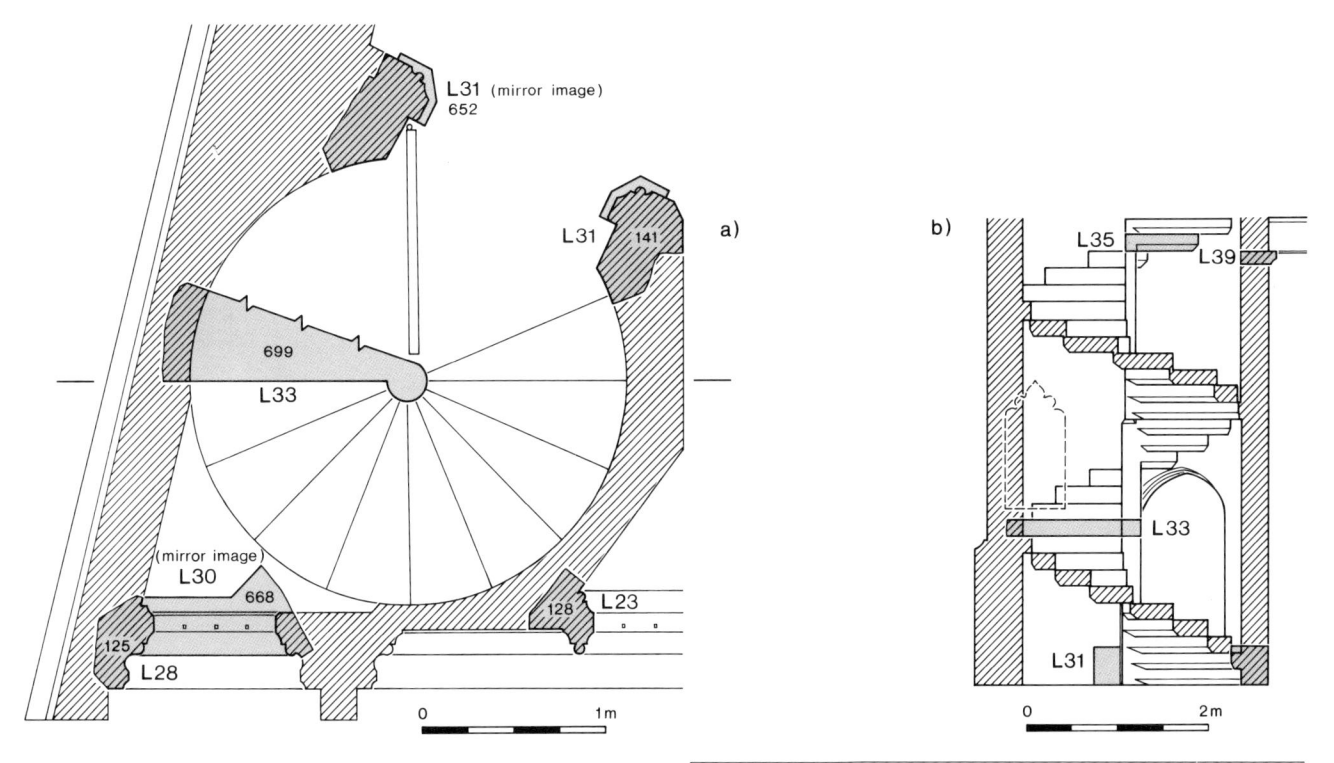

Reconstructing the medieval market at Leadenhall

ABOVE

Fig 45 Archive drawings of 15th-century moulded stones recovered from Leadenhall Court: a) spiral stair fragment and reconstruction of helix (L33) related to fragments of the associated stair turret (L23, L28, L30, L31). Scale 1: 40; b) cut-away elevation to show spiral stair in reconstruction of north-west corner tower of 15th-century Leadenhall Garner: cf. Fig 46. Scale 1: 80

Sketches and surveys
(Fig 47, Pl 32)

Our archaeological material could now be compared with surviving documents and plans of the Garner, some of which date back to the 16th century, together with a number of drawings made on the eve of demolition by 18th- and 19th-century topographical draughtsmen such as Nash, Carter and Smith. However, many of the surviving views cannot be treated like a modern photographic record. For example, the dilapidated chapel at Leadenhall was a popular subject for sketchers and only a certain amount of attention was paid to the grim old building it was attached to. Some, like Whichele, wished to prepare attractive engravings that would sell; he did not hesitate to beautify the subject matter by deliberately omitting lean-to shops and fish stalls and by unblocking windows. The Leadenhall chapel shown in his work is therefore displayed to its full advantage, but did it ever really look like that? Since

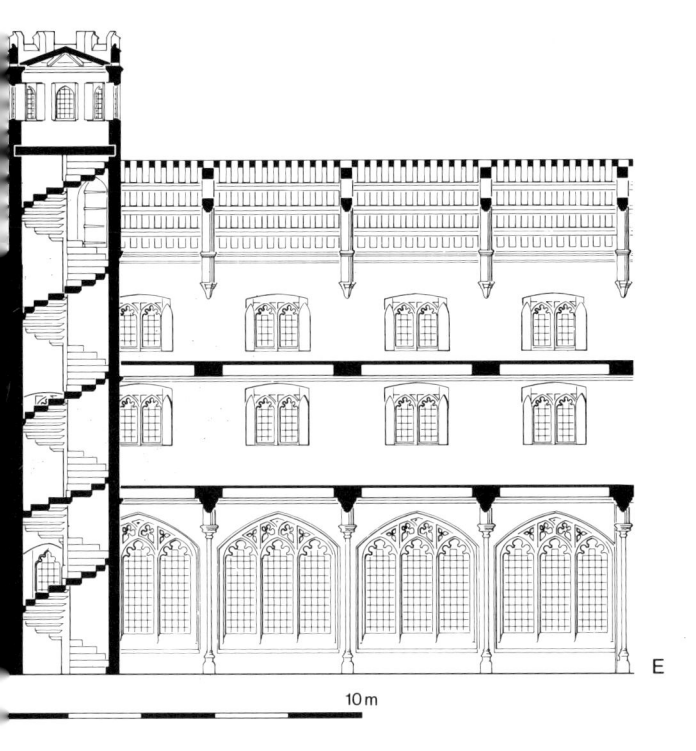

LEFT

Fig 46 15th-century Leadenhall Garner: part of a reconstruction of the north-facing facade with cut-away elevation of stair turret: cf. Fig 45. Scale 1: 200

Pl 32 The eve of destruction: Carter's late 18th-century engraving of the Leadenhall Garner's north facade, pictured just before demolition

the present-day notion of objective recording was unknown, it is only through careful judgement that such records can be used to assist reconstruction. The drawings of John Carter were of particular importance to the task, as he made a pencil sketch of the north facade in 1785, later worked up as an engraving (Pl 32), while Nash produced a pencil sketch of the Garner's courtyard. Both artists, in the corners of their original drawings, recorded additional architectural details of considerable importance. These details of mouldings show a real 'archaeological' interest on the part of the draughtsmen. They can therefore be accepted as accurate records and might have been done expressly for our benefit.

The survey undertaken by Leybourn in 1676 (Masters 1974) was long thought to have been the most detailed surviving plan. This was drawn to show the layout of the stalls for the purpose of assessing rentals rather than to record the architecture. However, during the course of research, a remarkable discovery was made in the Corporation of London Records Office, a discovery which proved as exciting and as rewarding as any made on the archaeological site. The document in question bore the unpromising title of *Design for Improving the Leather Market at Leadenhall, 1794* but inspection proved it to be a carefully surveyed and detailed ground plan of the Garner, immediately prior to the demolition of the north range.

The plan's accuracy was confirmed by comparison with the excavated evidence of the foundations from the north range; they shared exactly the same irregular spacing. However, the 1794 survey was mildly distorted by age. Nevertheless, it was now possible definitively to identify foundations recorded in the south-east of the site as part of the Leadenhall chapel. The great wall fragment could now be shown to have stood behind the eighth arch from the northern respond of the west arcade (Fig 23). The excavated evidence thus provided a series of 'controls' allowing the 1794 survey to be redrawn accurately (Fig 47).

We now had an accurate ground plan of the complex as originally built. The rectangular building comprised four ranges three storeys high; the arcaded ground floor opened out on to a central courtyard. The 1794 survey proved beyond doubt the unitary nature of the complex. Things were now going well.

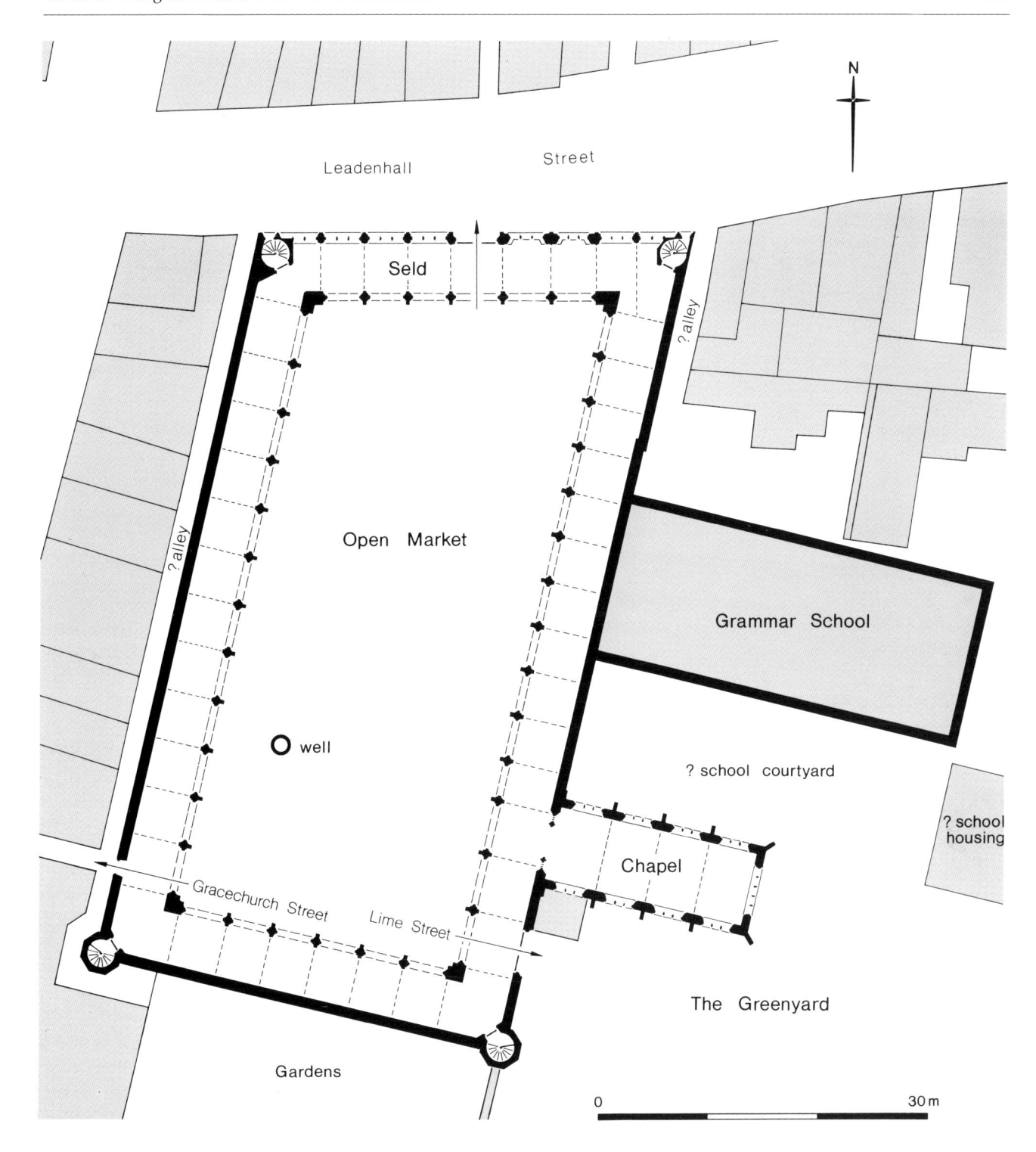

Reconstructing the medieval market at Leadenhall

Fig 47 Ground plan of 15th-century market and Garner at Leadenhall, as revealed by excavation and surveys conducted in 1677 and 1794. Scale 1: 500

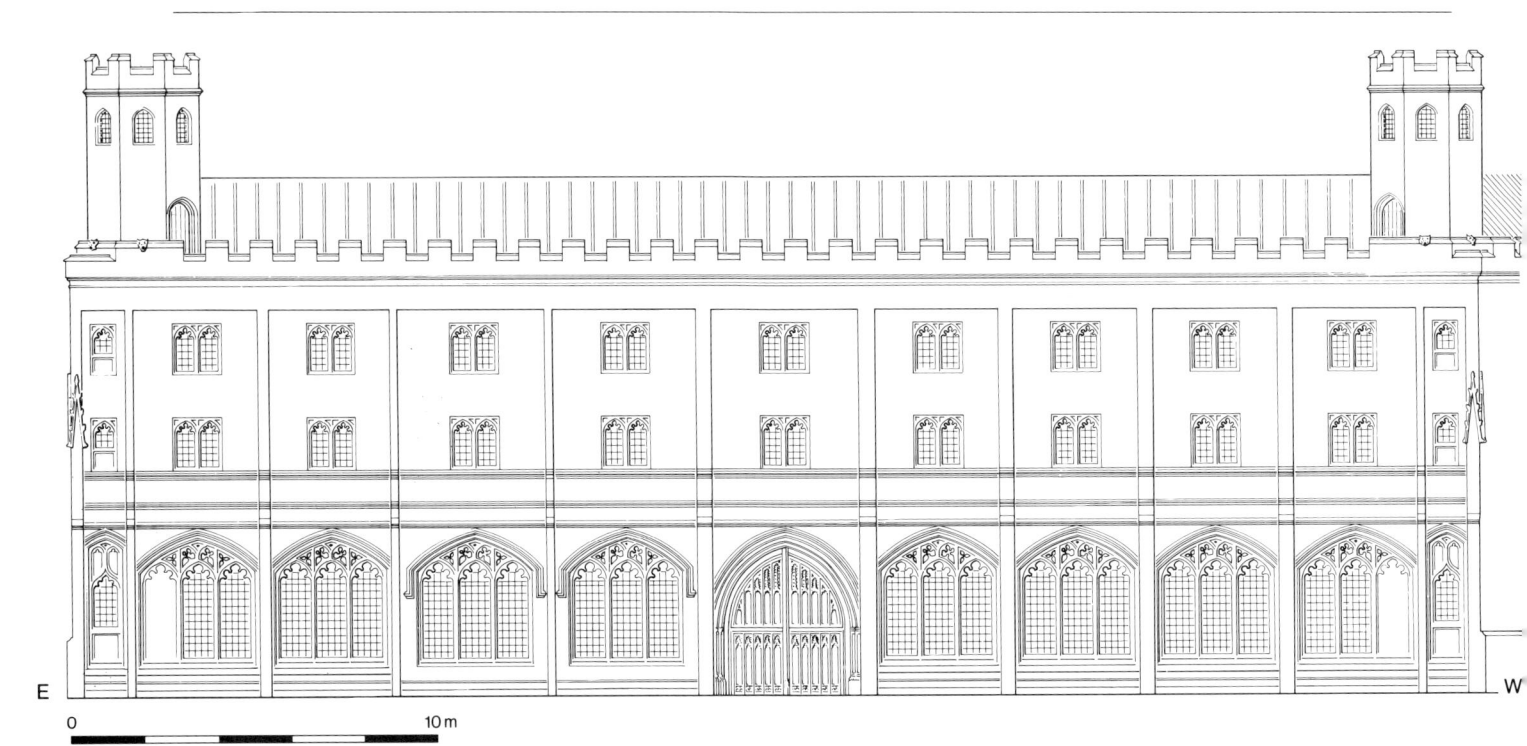

Fig 48 Reconstructed elevation of the north range of the 15th-century Garner which faced Leadenhall Street: cf. Figs 44 and 46. Scale 1: 200

Reconstructing the north range
(Fig 48, back cover illus)

Work could now commence on a reconstruction of the north range, the only wing of the complex provided with an elaborate, fenestrated facade – the reason being that it overlooked Leadenhall Street. Plans of the upper floors were created by combining information from the west wall fragment and the redrawn 18th-century survey. Piers had been reconstructed from the moulded stones, and the plan allowed these to be positioned. The arcade was formed by a series of piers supporting semi-elliptical arches. The complex form of these arches was achieved by using a sequence of voussoirs with different radii.

By identifying the parapet cornice on Carter's sketch, and assuming it to be the same height as the one recorded in the west range, the heights of the string courses, windows and other features could be calculated. The form and size of the three- and two-light windows were based partially on the recovered stones, their apparent dimensions in the old pictures, and the heights of the floors. Most of the three-light windows on the ground floor were open to the weather, though heavily barred with iron; there was no glass. However, at least one of the windows was provided with shutters. It is possible that, since the north range was the main entrance to the market, the bays next to the main entrance may have housed a market official or constable whose office required additional weather protection.

An engraving published in 1825 shows the Reigate stone two-light windows, of which there were nearly 100, overlooking the courtyard from the first and second floors of all the ranges, and also overlooking Leadenhall Street. These unglazed windows were barred and shuttered.

A mid-16th-century view of the Garner shows that there were tall stair turrets at the western and eastern corners of the north range. They had been partially removed before Carter produced his drawing in 1785. Some of the stone stair treads were recovered in 1985-6. They fell into four categories: each spiral stair tread revolved through either 22.5 degrees or 30 degrees of a circle; they were also 'handed' either to right or left. Four types of spiral stair were therefore used in the Garner. The plan of the north–eastern corner made for a deed in 1716 shows the position of the first tread and also the spiral's clockwise ascent. The symmetry of the north range indicates that the north–western stair revolved in the opposite (anti-clockwise) direction. It is possible that the 22.5 degree helix was used for the first 16 treads, while the more gently ascending 30 degree treads would bring the stairs to the level of the first floor door sill. By thus combining the reconstructed helix with the known levels of the upper floors and roof wall-walk, the stair turret was reconstructed. Internally the details are conjectural: the reconstruction shows one possible arrangement (Figs 45 and 46).

Carter's engraving shows that doors led from the turret on to the roof wall-walk. Nicely appropriate jambs from small Reigate stone doorways were recovered from the excavation. These could well come from the doors '...about three foot four inches wide, from the turret to the leads...' mentioned in a lease of 1679. The jambs had been burnt; perhaps in the serious fire which, as Stow records, badly damaged the Garner in 1484 (Wheatley 1956, 140).

The sockets and cornices that survived in the wall fragment enabled the floors to be reconstructed with some confidence, while the positions of the hammerbeam corbels were crucial evidence for the roof's construction. An engraving by J T Smith proves that the roof trusses were of hammerbeam construction. The roof pitch appears to have been shallow: the lead to cover it was obtained by a licence granted in 1443 and is depicted on the 16th-century 'Copperplate' map, where the engraver used the convention of vertical strokes to represent the seams between the lead sheets (Pl 20). By the 18th century, the lead had been replaced by cheaper tiles.

Masons and designs

In 1442 two masons filed a joint request to be discharged from jury service since they were '...gretely occupied as wele by the commandement of the maire for the tyme beyng...about a gretc werk that they have spedely for to make at Ledenhall for the Common wele and profit of this citee' (Cal LB, K, 206). The two men were the elderly John Croxtone and his partner John Hardy. A certain amount is known about the former; a supremely talented mason who gained the prestigious commission to redesign Guildhall in 1411, when he would have been in his late twenties. While working on the Guildhall Chapel, he had 'counseilled the moldes therof'. This must have involved the drawing of full-size designs, both for costing and probably also for the cutting of the dressings at the quarry, thereby reducing carriage costs (Salzman 1952,123). His career would have begun with work on stone-cutting, but he must soon have learnt all aspects of design and construction supervision. His role was that of an architect, although that term was not used until much later. After a lifetime of hard work combining the unofficial roles of what today would be called the 'City Architect' and 'Head of the Board of Works', he was reduced to petitioning the Corporation in 1446. With relief, one learns that his wages were doubled and he was reimbursed for paying his workmen labouring on the Guildhall chapel out of his own pocket.

Although it seems certain that Croxtone was responsible for much of the design of the Leadenhall Garner, he died before the work was finished and so responsibility for its completion presumably rests with his partner. John Hardy was more typical of the successful masons of the time, owning ships to hire out for the carriage of stone, and with the money to speculate in property. He even took a 50-year lease on one of the newly cleared properties next to the Garner, on condition that he built a new timber house upon the site within five years (Harvey 1954, 79). Since he was elected Senior Warden of the London Masons Company in 1441, he cannot have been much younger than Croxtone.

Although we know so little about their lives, we are now in a position to evaluate their 'grete werk' at Leadenhall. It was one of the most important civic buildings in the late medieval City. Its role was to provide free-standing for non-citizen food vendors at ground level, while the upper floors acted as storehouses for grain. The former market courtyard was greatly enlarged by the provision of a covered arcade (seld) to keep the market people and their wares dry. By enlarging the market and supplying it with free shelter, a well and chapel, the supply of food from the country for the City would have been increased and prices lowered. Recent excavations and research suggest that the complex had an additional eastern arm to the north end of the chapel which briefly housed Simon Eyre's school of grammar and song (Samuel, in preparation).

The first and second floors were well suited to the storage of grain. The Reigate stone ashlar facing of the galleries and the many ventilators served to keep the environment dry and airy. The ventilators could be closed in wet weather to reduce the risk of mildew. The stone walls would have discouraged rats and mice. The long galleries ran around the quadrangle without interruption, but access was restricted to the spiral stairs. The wide and shallow stairs imply that grain was carried in sacks by men rather than by beasts of burden. Having a stair at each corner would have eased the maintenance of the stockpile, since old grain could be removed in the opposite direction to that in which it was brought. In addition, the solid outer wall and the minimum of entrances meant that the building could be secured against riots in the event of civil unrest, a point commented upon by Stow (Wheatley 1956, 143).

The building was constructed in the style now known as the London Perpendicular. This style is a sober variant of the late medieval Perpendicular form of Gothic architecture. It has a rigid geometrical grammar allowing very little freehand embellishment or sculpture. The precision of this framework rivalled that of classical Greek architecture. With a sound knowledge of the style, it is possible to predict the architectural context of every element: this is most useful when trying to reconstruct an entire building from a limited number of moulded stones. Croxtone worked with moulding templates presumably cut from wood or metal. His skill was to transform this limited repertoire of 'notes' into new and complex 'harmonies'. He liked to cover the whole building in panel tracery, and the interior of Guildhall still displays his virtuosity in this field. Due to its expense, such panel tracery was only applied where it would be clearly visible. For example, the exterior of Guildhall was mostly of plain ashlar, save for such areas as the south porch and the entrance to the undercroft at the east of it. However, with the construction of Guildhall Chapel, he was able to extend a continuous screen of panel tracery around the east side of the yard.

This restricted use of panel tracery occurred at the Garner. Of all the four ranges at Leadenhall, only the northern facade was decorated beyond the bare minimum, since this alone was visible from the street. Croxtone's design incorporated large three-light openings rather than panel tracery, allowing the internal arcading to be seen from without. The barred screen was a purely ornamental set-piece to relieve the otherwise stark functionalism of the rest of the Garner. Its nearest equivalent is the screen separating King's College from King's Parade, Cambridge.

The dressings on the ground floor arcade were in Caen stone, an attractive yellowish stone capable of taking on an ivory-like sheen when polished. It was imported from France and used extensively in London in the 11th and 12th centuries. The gradual adoption of more local building stones meant that Caen stone was used more rarely, and its expense and fine quality meant that it was only used by the most wealthy patrons for the purpose of display. Its use at Leadenhall was principally to impress passers-by with the wealth of the City. Above the ground storey, the rest of the Garner was built from grey Kentish ragstone, while the piers were laboriously dressed from this extremely hard and brittle stone. However, the pier mouldings were not designed specifically for this new building, since similar piers can still be seen forming the crossing of St Alphege's, London Wall. Even the ventilators in the upper floors were conventional two-light windows of a type often seen in a domestic setting. In both cases, the mouldings were probably dressed *en masse* at the quarries using cheap Reigate stone. Although Croxtone had died by 1451, before the chapel was built, it now seems that the chapel and school must have been part of the original design for the chapel's entrance was integral with the Garner wall. It is indistinguishable in style from Croxtone's work, but must in fact have been executed by Hardy or some younger mason. The tracery pattern used for the fenestrated arcade was much the same as that used by Croxtone in the clerestory of the Guildhall chapel (Barron 1974, pl 27a). A sketch by John Carter shows how a favoured motif of Croxtone's, a large cinquefoil with two trefoil panels gracefully flanking its head, was here employed to form a window at either end of the range. The same motif was used to flank the piers of Guildhall 30 years earlier. The London Perpendicular style did not lend itself to expressions of individuality, and thus work should not be attributed to any one mason without good cause, though no doubt Hardy was competent to carry on the work in the same style as his mentor. The school was demolished long before the remainder of the complex, and nothing is known of its appearance.

The techniques employed in the Garner display the confidence and economy with which the masons tackled their work. Study of the putlog holes shows that they worked to a height of five lifts before creating a new platform entirely supported on beams passed through the wall, rather than on a free-standing timber scaffold, a practice which greatly economised on timber.

The building seems to have risen at a uniform rate on all sides. It is clear that both internal and external walls must have been erected simultaneously, since the ends of the principal floor joists were sealed by the next lift. This uniform method of construction meant that at any one moment the workforce was engaged in the same task, be it the lowering of all the first floor principal joists into position or the setting of 200 floor cornice mouldings. Since the building was designed to employ as many standard dimensions, mouldings and construction techniques as possible, the head mason's administrative burden would have been greatly lightened. As a consequence, the Garner would have been built as quickly and as efficiently as possible. The foundations seem to have been completed by 1445, and the Garner, seld and school were completed just 10 years later.

A unique civic building

There was no close contemporary parallel for this multi-purpose civic building in Britain or Europe, although composite buildings, such as the town hall in Thorn (Poland), incorporated courtyards, a vital feature of a market. However, there is a truly striking resemblance of the Leadenhall Garner to later bourses or exchanges where banking, trade and marketing could all be conducted under one roof. Stow records that the London merchants found the Garner a congenial place in which to assemble, and unsuccessfully petitioned Common Council to have it converted into a 'burse' in 1534 (Wheatley 1956, 144). It was in this period that the first custom-built exchange in northern Europe was built, in Antwerp, some 90 years later than the Garner and sharing many features with it. The new exchange was contained within a solid outer wall and had a quadrangular arcade surrounding a courtyard with warehousing on the upper floor. London built its own Royal Exchange in 1566 to a design which ostensibly owed much to the Antwerp bourse, although its initial inspiration was arguably Croxtone's Garner.

Thus our study of the 15th-century civic complex at Leadenhall has thrown much light on the design and construction of a remarkable public utility which was built by a civic authority and a public benefactor for the common good. The techniques and methods of the medieval mason have been examined, together with the detailed planning and rigid organisation developed for such major works. This aspect of the head mason's work is not apparent in such meagre documentary records as survive. The unusual design of the Garner shows how experienced head masons could rearrange familiar mouldings in a boldly innovatory manner to answer the need for a remarkable building outside their usual repertoire. Our study, when combined with consideration of the abundant cartographic and topographical records held in Guildhall Library, has also rectified some common misconceptions about the complex, such as the suggestion that the 13th-century Leadenhall was not demolished in the 15th century, but was incorporated in the new Garner (Masters 1974, 21). In addition the recent publication of an erroneous plan of the market as it appeared in 1520 can be corrected (Lobel 1989). Thus analysis of the archaeological data from the Leadenhall Court site together with records from Guildhall has made possible a major reinterpretation of associated documentary and topographical evidence. As a consequence, an episode in the civic history of medieval London has been clarified.

12 London viewed from Leadenhall

Trevor Brigham, Gustav Milne and Mark Samuel

In this chapter, attempts are made to see how research on the Leadenhall Court project provides new insights into the history and development of the City as a whole. For example, our understanding of the manner and chronology of the development of the Roman town has been clarified by the recent work, as has been shown in Chapters 2 and 6. But how might we account for such changes in fortune: why did London take the shape that it did? Who or what was responsible for the growth and administration of the City? Since military history can be studied through the development of fortifications, and mercantile history through the development of ships and harbours, the history of the City's administration can be studied though examination of its public buildings and the facilities provided. In this chapter, new insights into the governance of London are attempted by comparing and contrasting the evidence from the Roman Basilica and the 15th-century Garner. Both buildings were constructed in optimism as prestigious structures, notable and unique architectural achievements. Both suffered ignominious fates as harsh reality overtook them. The history of these buildings therefore seems to crystallise the changing attitudes of the City's administration as it coped with a changing world. In the final section of this chapter, some of the other results of the Leadenhall Court project are summarised, and pointers for further study indicated.

The legal status of Londinium

At the time of its foundation, Londinium fitted none of the main categories of Roman town. It was not a *colonia* of Roman citizens like Camulodunum (Colchester), nor was it the centre of a *civitas*, like Verulamium (St Albans). Merrifield considered that the town initially ranked as a *vicus*, a minor settlement attached in this instance to a port (Merrifield 1983, 61), set on a navigable river where several important overland routes met. These roads were developed originally as supply corridors for the army, which may have provided the initial economic impetus required to ensure the success of the fledgling settlement. Such a trading centre at a crucial position in the communications network approximates to the type of settlement referred to as a *forum*, and was known in Italy itself and other imperial provinces: Forum Gallorum in Spain and Forum Segusiavorum near Lyon, for example. The term should not to be confused with the more normal usage, although both are concerned with markets. This type of settlement may have been legally identical to the *vicus*. In Britain, *forum* seems to be identified with the Celtic placename element *Venta* or *-venta* (Rivet & Smith 1979, 262–5). A *forum* was a small planned centre for organised trade, in contrast to the uncontrolled growth stimulated by a collection of merchants and ancillary traders. Although as a minor settlement it had no government of its own at this stage, early Londinium would have boasted some of the elements of an urban plan; the regular layout of streets on the eastern hill extending down to the river, and an open metalled space at the northern edge of the settlement, adjoining the main crossroads, may reflect this. The metalled area was to develop into the first forum once self-government was established. The settlement could therefore be classed as a 'small town' of Burnham's Group V: one having an original or added planned street system based around a road junction (Burnham 1987). Its position at a crossroads was clearly carefully chosen; crossroads *(compita)* were of special significance in the Roman world, and influenced the siting of many settlements, for religious as well as for practical reasons.

Merrifield suggests that the switching of the procurator's office from Camulodunum to Londinium some time shortly after the Boudiccan revolt merited a promotion in status to the rank of *municipium*. This could have been marked by the construction of the first small forum-basilica, and substantial harbour facilities, including quays and warehousing, either side of the street which linked the bridge and forum. Merrifield also proposed that the construction of the second Forum-Basilica marked Londinium's further elevation to *colonia*, a rank extended to the town in recognition of its status as provincial capital by AD 100 (Merrifield 1983).

One possible implication of this gradual elevation in status is that Roman London did not become the capital in AD 70, but that Camulodunum continued to be the seat of provincial government for at least two decades after the uprising of c.AD 60. This in turn suggests a major reorganisation of the province in the late 1st century, presumably some time after the battle of Mons Graupius, which saw the defeat of the Caledonian tribes in the bellicose north in AD 84. This was a time for taking stock, since it was only after this date that the size and potential of the hard-won province could be fully appreciated. Only now, after the true extent of the island had finally been established and its inhabitants duly pacified, could a lasting plan be drawn up for the administration of the enlarged province. It seems that Londinium was to loom large in this reorganisation, set as it was in the heart of the safe south, within easy reach of the Channel and the North Sea, but astride the main land route north. The enlarged Basilica could therefore be seen as a reflection of the increased importance of Roman London in the new scheme for the development of the province as a whole. By way of a footnote, it is worth recording that Londinium was not the only British town which witnessed a major upgrading of its forum. There is now evidence that the civic centre in Silchester was initially built in timber, but was rebuilt in stone, a pattern which may have been repeated in other towns such as Lincoln.

Urbs et ordo: the administration of Londinium

Forum or *vicus* status would have meant that the new settlement had no town zone *(territorium)* under its direct control, until the granting of a rank equivalent to a *colonia* or *civitas* capital (Merrifield 1983, 127–34). In this regard it is notable that the position of Londinium at or near the suggested junction of four of the five mid-1st-century *civitates* – the South Catuvellauni, Trinovantes, Cantiaci and South Atrebates (later the Regnenses) – prevented it from being monopolised by any one, although Ptolemy, writing in the mid-2nd century, described it as a *polis* of the Cantiaci. Londinium was in addition directly connected by road to the *civitas* capitals of all four.

The function of the ruling council, the *ordo*, in most *civitas* capitals presumably went some way towards replacing that of the original tribal government, although it is likely that the latter retained influence in areas of civilian life with which the Roman administration was not concerned. Londinium, however, had no dependent *civitas*, and the jurisdiction of the *ordo* must have been limited to the administration, maintenance and taxation of the town itself. This would have been added to after the granting of *colonia* status by the administration of the affairs of a *territorium* which may have been carved in equal measure from the adjacent *civitates* (Merrifield 1983, 127–35). However, the lack of a large territorial area to administer and tax would have been balanced by administrative and legislative activity related to the regulation of trade by land and sea, and the exaction for the emperor of tolls and customs dues from imported goods. The importance of trade and financial transactions to the town was reflected in the enormous size of the meeting area and commercial sectors of the Forum and Basilica compared with the administrative areas, and in the expansion of the harbour facilities from the later 1st to the mid-3rd centuries. It could be argued that the eventual failure of this trade holds the key to the decline of Londinium, since an entrepot with, at best, shallow roots in the surrounding hinterland must always be at the mercy of events beyond its control.

The wealth of Londinium

Much of Londinium's wealth in the 1st and early 2nd centuries must have been derived from traffic arriving at or passing through the port. The collection of taxes and customs dues as well as profit derived from this trade would have supported a large workforce dependent for their livelihoods on the continued prosperity and expansion of the wealth-creating classes, through the provision of goods and services. The presence of the provincial government would also have benefited the town in several ways, apart from the prestige which it conferred. It supplied *curiales* – men of decurional class – to the *ordo*, thus helping to ensure a supply of public funds, since it was incumbent on such men to provide both the government of the town and the wherewithal to maintain it. Normally these would have been drawn from the *civitas*; Merrifield has suggested that local landowners from the surrounding *civitates* may have been recruited into London's council, rather than from the councils of their own regional capitals (Merrifield 1983, 135). Extra trade was generated from the supply of goods and services to the provincial governor, his staff and his 1,000 strong bodyguard, housed in the fort at Cripplegate. Private donations and bequests would have furnished monuments and public works at no extra cost to the public purse other than maintenance, some of which may in any case have been provided for by the original or subsequent donors.

Function of the forum-basilica

For some 25 years at the start of the Roman occupation and for a century at the end of the period Londinium survived without a forum-basilica. This raises the question of how essential to the status or functioning of the town such facilities were. The laying out of roads, terraces, and drains all argue for the presence of some degree of central authority from AD 50 to 75; the fact that Londinium apparently survived without a recognisable civic centre in this period suggests that it was not strictly necessary for the existence of an administration. If early Londinium ranked as a 'small town' this is not too surprising, since few settlements of that class show much in the way of public buildings, and only one (Godmanchester) is so far known to have had a basilica. Despite this, they were clearly administered and maintained by a local authority. This evidence, combined with the continued existence of Londinium for 100 years after the demolition of its forum-basilica, demonstrates that urban government was able to exist without being housed in a building recognisable as a basilica, although the form such a government took in the 3rd and 4th centuries is unclear. Thus while the presence of a forum-basilica positively indicates the presence of a self-governing community, the absence of such facilities does not necessarily signify the absence of one. The presence of an active administration must therefore be looked for in the provision, maintenance, or replacement of public facilities, rather than solely in the basilica itself.

The same could be said of the second main function of the forum-basilica as the centre of economic activity: a meeting place for merchants as well as a market for tradesmen. 'The forum-basilica, found in any Roman town, was but a covered extension of the adjoining market-place – a hall to transact business and to exchange town gossip and news from the Empire, a souk to display wares, much like the galleria in any modern Italian town' (Krautheimer 1986, 42). Bankers were also based in the forum; Vitruvius suggested that 'round about in the colonnades put the bankers' offices' (Morgan 1914, V, i.2). Of the site to be chosen he stipulated that 'basilicas should be constructed on a site adjoining the forum and in the warmest possible quarter, so that in winter businessmen may gather in them without being troubled by the weather' (Morgan 1914, V, i.4). Although 'a formal market place is not necessary for trade to take place' (Arnold 1984, 33), and a considerable volume of commerce already existed in Londinium before the first forum-basilica was constructed, the demolition of the second civic centre alone cannot necessarily be taken to imply either the decline of trade, or that it still flourished independently. There was more than one basilica in some larger towns, which 'might be assigned different functions: stock and money exchanges, clothing bazaars, florists' arcades, special law courts, each designated by an explanatory epithet' (Krautheimer 1986, 42).

The final function of the forum was as a general meeting place for the public as a whole. Again it is Vitruvius who informs us that it was a Roman custom 'handed down from our ancestors that gladiatorial shows should be given in the forum' (Morgan 1914, V, i.1). The *compitalia*, a festival traditionally held at important crossroads, may also have been held in the courtyard, which was at the centre of a major road junction.

Town and Basilica: demise and demolition

The division of Britannia into two provinces in the early 3rd century may have led to some reduction in activity, although Londinium had a *consular* governor, whereas its northern counterpart York had only a *praetorian* governor. Duplication of offices — rife in the later Empire – probably meant that London's economy was little affected by the change, even if its status suffered. Political upheavals in the later 3rd century, culminating in the Carausius/Allectus episode, probably also had little effect, since London became the base of a new mint in AD 286. The regaining of Britain from the rebel Allectus by the Empire in AD 296 was shortly followed by subdivision into four new provinces by Diocletian; Londinium's senior status was reinforced as it became the base of the *vicarius Britanniarum*, with its own province later promoted to seniority under a consular governor. Londinium seems to have emerged at the end of the 4th century as the dominant town politically, just as it had been in the later 1st, but with the honorific title 'Augusta', which has often been taken to reflect imperial interest. If that is accepted, then the marked decline in the town's population cannot be ascribed directly to political causes.

The Londinium of the later 2nd century onwards was a very different place from that of the 1st and earlier 2nd centuries. To the later period belongs the apparent abandonment of large areas of the town represented by the accumulation of extensive spreads of dark grey silt deposits (but see Yule 1990), and most significantly, the dismantling of the port and the Basilica. Similar phenomena recorded throughout Britain, Gaul and many other provinces can be attributed to the failure of the imperial economy. The reasons for this are many, but seem to have had their roots in the rapid expansion of the Empire under Trajan (AD 98–117) and the subsequent retrenchment under his successor Hadrian (AD 117–38). As the economy stagnated under the cost of maintaining the new imperial territorial acquisitions, the initial wealth which they brought evaporated and private indebtedness spread.

The problems of the economy were manifested in high inflation, which made the provision of goods and services expensive. As a result, there was a severe downturn in bulk trade and investment in industry. Many former traders probably invested their capital in agricultural land instead, thus removing much of the wealth and wealth-creating capacity from the towns. Those who had both town and country properties concentrated their capital in the improvement of their villa-estates. The larger estates also attempted to become self-sufficient, employing craftsmen who may have been tempted from the emptying towns. There is also a strong possibility that the burden of inflation, taxation, duty and public expenditure fell so heavily on the remaining *curiales* that they abandoned the town in favour of their country estates, although it is unclear whether they were allowed to avoid their duties simply by being *in absentia*.

Despite the construction of a new port facility in the 230s, trade in Londinium seems to have dwindled to the point where, shortly after the middle of the 3rd century, the waterfront was almost completely dismantled (Brigham 1990b; Milne 1985). Overseas trade must have effectively ceased, apart from the importation of a small quantity of high-quality goods and exotic foodstuffs unobtainable in Britain. For London, commercial disaster accelerated the decline in the population, which had begun in the mid-2nd century. This is marked by a gradual contraction of the occupied area, with many of the brickearth strip buildings dismantled and not replaced, and local service roads falling into disuse. Some of the high-quality townhouses were abandoned, as at Milk Street (Perring & Roskams 1991), while others continued to function in the otherwise largely abandoned western and northern parts of the town. These were surrounded by dark silt deposits, possibly representing gardens or orchards, covering the otherwise empty insulae. The trading and dependent artisan and labouring classes must have moved on to more lucrative areas or simply returned to the kind of non-urban life their ancestors had followed and most of their contemporaries still did.

The real wealth was gone, possibly drained by large-scale public projects, such as the provision of the landward and riverside defensive walls and maintenance of the harbour. Merrifield noted that inscribed public monuments of the 3rd century record the restoration of two temples with donations by individuals associated with the provincial government (Merrifield 1983, 173–83). When the late Roman riverside wall was constructed, even these restored temples together with other public monuments had to be dismantled. Roof tiles from demolished buildings were also used in the thickening of the fort wall, and tombstones incorporated into the 4th-century bastions attached to the eastern landwall. The evidence from late Roman London is therefore highly suggestive of a community which lacked the funds even for routine maintenance work. It also implies that the need for the riverside wall and strengthening of the existing defences was an urgent one.

It was around the end of the 3rd or early in the 4th century that the Basilica was demolished. It could be argued that the demolition of that once prestigious building was a political act, as when the Greater London Council's County Hall was closed down by

Act of Parliament in 1986. The usurper Allectus, who was killed in AD 296, may have used Londinium as his power base, and the Basilica may have been symbolically identified with his cause by the avenging emperor, Constantius I (293–306). Such punitive measures are not unknown in the Roman world: the total destruction of Carthage in 146 BC is an example that springs readily to mind. A measure of support for this suggestion is provided by a site near Peters Hill in the west of the City, where a major masonry building which incorporated wooden piles from trees felled in AD 293, 294 or 295 seems never to have been completed (Williams forthcoming). However, a more prosaic economic argument suggests that, with a shrunken population and few traders, most of the functions of the town's Basilica could best be transferred to a smaller, less expensive building. There is some evidence to suggest that the Apse remained standing longer than the rest of the Basilica, in which case it may have retained some form of status or function. Alternatively, the necessary administrative activities may have been conducted in a quite separate building, yet to be identified.

In Chapter 10 it was suggested that the Forum-Basilica had been planned in relation to the projected size of Londinium. However, it is now known that the population never reached the levels anticipated: indeed the town was unable to maintain the levels it had already reached in the early 2nd century. The expectations of that optimistic period are exemplified in the plan of the enlarged forum, while the contractions of the subsequent century are represented in the Basilica itself by periods of neglect, eventual demolition and the presumed incorporation of its building materials into public projects such as the construction of the riverside wall. Thus the **size** of the proposed 2nd-century Basilica encapsulates the contemporary expectation of a prosperous future, but the **sequence** documented by the archaeologists within that building records the harsher reality of what actually happened.

A common market

To understand why the Garner and market were built on the Leadenhall site in the 15th century, an understanding of London's relationship with the king, with mainland Britain and with Europe is required; also of the conflict between the Common Council (representing the commonalty or citizen body) and the Mayor and Aldermen (who controlled economic life through the supervision of the crafts and trade guilds). Since mayors and aldermen were elected exclusively from the guilds, conflicts amongst those powerful organisations determined the political hierarchy.

London, the chief of the realm

As long as London paid substantial taxes, the king did not interfere with the town's economic or political operations. Although London never enjoyed the feudal and fiscal independence of the greater communes of the continent (Williams 1963, 7), the special circumstances of the early 15th century allowed London a high degree of independence. Henry IV spent most of his reign beating down challenges in the north of England, while little was seen of Henry V until the wild celebrations of his victory at Agincourt in 1415. London lent generously to both monarchs, presumably to enable them to continue fighting as far away as possible.

While kings fought, the City embarked upon a rebuilding programme. Several churches were rebuilt in the London Perpendicular style, and this wave of redevelopment was probably reflected in domestic architecture as well. Such conspicuous consumption implies that many new fortunes had been made on such enterprises as the wool and cloth trades, and were now seeking an outlet. By the 1450s much of London must have been as uniform in style as Georgian London in its heyday. Of all these new buildings, the early 15th-century Guildhall is the most famous (Barron 1974). It was comparable in scale to equivalent buildings in Bruges and Ypres, and unparalleled in the British Isles.

In size and wealth, the port of London was exceptional among English medieval cities: in the mid-14th century, it was assessed for £733 taxation, while Bristol, its nearest rival, was assessed for a mere £220. By 1500, London's population of 75,000 was larger than any German city, although not as large as Paris (Baker 1970, 139). However, Venice had a population of 220,000 by 1332 (Norwich 1977, 206) and her supremacy must have seemed unassailable. Nevertheless, her intelligence gatherers considered London to be a city comparable to Rome or Florence.

The differing fates of Venice and London disguise their similarities in the 15th century: both cities housed branches of the German Hanseatic merchants, the bankers of Lombardy and the other great trading groups of Europe. A Venetian wool trader would have felt at home in London, travelling from house to office or warehouse by boat along the Thames. Crowds of merchants may have spent part of the day haggling and gossiping on the London waterfront just as Carpaccio records them doing by the Rialto. In her 15th-century heyday, Venice was not, as she is today, a beautiful anachronism, but a model to copy. Her civic installations were admired and coveted throughout Christendom, and would have been well-known to wealthier Londoners, such as Simon Eyre.

Simon Eyre, Alderman and Mayor

In 1394, re-election for aldermen in London was dropped, and they now held their posts for life, on average a term of some 12 years. From 1397, they extended their control over the influx of new aldermen. Prior to that date, they had been directly elected by the citizens, but now two men were nominated from each ward, and the aldermen themselves made the final choice: the administration took on the form it retains to this day. In 15th-century London a social mobility which would have horrified the Venetians was quite normal. One reason for this was the strong links between the City and south-east England. Once an alderman reached the pinnacle of his London career, he would often buy himself into the landed aristocracy, as Sir John de Pulteney did for example. Conversely, there was always room for the newcomer who wished to become the Mayor or an alderman merely by shouldering the expense of gaining popularity. A rich draper called Simon Eyre chose to do this by building a covered market, garner and grammar school. The first two were 'for the Commonalty on Common soil' (Cal LB K, 218v); while the latter was intended to provide a free education for citizens' children. Clearly the draper was one to hedge his bets.

Simon Eyre was thus a typical newcomer. He was born in the last decade of the 14th century, the son of John Eyre of Brandon, Suffolk, and obtained citizenship when admitted to the Upholders Guild, but succeeded in transferring himself to the more prestigious Drapers in 1419. There were some 111 separate guilds at this time, and the more expensive the commodity they dealt in, the more rich and powerful their members became. In 1444, Simon Eyre became an alderman: by promoting himself, he was also promoting his company, and may also have had private hopes of giving London a political power in keeping with its economic muscle. His promotion of the scheme at Leadenhall would gain popularity on several fronts as discussed in Chapter 4, providing welcome facilities such as a covered market and a school. Following his election as Mayor in 1445, Simon Eyre energetically oversaw its construction. Stow records the popular legend that Eyre built the Garner at his own expense (Wheatley 1956, 138–9). It certainly seems that he used his own wealth to prime the pump, although he had good reason to suppose that the City would eventually reimburse him once he became Mayor. Nevertheless, both the school and the chapel were built and endowed from his own purse. He married twice and had three grandchildren living when he drafted his will, the size of his legacies suggesting exceptional wealth. He died in 1458, having lived to what then passed for a ripe old age (Thrupp 1948, 339).

However, the executors of his will met with insuperable obstacles, since the school was never endowed and the Garner was soon used for every purpose but the storage of grain. It seems that even the courtyard and covered market became built up with permanent rented stalls, all quite contrary to Eyre's original wish. A petition presented by the Commonalty to the Common Council in 1519 expresses concern about this steady encroachment. It states that Eyre had willed that the non-citizen market people '...should have their free-standing within the said Leadenhall in wet weather, to keep themselves and their wares dry and thereby encourage them... to resort to the said City to victual the same' (Wheatley 1956, 143–4). Simon Eyre was remembered as a local hero.

Public buildings, private benefactors

While accepting the obvious differences between Londinium and 15th-century London, it is suggested that there are some significant similarities between the Garner and the much larger Roman Forum and Basilica. We are fortunate in being able to set the busy fine detail of historically documented medieval economic and political life against the material archaeology. By contrast the Basilica must be studied without such welcome support, since the vast repositories of Roman civic records have all vanished. But Londinium was just as complex an administrative organism as the 15th-century City, and both had comparable levels of technology. Roman London would have had its own groups of merchants, drapers, vintners and so forth who would have tried to control the political and economic life of the town through their wealth and influence. Like the medieval aldermen, the Roman *duovirs* intrigued, jockeyed for power and attempted to win popular support through their largesse and public works. There is a tendency among some archaeologists to attribute all large Roman buildings to imperial generosity, but such a benevolent attitude is not in keeping with what is known of the way the Empire was organised. However, it is fair to say that the actual construction of a building as large as the Basilica is evidence of a strong contemporary economy. The work required a large skilled work force, supported by well-established local industries providing, for example, brick in prodigious quantities, and no amount of imperial money could have produced the necessary infrastructure overnight. While it is possible that the Emperor approved or acted as a patron of the provincial capital's new Basilica, it was the strength of the then expanding local economy that brought it into being. No doubt some Romano-British Simon Eyre was the driving force behind it.

The future of Leadenhall's past

This volume has summarised some of the work of the Leadenhall Court project team. It has attempted to show how the evidence was collected and assessed and what developments seem to be represented on that site. It has then discussed how and why those discoveries have changed our understanding of the history of London as a whole. The developments recorded seem to show how Londinium grew from an undistinguished settlement in AD 50–70, represented by the widely-spaced Buildings 1–4, to a *municipium* with intensively occupied insulae in AD 75. The clearance of the vernacular buildings on the Leadenhall Court site to make way for the enlarged Forum began in the AD 90s, which implies that Roman London had acquired the status of *colonia* and provincial capital by that time. The confidence and optimism of those days is clearly reflected in the scale of the proposed new plan: however, the modifications to and the final fall of the Basilica in *c*.AD 300 show that such confidence did not last. The late-Saxon rebirth of London is also represented on the site, while the later energetic development and ignominious demise of the medieval market retains echoes of the Roman past. Nevertheless, the Saxon settlement which developed in the 10th and 11th centuries was ultimately more successful than its Roman predecessor. Indeed, much of the shape, if not the fabric, of the present-day City can be traced back to early English roots rather than to classical civilisation. For example, the great bulk of the Basilica has left no mark on the Leadenhall townscape, whereas the form of the the Saxon streets and even some of the first burgage plots have had a direct or indirect influence on even the most recent developments.

It must be stressed here that the study is by no means complete: indeed another major volume is in preparation which will examine the 1st-century material in more detail than was possible in this report, for such is the nature of research. We have collected a substantial quantity of archaeological data, but have barely begun to extract the wealth of information that lies locked within it. Even the very act of digging brings its own advances. As a result of large-scale excavation programmes such as those at Leadenhall Court, the archaeological recording system then in use was subsequently modified in the light of experience (MoL 1990): study of the large quantities of Roman pottery recovered from the site has helped refine the dating of such ceramic material, as reported in Chapter 6.

The more we learn, the more future excavation and conservation strategies must also change. For example, we now know that the isolated sections of the Roman Basilica which still survive, such as those beneath Whittington Avenue itself, merit careful preservation. In addition, the southern wall of the 15th-century Garner, hidden behind Leadenhall Market, should be scheduled now to prevent its needless destruction in any future redevelopments. Armed with such knowledge, we can begin to understand that part of the past we have revealed and care more conscientiously for that which lies safely unexposed.

As recently as 1985, Peter Marsden compiled a major study of the London forum. However, although that report was based on some 20 sites investigated over a 100-year period, he was unable to establish clear dates for the construction and demise of that major complex (Marsden 1987, 67, 76). The reason was simply that few of those sites had been supported with the resources of time, money and manpower needed to recover the necessary data. It is a measure of the success of the Leadenhall Court project that from just one site upon which resources were, if not lavished, at least expended in reasonable quantity, a dating framework for the London Basilica has finally emerged. There were many other notable advances in knowledge, not least with regard to the 15th-century Garner, the reconstruction of which is among the first major medieval building studies of its type attempted in London. Again, much if not all of the data used in that work could so easily have been lost had the redevelopment taken place in a less enlightened age. The Leadenhall Court project saw genuine co-operation between the Museum of London, a major City developer (Legal & General) and English Heritage, who worked together to rescue part of London's history. The detailed excavation of an urban site will never be cheap, but it can be worthwhile: we have tried to show the real value of such co-operative ventures, and hope this volume presents a constructive approach to the excavation and understanding of our common heritage, and one which others may wish to build on.

Appendices

A: Whittington Avenue excavations: a summary
Gary Brown and Brian Pye

The 30 × 40m site formerly occupied by the Post Office in Whittington Avenue lies some 10m east of Leadenhall Court, directly over the north–east corner of the 2nd-century Basilica. During the first phase of excavations, nine trenches were investigated in the basement of the standing structure between June 1988 and February 1989. Then the building was demolished and the site was cleared. In June 1989 the Museum team returned for three months and was able to excavate five more trenches while recording a number of features exposed during underpinning operations conducted by the contractors around the perimeter of the site. The archaeological work was directed by the authors, and was generously funded by the developers, the Corporation of London. Since work on the archive report is still in progress, it is not at present possible to integrate all of the site sequence with that of the neighbouring Leadenhall Court project. Nevertheless, it was felt that some comment on the more relevant levels would be of value. The following summary of the activity represented is based on a preliminary assessment of the field records made between September 1989 and June 1990: all dates quoted are therefore subject to revision in the light of further research.

AD 50–60
A truncated horizon of natural Brickearth was recorded at 11.8m OD in the north of the site sloping down to 11.6m OD in the south, showing that the area had been extensively de-turfed. The ground surface had then been raised by *c*.0.3m with the dumping of layers of redeposited brickearth. Over this a 5m-wide road was constructed with rammed gravel and sand. It ran north–south across the centre of the site and was lined with clay and timber buildings which had been burnt down, presumably during the Boudiccan revolt *c*.AD 60.

AD 70–100
To the east of the street new buildings were erected, first with tile and cobble foundations, and subsequently with clay sills. However, the sequence to the west, i.e. facing Leadenhall Court, was different, for here the buildings were not replaced. Instead part of the area was turned over to cultivation, possibly using a plough, ard or spade, since narrow, shallow linear grooves were recorded on the underlying surface. This plot was subsequently covered by layers of interleaving rubbish or midden deposits.

AD 100–300
A major change in the development of the site in the early 2nd century saw the construction of the Basilica and an extension of the associated street system (Fig 49). Initially, the north–south road continued in use at its original width, but it was now met by the new east–west road laid out immediately north of the Basilica. After this new street had been resurfaced four times, the north–south road was increased in

Fig 49 Whittington Avenue excavations 1988–9 (WIV88): general site plan showing portico and east end of Basilica, with masonry buildings to east of road. Note water pipe (wp) on west side of street. Walls recorded on WIV88 shown in black; walls conjectured shown hatched; remainder of Basilica walls shown with grey tone

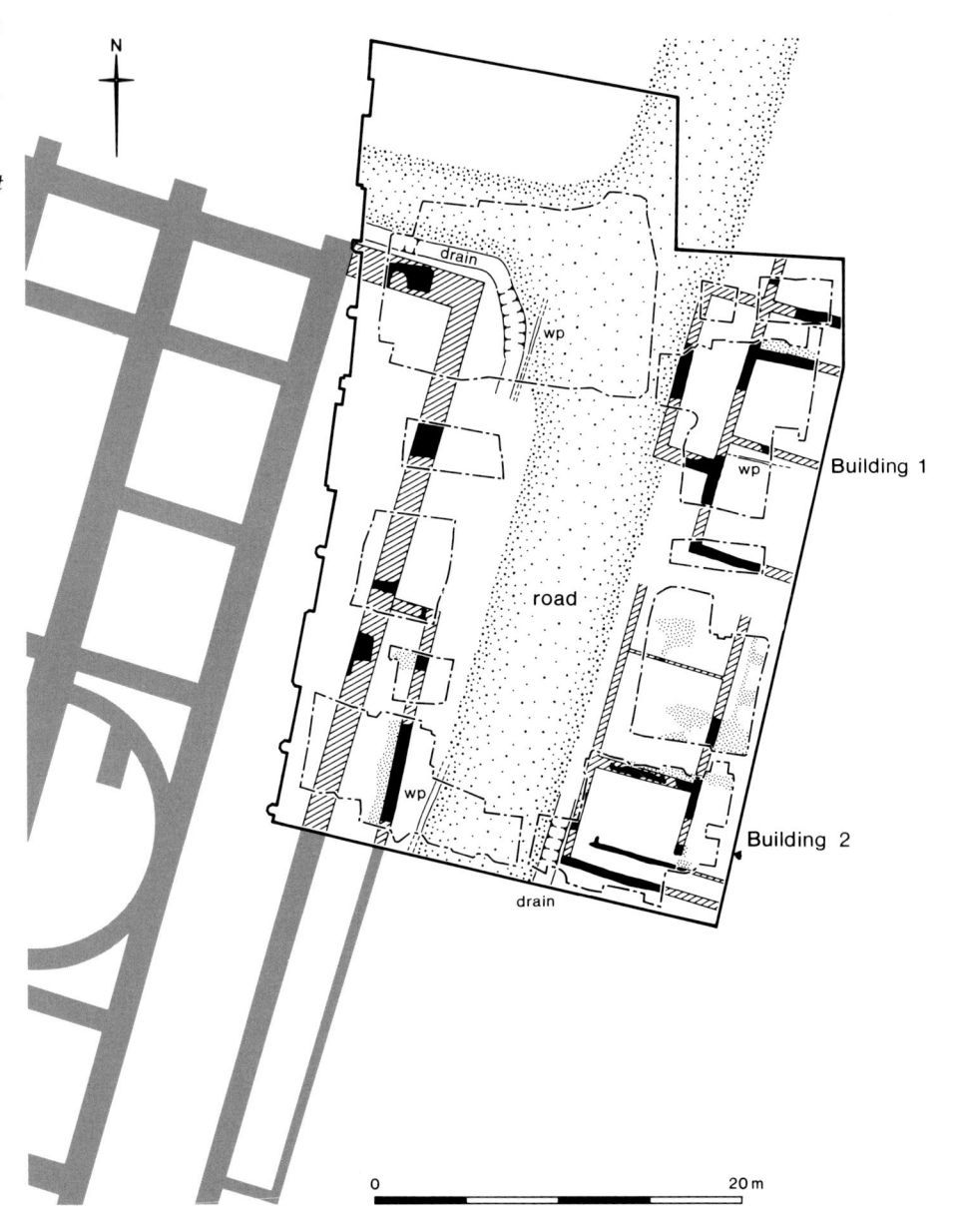

width to 9m. Timber-lined drains on the southern and eastern sides of the roads carried rainwater off the site. Within the streets lay wooden water pipes connected with iron collars which supplied water both to the Basilica and to the private buildings.

In the area enclosed to the west and south of the roads, the ground surface was raised and the substantial ragstone and mortar foundations of the north-east corner of the Basilica were laid. The floors recorded within this major public building were of poor quality mortar and of brickearth. In the mid-2nd century a large part of the building was damaged by fire. During the subsequent rebuilding a portico was added to the main external wall but confined to the area east of the Nave and its north and south aisles. It had a narrow dwarf wall at the front which presumably supported a colonnade. A thick layer of concrete formed the initial floor, but this was replaced by *opus spicatum*, a tile surface laid in a herringbone pattern (Col Pl H). By the mid-3rd century, the portico had been dismantled, although the remainder of the Basilica, the area around the Apse, seems to have continued in use, although for how long is

Pl 33 The marble plaque: fragments of a white marble wall plaque thought to be derived from the early 2nd-century Basilica

uncertain. Substantial fragments of a white marble plaque were recovered from a drain beneath the portico floor (Pl 33). The marble was probably derived from the first phase of the Basilica, before the portico was built.

In the mid-2nd century, to the east of the main north–south road opposite the Basilica, two substantial buildings replaced the earlier structures. The northern building, which had ragstone foundations, may have been used as a shop. It shared a party wall with the southern building, which was of brickearth and timber construction but contained tessellated floors, hot-air flues and painted wall plaster. Both these buildings appear to have fallen into disuse by the 3rd century, and were overlain by destruction debris and an horizon of dark grey silts.

Medieval features

Unfortunately the insertion of the deep 19th-century basement had destroyed most of the late Roman and post-Roman levels. However, the truncated bases of pits, robber trenches, wall foundations and other medieval features survived. A well which had been dug through the Basilica foundations was backfilled in c.AD 1100, after which the massive Roman foundations were extensively quarried for the ragstone rubble. In addition, two chalk lined cellars were recorded and the Victorian party wall on the north-east side of the site was found to incorporate an upstanding section of 14th-century masonry 2.2m in height and 5m wide, decorated in chequer-board fashion, white chalk blocks alternating with black flints.

Fragments were also recorded from later medieval buildings including part of the Greenyard Inn as well as the chapel and the school on the eastern side of the 15th-century Leadenhall Garner (Fig 23). A row of masonry foundations similar in composition, size, shape and spacing to those associated with the Garner is thought to represent the line of one wall of the 15th-century school, while an L-shaped robber trench and further foundations to the west are probably associated with it. Together they define part of a large rectangular building which was probably arcaded along its southern edge, and ran eastwards from the Garner.

B: Public Archaeology
Gustav Milne and Chrissie Milne

London's past does not belong to the Museum or to the owner of any particular historic site: it belongs to us all. The information recovered from archaeological sites in the City must therefore be shared as widely as possible. Initially this is achieved through site information boards, press releases and lectures, and then through summary reports, articles in learned journals, archive reports lodged in the Museum library and publications such as this. Wherever possible excavations are opened to the public, but this facility is becoming increasingly rare, since most of our short-term sites are squeezed into the basements of standing buildings or lie in the middle of building sites shared with contractors' noise and moving machinery.

The Leadenhall Court project was an exception to that rule, for here a programme of open area excavations took place on a cleared site in the heart of the City for just under a year. Appreciating the real and rare opportunity this situation offered, Legal & General were most supportive of the Museum's wish to let everybody see how the archaeologists of today record yesterday's London. Although people could not be allowed down on to the site itself for safety reasons, a viewing gallery with a small exhibition and shop was established in a portacabin on one side of the site, with a long viewing platform protected with open mesh on the other. From these two high-level vantage points, much of the site work could be seen in complete safety without disrupting the excavation itself.

Many thousands of people visited the site in 1986. Special tours were given to pre-booked parties and *in situ* lunch-time lectures were performed weekly. A team of loyal volunteers manned the gallery and were supplied with a selection of ancient artefacts which visitors were encouraged to handle. Answers also had to found for the remarkable range of questions which Londoners, tourists, overseas visitors, office workers and school children wished to ask. The majority of the comments which were entered in the visitor's book were favourable and warmly supportive; many, but by no means all, expressed gratitude towards Legal & General for funding the work. It is interesting to note that the heritage we were uncovering was not just that of Londoners: it was enthusiastically embraced by Americans and Australians, and even more proudly repossessed by our Italian friends. Other visitors had a special personal interest in the site: some had served in the shops or worked in the offices which once occupied it, and another, one Brian Philp, had mounted a major archaeological excavation on a neighbouring section of the Roman forum 20 years earlier. Looking to the future, to the next generation, we were pleased to learn that one of our younger visitors thought that the site was 'Soooper', while Rebecca Reeves gave us the accolade 'Better than school'.

Mass observations

To conclude, here is a selection of comments from our visitors book, compiled over a nine-month period in 1986:

K Vickey	London	*Thanks to Legal & General for this great opportunity*
Carol Forman	London	*Looks like hard work!*
J Siron	London	*Road in better condition than M1*
B Eastop	West London Archaeological Group	*Nicer than our gravel pits*
Michael Brett	London	*Fascinated at what was under Dixons!*

Appendix B

Eileen Eason	Brentwood	*Most interesting, excellent display*
R King	London	*Pity it can't be kept*
Viv Anderson	Wokingham	*Splendid, can't wait for the final results*
J Rose	London	*Well done, London Museum*
J Cheek	Melbourne, Australia	*The history we walk and build over*
C Bray	Luton	*A privilege to watch history: thanks!!*
B Dash	London	*Encouraging to see private companies helping to expand our knowledge*
I Sutton	London	*Why is it necessary to build over this site? Answer: money power exerts more influence than Heritage*
G Vagliano	London	*Reminds me of Greek excavations*
W Wright	Argentina	*Shame to destroy it!*
Clive Bishop	Surrey	*Full marks for enterprise*
Chris Castle	Cumbria	*Don't build on it!*
I Dinden	Trier, Germany	*Greetings from another Roman city (Augusta Trevesorium): encouraging work!*
J and K Milne	Banbury	*Great wonders come to light again*
A Lupi	Rome, Italy	*Happy to see a little piece of old (and of Rome!) in the City*
Martin Biddle	Oxford	*Well done!*
Brian Philp	Dover Castle	*Quite like old times!*
R Goodwin	Hull	*I came to look at Lloyds but spent longer here*
Elaine Solari	San Fransisco, USA	*Excellent presentation: especially impressed with Legal & General*
Dr Z Fetiman	Cape Town	*Your archaeologists are a bit rough, pickaxes etc?*
Sally Bacon	Queen Eleanor School	*Painstaking but fascinating: you've inspired a new generation of archaeologists*
Jeff Ellis	Australia	*Unbelievable, fifth visit, I'll support you all the way*
J Watts	Surrey	*Utter vandalism that this site should be destroyed for ever*
anon	Mexico City	*Please! Please build around the ruins*
A Falconi	Rome, Italy	*Good! Let us live again in London!*
B Anderson	Sweden	*Save the past for the future!*
Y Rapley	New Zealand	*History alive again, wonderful*
H Shepard	Essex	*Could have stayed for hours*
M Bettelli	Rome, Italy	*We builded London quite well, don't you think?*
D Bryan	Dagenham	*I fainted with excitement*
W Conoll	Theydon Bois	*I started work in the building on this site in 1937*
S Withers	Kent	*The whole thing brought to life by the enthusiasm and information of the people at the desk: thanks to everyone who has made this site live again*
M Wetherall	London	*Interesting to think 18 months ago I worked only a few feet above*
A Fornay	London	*Generous assistance from Legal & General!*
K Rawkins	Petts Wood	*Build legally and generally elsewhere*
B Dinilula	Ravenna, Italy	*Buon Lavoro!*
James Thomas	San Francisco, USA	*A time trip!*
H Haraquchi	Japan	*A great pity that it's to be destroyed soon*
G Baker	London	*One more office block?*
S Grahame	Canada	*Will the new building last as long as the old?*
P Branley	East Dulwich	*Is this the Roman GLC?*
I Jones	Essex	*Goodbye!*

Bibliography

Anderson, A C, & Anderson, A S, 1981 *Roman Pottery Research in Britain and North-west Europe*, BAR no S123, Oxford

Arnold, C J, 1984 *Roman Britain to Saxon England*, London & Sydney

Arthur, P, & Marsh, G (eds), 1978 *Early Fine Wares in Roman Britain*, BAR no 57, Oxford

Atkinson, D, 1942 *Report on the excavations at Wroxeter in the county of Shropshire, 1923–7*, Oxford, reprinted 1970

Baker, T, 1970 *Medieval London*, London

Banister Fletcher, 1943 *A History of Architecture on the Comparative Method*, London

Barker, P, 1977 *Techniques of Archaeological Excavation*, London

Barker, P, 1985 'Aspects of the Topography of Wroxeter (Viroconium Cornoviorum)' in Grew & Hobley 1985, 109–17

Barron, C, 1970 *The Government of London and its Relationship with the Crown 1400–1450*, unpublished PhD thesis, University of London

Barron, C, 1974 *The Medieval Guildhall of London*, London

Biddle, M, Heighway, C, & Hudson, D, 1973 *The Future of London's Past*, Worcester

Bidwell, P, 1979 *The Legionary Bath-house, Basilica and Forum at Exeter*, Exeter

Bird, J, Chapman, H, & Clark, J (eds), 1978 *Collectanea Londiniensia*, LAMAS Spec Pap no 2

Boon, G, 1974 *Silchester, the Roman town of Calleva*, Newton Abbot

Brewer, R, 1988 *Venta Silurum – Caerwent 1988: summary of results*, National Museum of Wales

Brigham, T, 1990a 'The London Basilica, AD 100–300: a reassessment', *Britannia*, 21, 53–97

Brigham, T, 1990b 'The Waterfront in Late Roman London', *Britannia*, 21, 99–183

Burnham, B, 1987 'The Morphology of Romano-British small towns', *Archaeological Journal*, 144, 156–90

Cal LB *Calendar of Letter-Books 1275–1498*, Books A to L, held in the archives of the Corporation of London

Carandini, A, & Panella, C, 1981 'The Trading Connections of Rome and Central Italy in the late 2nd and 3rd Centuries', in King & Henig 1981, 487–503

Castle, S, 1973 'Trial Excavations in Field 401 Brockley Hill', *London Archaeologist*, 2, no 2, 36–9

Crummy, P, 1984 'The Temple of Claudius at Colchester Reconsidered', *Britannia*, 15, 7–50

Davies, B, & Richardson, B, forthcoming *The Archaeology of Roman London, 5: a Dated Type Series of Roman pottery from London*, CBA Res Rep

Dillon, J, 1989 'A Roman timber building from Southwark', *Britannia*, 20, 229–31

Dunning, G, 1931 'Roman London in 1930', *Journal Roman Studies*, 21, 237

Dunning, G, 1945 'Two Fires of Roman London', *Antiquaries' Journal*, 25, 48–77

Frere, S, 1967 *Britannia: a history of Roman Britain*, London and Boston

Frere, S, 1971 'The Forum and Baths at Caistor by Norwich' *Britannia*, 2, 1–26

Frere, S, 1972 *Verulamium Excavations I*, Oxford

Frere, S, 1983 *Verulamium Excavations II*, London

Fulford, M, 1984 *Silchester: Excavations on the Defences 1974–80*, Britannia monograph 5

Fulford, M, 1985 'Excavations on the site of the Amphitheatre and Forum-Basilica at Silchester, Hants: an interim report', *Antiquaries' Journal* 65, 39–81.

Girouard, M, 1980 *Life in the English Country House: a social and architectural history*, London

Goodburn, D, 1990 'The earliest timber-framed buildings in Britain?', *Rescue News*, 50, 8

Goodchild, R G, 1946 'The Origins of the Romano-British Forum', *Antiquity*, 70–7

Green, H J M, 1975 'Roman Godmanchester', in W Rodwell & T Rowley (eds), *Small Towns of Roman Britain*, BAR 15, 183–210, Oxford

Grew, F, & Hobley, B (eds), 1985 *Roman Urban Topography in Britain and the Western Empire*, CBA Res Rep 59

Grimes, F, 1968 *The Excavation of Roman and Medieval London*, London

Harris, E, 1989 *Principles of Archaeological Stratigraphy*, London
Harvey, J, 1954 *English Medieval Architects*, London
Hebditch, M, & Mellor, J, 1973 'The Forum and Basilica of Roman Leicester', *Britannia*, 4, 1-83
Hill, C, Millet, M, & Blagg, T, 1980 *Roman Riverside Wall and Monumental Arch in London*, LAMAS Spec Pap no 3
Horsman, V, Milne, C, & Milne, G, 1988 *Aspects of Saxo-Norman London Vol 1*, LAMAS Spec Pap no 11
Hurst, H, 1972 'Excavations at Gloucester 1968-71', *Antiquaries' Journal*, 52, 24-69

James, P, 1987 '68 Cornhill, 1981-2' in Marsden 1987, 87-9
Johnson, A, 1983 *Roman Forts*, London
Jones, C, 1988 *Roman Mosaics*, Museum of London
Jones, M, & Gilmour, B, 1980 'Lincoln, Principia and Forum', *Britannia*, 11, 61-72

King, A, & Henig, M (eds), 1981 *The Roman West in the 3rd Century*, BAR no 109, Oxford
Krautheimer, R, 1986 *Early Christian and Byzantine Architecture*, 4th ed, Kingsport

Landels, J, 1978 *Engineering in the Ancient World*, London
Lethaby, W, 1923 *Londinium: architecture and the crafts*, London
Lobel, M, 1989 *The City of London from Prehistoric Times to 1520*, Oxford

Mackreth, D, 1987 'Roman Public Buildings' in J Schofield & R Leech (eds), *Urban Archaeology in Britain*, CBA Res Rep 61, 133-55
McWhirr, A, 1981 *Roman Gloucestershire*, Gloucester
Maloney, C, & de Moulins, D, 1990 *The Archaeology of Roman London, 1: the Upper Walbrook Valley*, CBA Res Rep 69
Maloney, J, 1983 'Recent Work on London's Defences', in J Maloney & B Hobley (eds), *Roman Urban Defences in the West*, CBA Res Rep 51, 96-117
Marsden, P, 1978 'The Discovery of the Civic Centre in Roman London', in J Bird et al. 1978, 89-103
Marsden, P, 1980 *Roman London*, London
Marsden, P, 1987 *The Roman Forum site in London: discoveries before 1985*, HMSO, London
Marsh, G, 1978 'Early 2nd-century fine wares in the London area', in Arthur & Marsh 1978, 119-223
Marsh, G, 1981 'London's Samian Supply and its Relationship to the Development of the Gallic Samian Industry', in Anderson & Anderson 1981, 173-238
Masters, B, 1974 *Public Markets of the City of London surveyed by W. Leybourn in 1677*, London Topographical Society, 117
Mattingly, H, Sydenham, E & others, 1923-1967 *The Roman Imperial Coinage*, vols 1-7, London
Merrifield, R, 1965 *The Roman City of London*, London
Merrifield, R, 1983 *London, City of the Romans*, London
Merrifield, R, 1987 *The Archaeology of Ritual and Magic*, London
Miller, L, Schofield, J, & Rhodes, M, 1986 *The Roman Quay at St Magnus House, London*, LAMAS Spec Pap no 8
Milne, G, 1985 *The Port of Roman London*, London
Milne, G, 1986 *The Great Fire of London*, New Barnet
Milne, G, 1990 'King Alfred's Plan for London', *London Archaeologist*, 6, no 8, 206-7
Milne, G, Bateman, N, & Milne, C, 1984 'Bank Deposits With Interest: excavations at 3-5 Bishopsgate, 1983', *London Archaeologist*, 4, no 15, 395-400
Milne, G, & Goodburn, D, 1990 'The early medieval port of London', *Antiquity* 64, 244, 629-36
Milne, G, & Wootton, P, 1990 'Roman Urban Development in London AD 50 to 120: excavations at Leadenhall Court 1985-6', *London Archaeologist*, 6, no 7, 179-87
MoL 1990 *Archaeological Site Manual*, Department of Urban Archaeology, Museum of London
Morgan, M (ed), 1914 *Vitruvius: Ten Books on Architecture*, reprinted 1960 New York

Neal, D, 1982 'Romano-British Villas: one or two storied?' in P Drury (ed), *Structural Reconstruction*, BAR no 110, 15-71, Oxford
Norwich, J, 1977 *Venice: the Rise to Empire*, London

Panella, C, 1973 'Appunti su un Gruppo di Anfore della prima, media e tarda eta Imperiale', *Ostia* III, 460-633
PCC Stockton, unpublished documents held in the Public Records Office, relating to the Prerogative Court of Canterbury
Peacock, D, & Williams, D F, 1986 *Amphorae and the Roman Economy*, London
Perring, D, & Roskams, S, 1991 *The Archaeology of Roman London 2: development of Roman London west of the Walbrook*, CBA Res Rep 70
Philp, B, 1977 'The Forum of Roman London', *Britannia*, 8, 1-64
Prockter, A, & Taylor, R, 1979 *The A-Z of Elizabethan London*, London Topographical Society, 122

RCHM, 1928 *London, 3: Roman*, Royal Commission Historical Monuments

Reece, R, 1981 'The Third Century; Crisis or Change?', in King & Henig 1981, 27–38

Richardson, B, 1986 'The Roman Pottery', in Miller et al. 1986, 96–138

Richardson, B, & Tyers, P, 1984 'North Gaulish Coarse wares in Britain', *Britannia*, 15, 133–41

Rivet, A F, & Smith, C, 1979 *The Place Names of Roman Britain*, London

Roxan, M, 1983 'A Roman Military Diploma from London', LAMAS, 34, 67–72

Salzman, L, 1952 *Building in England down to 1540*, Oxford

Samuel, M, 1989 'The 15th-century Garner at Leadenhall, London', *Antiquaries' Journal*, 69, 119–53

Schofield, J, 1984 *The Building of London from the Conquest to the Great Fire*, London

Sear, F, 1982 *Roman Architecture*, London

Smith, J T, 1815 *Ancient Topography of London*, London

Spence, C (ed), 1989 *Digging in the City: the annual review 1988*, Museum of London

Spence, C, & Grew, F, 1990 *The Annual Review 1989*, Museum of London

Stevens, J, 1970 *The Venerable Bede: the ecclesiastical history of the English nation*, revised edition, London

Thomas, A, 1923 'Notes on the History of the Leadenhall, 1195–1488', *London Topographical Record*, 13, 1–23

Thrupp, S, 1948 *The Merchant Class of Medieval London, 1300–1500*, Chicago

Todd, M, 1985 'Forum and Capitolium in the Early Empire', in Grew & Hobley 1985, 56–66

Todd, M (ed), 1989a *Research in Roman Britain 1960–89*, Britannia monograph 11

Todd, M, 1989b 'The Early Cities' in Todd 1989a, 75–89

Tyers, P, 1984 'An Assemblage of Roman Ceramics from London', *London Archaeologist*, 4, no 14, 367–74

Tyers, P, & Vince, A, 1983, 'Computing the DUA Pottery' London Archaeologist, 4, no 11, 299–305

Tyers, P, & Vince, A, 1984 *Pottery Archive Users Handbook*, Museum of London

Vince, A, 1990 *Saxon London*, London

Vince, A, forthcoming, *Aspects of Saxo-Norman London Vol 2*, LAMAS Spec Pap no 12

Vincent, T, 1667 *God's Terrible Voice in the City*, London

Wacher, J, 1974 *The Towns of Roman Britain*, London

Wacher, J, 1978 'The Water Supply of Londinium', in Bird et al. 1978, 104–8

Wheatley, H (ed), 1956 *Stow's Survey of London*, London and New York

Wightman, E, 1985 *Gallia Belgica*, London

Williams, G, 1963 *Medieval London: from Commune to Capital*, London

Williams, T, 1984 'Excavations at 25–6 Lime Street', *London Archaeologist*, 4, no 16, 426–30

Williams, T (ed), forthcoming *The Archaeology of Roman London 4: the development of Roman London east of the Walbrook*, CBA Res Rep

Yule, B, 1990 'The "dark earth" and late Roman London', *Antiquity* 64, no 244, 620–8

Explanatory notes

BAR = British Archaeological Report
CBA = Council for British Archaeology
LAMAS = London and Middlesex Archaeological Society
Res Rep = Research Report
Spec Pap = Special Paper

Unpublished archive reports

All may be consulted in the Museum of London Library, by written request.

Site reports

LCT84: Excavations at Leadenhall Court 1984–6
- Introduction — G Milne
- Areas D and M — P Wootton
- Area N — G and C Milne
- Area S — T Brigham
- Area W — G Brown
- The Building Materials — I Betts and N Crowley
- Discussion of Dating Evidence — B Davies
- Finds Appraisal — J Groves
- The Coins — J Hall
- The Glass — J Shepherd
- The Faunal Remains — B West
- Moulded Stones — M Samuel

WIV88: Excavations at Whittington Avenue 1988–9 — G Brown and B Pye

Pottery reports

Chadburn, A, & Tyers, P, 1984 — *Roman Ceramics from Fenchurch Street*

Davies, B, 1983 — *Highgate 'C' Fabrics from London*

Davies, B, 1984 — *Imported & Romano-British Finewares*

Davies, B, Grew, F, & Richardson, B, 1984 — *Roman Lamps from Excavations in the City*

Davies, B, & Tyers, P, 1983a — *Early Neronian Pottery from London*

Davies, B & Tyers, P, 1983b — *Highgate 'B' & Allied Fabrics from London*